Trophy of Grace

Bronwen Healy

Copyright © 2004 by Bronwen Healy
P.O Box 265
Mt Gravatt Plaza
Mt Gravatt 4122

FIRST EDITION (2004)
REPRINTED 2005
2ND REPRINT 2006 (USA)

Website: www.trophyofgrace.com

ISBN 0-9752025-0-2

The names of certain persons and places mentioned in this book have been changed in order to protect the privacy of the individuals involved.

Desktop Publishing by PostHaste, Coorparoo, Brisbane.

Front cover design by Jason Healy

Photographs on back cover: "then" by Fred, "now" by Deanna

Printed and bound in Brisbane by Bethany Press International

Endorsements

"The story of Bronwen Healy is a truly amazing story that really shows how great the love of God is for each one of us. He doesn't see us as we are; down in sin, behaving like animals. He sees us through His eyes; like the ones that we will become, when He has done His work in us."

– Pastor Matthew Barnett – Senior Pastor, Los Angeles Dream Center.

"Bronwen makes people feel bigger. She will make you dream again. She's turned her nightmare into a dream. She empowers and fills people with hope through her testimony. You start to believe you can do anything and dream massive when you read through the black and white print. Her life is a reflection of her not being content with staying in the same place. She walks the talk... and knows how God can do a miracle in a moment of time."

– Deb Malcolm – Mercy Ministries, preacher and friend.

"Bronwen's story is what the gospel is all about. This story underlines the fact that Jesus came to see lives transformed; that following Jesus brings colour, joy and meaning to the individual. God stories such as Bronwen's need to be told and re-told so that people realise that God is not found in the musty study alone, but in the lives of all those who have embraced this wonderful grace-filled message."

– Phil Baker – Senior Pastor, Riverview Church Perth Aus; author and speaker.

"Bronwen's story is one of great victory and breakthrough. Her life was a huge mess, but she just kept looking until she found her answer. Her answer was finding the truth and the life that lies in Jesus Christ. Her life, now changed for good and forever, is a testimony of the true life changing power of the gospel. With man some things are possible, but with God all things are possible."

– Pastor Mark Ramsey – Senior Pastor, Citipointe COC Brisbane Aus; speaker.

"I found your testimony to be a great encouragement and an affirmation of the miracle of a 'new creation in Christ'. Bronwen, your book is an inspiration and a reminder to people like me that the age of miracles is far from past! You are a living witness to His healing and transforming power."

– Major Brian Watters AO – Member, International Narcotics Control Board.

"Reading of the experiences that Bronwen Healy has encountered, one meets the power of God head-on that is released in a person's life upon being united with Christ. What a journey! 'Trophy of Grace' is confronting and care-fronting, challenging and encouraging, gripping and releasing. But most of all it a testimony of the grace of the Lord Jesus, evident in a life broken before Him."

– Rev Dr David Loder – General Superintendent, Queensland Baptists.

"Speaking with authority and experience as an insider and a survivor saved by grace; Bronwen offers us a different perspective to popular culture. With disarming honesty and the courage to bare her soul, she gives a frank account of her deepest secrets, her failings and her sins. As Bronwen narrates it, the salvation of this lost generation truly lies in doing His works and walking and abiding in His love. She is proof."

– Dr Stuart Reece – Naltrexone doctor, researcher, carer and friend.

"This book is a frank and candid window on the pathway to an addiction-based lifestyle of a typical Brisbane teenager. Bronwen's story gives you a graphic insight to what life is really like in schools, youth culture, drug sub-culture and the sex trade and needs to be read and heard by anyone who is interested in what really goes on. This book is a pungent and unique contribution to the resources available for those who want to understand addiction and the way to freedom from the voice of one who has experienced it from the inside and found real and lasting freedom."

– Dr David Hunt – Naltrexone doctor, Pastor and friend.

"Bronwen is a walking miracle. By rights she should be dead and buried, for that is where her drug addiction and lifestyle were surely dragging her. Instead she is a vivacious mother of two, a warm and persuasive communicator, and a devout Christian. I suppose she is just glad to be alive. Her book is charged with hope and love."

– Father Gregory Jordan, S.J.

" 'Trophy of Grace' is a courageous offering to help others who have lost their way. As a close observer of her changed life, I would endorse her desire to use her experience as a warning and a hope for others who have travelled down the same path. As a pastor I am so proud of her book, and even more thrilled by the life she leads as proof of the truth of her written words."

– Pastor Jan Campbell – Citipointe COC, Brisbane Aus.

" 'Trophy of Grace' will take you on the very personal journey of Bronwen Healy's life. With a vulnerable and open heart Bronwen shares the intricate details of her struggles and triumphs. The personable approach she takes to the book places you inside her world. It is here that you will identify with some of your own struggles and take comfort in the answers and the hope she shares."

– Pastor Brian Mulheran – Associate Pastor, Citipointe COC, Brisbane Aus.

"Bronwen Healy's journey from self-destruction to life-giving ministry is a beacon of hope that all can never be lost. Her words are filled with candour, absorbing detail, poignant meditation, and a saintly hunger to walk with God, with relentless discernment, ponderance and resplendence along the way. A remarkable soul, whose story should be read, re-read and spread."

– Alistair Barros – Qld State President, Australian Family Association.

Book Dedication

I would like to dedicate this book to my best friend and my strength, my Lord and Saviour Jesus Christ.

I need to thank my very precious husband Jason for being the patient and loving man of integrity that he is to me.

My miracle daughter Grace for being such an amazing blessing in my life, I love you so very much my precious girl.

To my precious blessing from above, Rebekah Joy; for the light that you are to my life.

To our treasured Lauryn, you have come into our world and blessed us over and abundantly. We adore you little one!

To all three of our girls - God has a big and mighty plan for each one of you and it is my honour to stand beside you, as your mum, and cheer you on. Every day I look at you and I am reminded of His love, grace and mercy. I love you!

Thank Yous

There are so many people whose love, prayers and support for me and my family have helped to make this book all that it is. To all of you I pray God's richest blessing over your lives and the lives of your families. May you prosper just as your souls prosper.

To my very special parents Margaret and John thank you for being who you are and loving me through to become the woman that I am today, and for being such awesome grandparents to Grace and Rebekah, I love you more than words can say.

To Deanna and your precious family, thank you for being the creative inspiration that you are to me, for your honesty and encouragement, for being in my life in the right place at the right time, I love you so much my special friend. Damian, a special thank you to you and your amazing staff. Thank you for your wisdom and your patience with me. Your work on this project has been so priceless, and so appreciated. Bless you for all that you are and all that you have done.

To Rhonda and Ian, thank you for being fantastic in-laws to me and wonderful grandparents to Grace and Rebekah, your words of encouragement have inspired me to reach out to God in a new way and to be all that He created me to be.

To the awesome Prayer Team for "Trophy of Grace", you have all been so amazing and giving of your prayers, time and commitment and for that I thank you. Thank you for being such willing and abiding prayer warriors – you have given us an indescribable gift. We honestly could not have made it through without you – each and every one of you is so precious to us. Thanks for standing with us!

To Becky Lucas, thank you and Aaron for believing in my testimony enough to encourage me to put it on paper, your words are always so refreshing to me and my soul, you sing straight into my spirit and for that I thank you.

To Nadine, and your wonderful husband Mike, thank you both so much for believing in me, and my family, and for your constant encouragement and the blessing of your time for us. Nadine thank you for taking my good book and turning it into a great book. I know that your time and efforts will be richly rewarded. You are amazing.

To Brian, and your precious wife Viv, you have been such a source of wisdom and guidance for me with this project. You have been so patient and understanding with me and so willing to vouch for me. Your ideas and suggestions have been priceless. I know that God will bless you for your input into my life and into this book. You are great.

To precious Jan, and wonderful Peter, thank you so much for your love and encouragement with this project and our whole lives. Jan thank you for your wisdom and counsel and for helping me to make this a book of real integrity. Be blessed.

To Dr Stuart Reece, thank you for your unfailing support and prayers, and for believing in me from the day that I met you, you have helped to give me a new life – and for that I will be eternally grateful.

To Aureole, thank you and Tony, for being the woman that spoke the title of this book into my spirit, for your wisdom and for always knowing when all I needed was a cuddle, you are so special to me.

To Kylie, thank you Michael and Harmony, for being my friend, for standing by me when no-one else would, for speaking out on my behalf, for loaning me the computer that made me able to make this dream a reality. God will honour you for all that you are and all that you have done for me.

To Eliana, thank you so much for believing in me and for encouraging me to follow through with the destiny that the Lord has planned for me, you are so special to me!

To my brother Adam, thank you for always loving me despite of my circumstances, you are the best brother that God could have chosen for me and I love you, and miss you, very much.

To Arlene, thank you for never letting me go and for always standing by me, for being the first person who spoke real words of life into my dying spirit, I will never forget your love and your prayers for me.

To Ben, thank you for always believing in me and standing by me and my dreams. For stepping up and sowing in to the vision of this book and this ministry. Love you heaps.

To my precious friend Viv, and to your beautiful family, thank you for loving me and for listening to me when all I needed to do was talk, for your wonderful cuddles and our special times of just laughing together, I love you my special friend.

To all of the ladies that have been a part of the 'Be Blessed Ladies Group'. You girls are so awesome. Thank you for your unceasing prayer and support, never ending love and kindness. You all mean so much to me – thanks for helping to stretch me into the woman that God has called me to be.

To every person that chose to step out of the boat and on to the water with me. Without your support, prayers, gifts and belief in this project it would not be. I thank you all for helping to make this dream a reality. I pray that God will multiply all that you have sown into me and this book. You are amazing.

A special thank you to all of the people that appear in my book; for sharing with me a story that needs to be told!

Genesis 50:20 – "But as for you, you meant evil against me; but God meant it for good, in order to bring it about as it is this day, to save many people alive" (NKJV)

Revelation 12:11 – "And they have overcome (conquered) him by means of the blood of the Lamb and by the utterance of their testimony, for they did not love and cling to life even when faced with death" (AMP)

Contents

Foreword

Very soon after the situation with Kent I moved into a one bedroom flat on the other side of town; in New Farm. I saw it as a completely fresh start, after the fire and everything else I just wanted something new that I could call my own. I had been living at 'Rodmaun' for over 18 months, which seemed like a long time to me then. The place that I moved to was very old and funky; not unlike the feel that 'Rodmaun' had. The block had young and creative-types living in it. There was a fashion designer, a DJ, a photographer, and an artist; and there was me. A semi-depressed, part-time cinema worker, part-time model, whose boyfriend was a junkie, who had just had an abortion, whose house had just burned down and who had just had a mini-affair with her best friend. My life seemed to be so disastrous. I was unsure of where I was going or what I was doing. I spent most of my life stoned on pot; trying very hard for my reality to blur into some kind of non-existence. I found what I thought to be the perfect answer in Jack: heroin.

Now all that I had to do was convince Jack that he needed to give me some. He kept refusing. He and I had been together for almost a year and a half and he had been using heroin everyday; although I was still yet to use any, and at the time nothing that anybody said to me would have made me change my mind. I was determined to try some heroin. I had seen most of my current friends and friends that had disappeared from my life using it and thought that the numbness they all seemed to experience was exactly what I needed at the time. I gave no thought to the fact that everybody that I had seen try it was now addicted to it; that thought never even entered my mind.

It is so plain to see now just how deceived I was at the time.

My so-called "break" finally came one Saturday after Jack had been to the stall at the Valley Markets with his dad, Alan, which happened to be just down the road from where I was living. He and Will came over to my place and asked me if they could borrow some money. Jack had already spent the money that he had earned that day at the stall and they needed more money to 'get on' to more heroin. They both knew that I had been bugging Jack to get some for me, but even that night he kept saying that he never wanted me to have any. I ended up telling them that they could have $200 so long as they gave me some. They, and their addictions, eventually gave in to me and my money. Little did I know that I would only need a small amount. Even $10 worth would have been enough. As it was, because they had been able to buy so much with the money that I had given them, they ended up giving me almost $50 worth.

As I had already shot up speed and ecstasy in the past, the actual experience of shooting up wasn't strange for me. But the tingling sensation that I got immediately as the liquid entered my vein was all consuming. By giving me $50 worth of the drug, Jack had given me enough to make me very 'stoned' and also very sick. Heroin, in large amounts, makes people vomit a lot. In time I would come to know that either too much or not enough of the drug gives your body the same reaction. As it was I spent most of the night feeling very nauseated, lying on the couch trying to watch videos between 'nodding off' (the desired effect from taking heroin being a semi sleep state) and vomiting. Not a pleasurable experience to say the least. Unfortunately for me I saw it as 'the best vomit' that I had ever had. I had no idea at the time just how deceived I was. Jack and Will had been hoping that by giving me such a large amount and me being so sick that it would put me off heroin; but it had the opposite effect. A week later I wanted more. Jack gave in and soon gave in to me every few days after all every time he got some for me he got some himself. How foolish I was not to be able to see what was going on. I was so blinded by my deep (and unhealthy) love for Jack and my newfound love for this drug called heroin.

Introduction

A very special friend of mine once introduced me to a friend of hers by saying, "This is Bronwen, she is a trophy of grace". At the time I was in need of some encouragement about the writing of this book and as soon as she had said it I knew that the Lord had given me the title in those three very precious words. It is now up to me to seek God and believe for Him to bless the words that are to follow that they in turn can be a blessing to all of the people that are going to read this book. I believe that people will read this book and their lives will be changed by the true account that I am going to share.

The word trophy means; thing kept as a prize or memento of any contest or success; pile of enemy spoil set up after victory. The word grace means; favour of God, divine regenerating and inspiring influence (The Australian Pocket Oxford Dictionary, Oxford University Press, Melbourne). These words best describe who I am now and the aim of this book is to give you some insight as to why this is such a truth in my life today. If I were to describe to you my life today you would have no understanding of the true meaning of the title. Therefore, I am going to go back so that you can gain an understanding of where I am coming from.

Chapter 1

Planted In My Memory

I was born on the 19th of April in the year 1975. I don't really remember too much from my early childhood. I know that my dad was an alcoholic and that my mum decided to get pregnant for a second time as a means of trying to tame his ways. As to be expected this wasn't the case. When I was about two and a half my mum left dad. One day she just came in and told my brother Adam, who is five years older than me, to pack his and my things and that we were going to stay at one of her friend's places. I don't know how long we stayed there but I do know that when my dad did make contact with her again that he had joined Alcoholics Anonymous and was working hard at staying sober. After a while of him continuing to stay sober we returned home. My mum joined Al-Anon for the families and friends of alcoholics, and all of our lives would never be the same again.

One of my earliest memories is of sitting under the table at mum's Al-Anon meetings and reciting the serenity prayer at the closing of the meeting. I would have been almost four years of age. "God grant me the serenity to accept the things I cannot change, courage to change the things I can and the wisdom to know the difference". I would sit under the table and draw or read books but I always joined in when it was time for the closing prayer. There is so much wisdom in those words and there was so much inspiration in the prayer for both of my parents. My mum collected the prayer in all forms such as on plates, magnets and stickers. You name it, we had it. They were all over the house everywhere you looked. They were words to live by for her and for dad.

When I turned five I was old enough to join Alateen, a group for the children of alcoholics. I wasn't really old enough to join in but I would sit and flick through the comics that they had, literature for children. A very special lady named Joanie King was our sponsor and in charge of the meetings. She would always give me the biggest hugs and let me sit on her lap; gifts that I will never forget and will always treasure.

As time went by my mum got more and more involved in the fellowship and the loving family that she had discovered and we would always have people in our home: people in need of love, acceptance (and, of course, a cup of tea). I know now that at the time it was the best thing possible for both mum and dad, they needed the special love that was being shared to totally fill their lives. They needed to fill the void that years of active alcoholism had created inside of them. It seemed to be their way of filling in the gaps.

It seemed as though we were always having get-togethers of some kind. Picnics and barbeques, either at someone's house or at Queens Park in Moonee Ponds or at Brimbank Park; of course my mum was always the coordinator. I remember that they were always so much fun. I had a lot of friends in the group and we would run around or go swimming. I especially remember that we were always laughing. Laughter is such important medicine for all children but especially for the children of alcoholics who have experienced such fear and brokenness. The Christmas parties were great; Father Christmas was always there with gifts and lollies for all of us kids, truly a time to remember.

From a young age I always loved school. Even before regular school started I went to kindergarten and I loved it there. We were always making things for me to take home. Paintings, drawings and jewellery made from pasta for my mum to wear. One of the things that I made to take home was a bookmark that I had decorated and my teacher wrote on for me. It said; To Mummy love Bronwen. My mum still cherishes it to this day. We were always playing in the small playground that they had there. In the sandpit or in the wooden castle I never minded where I was so long as I could play and have a good time. I loved story time at kindy; a time to escape into another place, another time – some things never change. I made some very special friends at kindy; people that I would share my formative years with, people that I will never forget.

Strangely enough in the time that I was at kindy I made friends with some people that I would continue to be close friends with for a very long time Darren, Ross, Nathan and Kerry. The five of us would spend all of our playtime together, doing whatever. Darren was the most helpless of us all; he had asthma and was quite weak and was also very sensitive, and I became closer to him than to any of the others. I would sit with him when he was having an attack so that he didn't have to be alone. I liked that he felt comfortable enough with me to let me help him. Even at four years of age I knew that I wanted to help people in need, I just didn't know how it would become real for me. We all just loved being kids having lots of fun and monkeying around with each other at any given opportunity. We had no idea at the time just how important friendship was, but we would all soon discover how important we were to each other.

We all went into Moonee Ponds Central School. Starting off in grade prep, I was almost five years old. I am glad that I already had friends that I knew from kindy or it would have been much more daunting. I always enjoyed the challenges that I was faced with at school, even from a very early age. The whole concept of learning was very exciting to me. Learning to read and write were my favourite things to do because then I could step into the same escapism that I had loved at story-time whenever I chose to; which seemed to be most of the time. From the time I was about seven I used to turn my bedroom light off at night and say that I was going to sleep but, instead, I would read under the covers with a torch. One night my mum cottoned on to what I was doing and warned me that I was destroying my eyes and that one day I would need glasses if I didn't stop doing it. I didn't listen and at the age of thirteen was fitted for my first pair of glasses, which I still need to see properly to this very day.

The years passed by at school so quickly. I was very active in school life and out of school doing a variety of things such as Little Athletics, jazz ballet, callisthenics and playing sports such as softball and netball. I loved the challenge of learning new skills and trying to master them. I even tried to learn the flute at one stage, but no matter how much I enjoyed listening to music I was never very good at making my own. I loved going to the library and I saw it not only as a place of knowledge, but somewhere quiet where I could go to just be me.

Although one of the things we did in the library as part of the school curriculum was R.E (religious education). I don't know why but I hated it and the only way I could get out of it was to ask my mum to write me a note that we weren't religious people and therefore I didn't have to attend. Instead I got free time in the library. Because of the fellowship and knowledge that I was receiving from the Alateen meetings mum wrote the note and did so every year so I never had to attend R.E again. It just seemed so boring and pointless talking about a God who seemed so unreal to me.

When I was about ten years old one of my relatives had a baby girl, Simone. I thought that she was just the most special little girl. I would walk the long way home almost everyday to stop in at Nance's place just to help out with Simone. I would change her nappy, bathe and feed her. At the weekends I would go there with my friends; either Rani, Jade or Tammy, and we would stay there to help out with Simone. We would crash out in the lounge room watching music videos and make a huge mess in the kitchen; we always had so much fun.

The girlfriends that I made at that time of my life were of such importance to me. They helped to shape the woman that I was to become. There were five of us that spent all of our time together; Anna, Jade, Rani, Tammy and I. But there was one of them that I became closer to than any of the others, Rani. Rani and I were very similar in so many ways. We were both tomboys who also enjoyed being girls. We were both very sporty and we both loved music. When we would walk down the street together people would ask us if we were sisters; we did look alike in that we both had blond hair and blue eyes. We liked the same things and even had the same taste in the boys that we liked. I loved my time with her; we could just be in each other's company, without speaking, and I would feel as though it was time well spent. I had no idea the full impact that we would have on one another's lives or to what extent our friendship would matter to either of us, but in time I would definitely find out.

For the Christmas holidays we started going to a place on the Victorian Peninsula called Tootgarook. A family we had been friends with since I had started kindy always went there and one year we went with them and from then on it seemed to become a bit of a tradition. It was always such a good time. There were so many kids. We would spend our days doing things such as swimming in the passage through the seaweed out to the sandbanks to make special sandcastles, playing cricket on the beach, catching crabs and sometimes we would go roller-skating. I will never forget those holidays; they will be forever planted in my memory.

Our whole family would go to Tootgarook. My brother Adam would sometimes bring a friend with him and they would sometimes get up to quite a bit of mischief. One year when I was about ten and Adam was fifteen, he went missing one night. The next morning he told mum and dad that he had been picked up by a bunch of skinheads in a car. He even drew pictures of what they apparently looked like. It turned out that he had met a girl and spent the night with her but didn't want to get into trouble. My brother was always funny like that.

New Years Eve in Tootgarook was always a blast. We were such hooligans we would do things like wrap wet toilet paper around the traffic lights so that every car drove through them. We would run up and down the road with anything that made a noise, making as big a one as possible. We would try and stay up as late as we could. Such innocence, such fun, such memories. An average night would find us playing games of some kind; Trivial Pursuit, Monopoly and Uno were our favourites. We would play until we couldn't keep our eyes open any more or until a stray mosquito would find its way into the tent and annoy us all enough that we would go to bed. I will never forget one night a mosquito stung me on both eyelids and; because I am allergic to them, my eyes swelled up so much that I couldn't open them. Looking back it must've been so funny to look at me, but at the time I was really upset. Actually, I think that was the last year that we went down there for Christmas, not because of the mosquito episode, but because our lives were all starting to take a change.

When I finished Grade 6 the headmaster of the school called me to her office; I knew I wasn't in trouble because I hadn't done anything wrong, but that didn't stop me feeling quite anxious about the meeting with her. When I sat down she started to tell me how proud she was of all of my efforts throughout my time at the school and how she felt honoured to know a young girl of such strength of character. I was embarrassed; it was the first time that someone of such high authority in my life had ever spoken words like that into my life. Any comment that any of my teachers made were always about my academic achievements, not my character. She told me that at awards night they were going to be giving three students citizenship awards for all that they had done at the school and for the school, and that I was going to be one of the recipients. I felt so proud that just being who I was seemed to be something special and that other people recognised as special also. My parents were so excited for me and so proud that after the early childhood that I had I seemed to have grown into a beautiful and caring young girl; I was so happy.

The change from primary to secondary school was not that bad for me because I stayed on at the same school. Moonee Ponds Central offered the first two years of high school as a means of helping students adjust to the big move gradually. So all of the friends that I had in primary school stayed together anyway. I made lots of new friends too and in that sense the dynamics of my life altered. Having new friends and trying to get used to changing classrooms for every new lesson was slightly confusing at first, but I soon got into the swing of it and started to really love all the new things that I was learning. My favourite subjects were English and Spanish. I loved the whole concept of language and all of the description and beauty that we have in the words that we express. The whole idea of learning a new language excited me, especially Spanish which is such a beautiful language. Sadly, now all I remember is hello and what's your name. Isn't it funny the way we can enjoy something so much at one stage of our lives and as we grow different things become important to us?

It was the first year of high school for me, Grade 7, and I was very excited. I had my very first job! One of my mum's friends owned a fast food convenience store that was a 10-minute tram ride from school. Her name was Jill; she was and always will be a very special lady and a great friend to my mum. She knew that I was a keen worker around the home and that I was very focused with my school work and so she asked me if I wanted to go and work at the store 3 afternoons a week. I was trying to save up for my own portable stereo and so I jumped at the opportunity. I loved working there, I felt like such a big person. I would clean the place from top to bottom, stack the shelves and the fridges and when I had been there for a while I was even allowed to serve customers. It was one of the first times that anybody had ever placed that much trust in me and I appreciated the opportunity so much. I will always remember my time there as being very special, helping me to grow and teaching me the ethics of being a solid and strong worker; something that I have never forgotten.

For the school holidays of 1987 I went up to Queensland. I travelled on a plane by myself and was staying with friends. Mum and dad were going somewhere else on an adventure of their own and Adam was then old enough to be doing his own thing. About two weeks before I was due to return I got a call from mum that the place that they had gone to had flooded and that they were heading up to Queensland for the remainder of their holidays. As a family we all fell in love with Queensland and when we returned to Melbourne mum and dad put the house on the market and we decided to move there permanently.

Saying good-bye to my friends in Melbourne was difficult; many of them I had known since I was really young. For me it was especially difficult saying good-bye to my boyfriend of that time. His name was Matthew and he and I had been seeing each other for over a year. I remember feeling as though someone had ripped my heart out and jumped up and down on it. All this and I wasn't even thirteen yet. Matthew was a really special part of my life; kind, gentle and understanding; and unlike most of the males that I had grown up with. My friends were all full of good wishes for my future but I couldn't help but feel as though I was leaving a part of myself there with them in Moonee Ponds. It was strange to pack up our house there as it was the only place I had ever known to live. I really loved that home in Stuart Street and will always remember it fondly.

My brother Adam decided to stay behind to follow through on his panel beating apprenticeship and he kept our family dog, Rocky, there with him also. Saying good-bye to both of them was very emotional. We may not have been the closest of siblings but he was the only brother I would ever know and he had given me many memories to hold on to, both good and bad.

When we first arrived in Brisbane we stayed with my dad's brother Peter and his family while we were looking for somewhere to live. I don't remember how long we were there but I do know that we looked at a lot of different houses before we found the ultimate Brisbane family home for us. It was in the suburb of Ferny Hills, which is about half an hour on the train to the city. It was awesome. We all loved it from the moment that we first saw it. It was a three bedroom, double storey home with a pool and a huge room downstairs that had been a playroom for children, but the moment I walked into it I claimed it as my bedroom and, thankfully, my parents agreed.

Chapter 2

Keeping it Together

One of the most important chapters of my life occurred at around this time of us moving to Brisbane in that I then had to decide which school I was going to attend. As I had always been at the same school in Melbourne, with the same friends, it was a thoroughly nerve racking experience for me. We had some family friends that had moved up to Brisbane a couple of years before us and their girls had gone to Brisbane Girls' Grammar School so it seemed like the obvious choice. We had to go for an interview with the principal of the school so that she could check my school records and probably to make sure that my parents could afford to pay the fees. Girls' Grammar at the time was the most affluent of girls' schools in Brisbane and also the most expensive. I know that my parents couldn't really afford it but they did want what was best for me and so they agreed to pay the amount that was asked.

It was so difficult for me to start at a new school, not only because it was worlds away from Moonee Ponds Central School but also because I was starting in the second term of Grade eight. This meant that everyone had already had a full term to get to know each other and form friendship groups that I presumed would be hard to break into. Thankfully, my presumptions proved me wrong and the form class that I was put into was full of some really special girls and they soon accepted me. I made friends with a group very quickly. We were all very sporty and creative so we seemingly had a lot in common. I very soon became involved with athletics, netball, softball and speech and drama groups; where I also made many more friends. The comfort that I found in these friendships made the transition from Melbourne much easier but I still couldn't help but feel that I didn't really belong.

At the time Expo '88 was on in Brisbane and my dad was working there so we had season passes, so that we could go as often as possible. I would go almost every afternoon after school; it was one of the most amazing experiences of my life. It was almost like going to the countries without having to travel. I gained so much knowledge there. My mum would often come in and meet me and we would explore different parts of the world together. It was a real time of bonding for us. Our worlds had just experienced a big upheaval with the move and those times at Expo were a chance for us to get used to our new lives in a very exciting way. We spent a lot of time just talking and walking; it was really special to me.

Just after we arrived in Brisbane and I had settled in at Girls' Grammar I started going out with a guy who was in grade ten at Nudgee College – an all boy school. His name was Ben. It was a really strange relationship in that we would only ever see each other on weekends, at Expo normally. We talked a lot at first, as you do. Then he wanted to go further physically and I wasn't interested in that, so he dumped me. This was one of my first "grown up" experiences with rejection of that variety; but it certainly would not be my last.

The girls that I had made friends with at Grammar were some of the most popular in Grade eight, not only within the school itself but also with the boys in the private school circle. It wasn't long before we were attending dances at the boy's schools; the most popular of these being the Churchie (Church of England Grammar School) dances. We would see a group of Churchie boys from these dances on weekends and we would also meet up with them in the Fun Park at Expo. The times that we all shared were so innocent, we would just hang around, talking and laughing; they were really good times for me. I had grown up with a couple of really special friends that were males, so it seemed natural to me to be surrounded by male friends again.

I also had the opportunity to make friends with some of the girls from other private schools because I would see them at Expo also and we would often congregate on the platform at Central Station after school. A few of the girls from St Margarets used to catch the same train as me and so we quickly became quite close. Their names were Jacqui, Melinda and Lucinda. I immediately connected with Melinda; she and I were very similar in many ways. I used to love just talking to her about things; we would talk about whatever came to mind at the time. We would spend hours just talking about the universe and about what we thought about spiritual things. I would tell her that I knew there was a power bigger than me watching out for us but that I couldn't say for sure that it was God. We would talk about it and laugh about the whole concept of creation and how amazing life really was to us; just how precious we really were. I loved my special time with her and knew that she would always be very special to me, and she was.

The girls were all so different to me and to the friends that I had grown up with in Melbourne. The first true and real friend that I made at Grammar was a girl named Juel. She started school there in the first term of grade nine and we caught the same train home and got talking on the first day. We were so close; she was like a sister to me. It was strange because we were in none of the same classes but spent as much time together as we could. This, of course, got the rumour-mill running at school that we were 'lesbians', which was really funny actually, because at the time we both had steady boyfriends and often double-dated on weekends. Juel and I had a lot in common other than our mutual love of speech and drama. Our musical tastes were so different to those of the rest of the group in that we loved rap and hip-hop music; bands like Run D.M.C, Public Enemy and the Beastie Boys. I am sure that my musical tastes of the time were influenced by one of my brothers many stages, that of break-dancing in the mid-'80's. One of our favourite songs of the time was by a band called Soul to Soul and it was called 'Get a Life'. We would sing in it my room at Ferny Hills at the top of our lungs and I'm sure my parents despised it within the first week.

For my fourteenth birthday my parents let me have a party at our house. I'm sure they presumed that a household of private school kids couldn't cause too much damage. Well, many of the boys brought bottles of alcohol and many of them had been drinking before they even arrived. My mum had laid out a huge spread of food and soft drink, which was soon devoured. My parents, to their credit, gave us the downstairs area to have the party and it was only when they heard bottles being smashed on the road that they intervened. Soon the neighbours called the police and the party was brought to a very abrupt end. Most of my girl friends were sleeping over and hadn't been drinking so they were allowed to stay, but mum called all of the boys parents and they were sent home. At the time I was a mixture of emotions; embarrassed for myself, sad for my parents and angry at the boys for spoiling my first, and last, party at that house. My parents were understandably angry with me mainly for thinking that I had orchestrated the whole thing (which I hadn't). They grounded me for a month after that, for the first time ever.

Another of the things that Juel and I shared together was our desire to start smoking cigarettes. Just after I turned 14 we got one of her friends, who was 16, to buy our first packet of them – Peter Jackson Extra Mild 20's; I will never forget them. Juel had already smoked a few cigarettes in her time and so she showed me how to inhale. I felt so foolish and I must have looked ridiculous to her, but I was determined and within a few weekends of trying I finally got it right and they stopped giving me headaches. Both of my parents smoked and so I had no fear of them ever smelling it on either of us, so we spent most of our weekends at my house. We would walk around to the local school and smoke and then go home.

One of my special friends Jordan would sometimes come over on the weekends and hang out with us as well. He had a crush on Juel at the time and for a long time after. Jordan was one of those male friends of mine that was just like a brother to me. Our friendship was one of mutual respect and honesty and we were very loyal friends for many years. I would talk to him about all of my boyfriend troubles and he would very patiently listen to me for hours on end. I admired him so much for being so real with me at all times and I loved spending time with him. He stood by me for many years, through many troubles, and I will always love him for that.

During that year, 1989, my brother and his soon-to-be fiancee Lynda moved up to Brisbane to live with us. Adam and I had never really gotten along very well and it was only at this time that we both made an effort to work on our relationship. I guess it helped that we were both that little bit older, and had spent nearly 18 months living apart, which made us both realise that we were going to be brother and sister forever and it was time to do something about it. We were spending a lot of time together driving around in his car listening to Guns 'n' Roses blaring, going to the drive-ins with Lynda and watching videos. One weekend they took me to the Gold Coast with them and we stayed in a cabin. It was that weekend that we all got very drunk together and Adam taught me how to blow smoke rings – a grand achievement in any smokers' life. We never really discussed our childhood much but seemed to have made a decision to start afresh. I am so glad for the time that they lived with us as it gave me memories of my brother that I will always cherish; something that had been lacking up until that time.

During my fifteenth year many changes took place in my life. Noticeably, I got glasses for my poor eyesight and braces for my bad teeth. Both were horrifying for me at first, but something that I soon got used to and am now grateful for. My parents worked so hard to give me everything that I needed, including the huge cost of the braces which they were still paying for months after I got them off two and a half years later. I don't think that I showed them enough appreciation for all those things they did for me then.

I was very close to my mum and we would do a lot of things together and I would often tell her that I loved her. My dad and I had a different type of relationship. We were always so excited just to catch the train home together in the afternoons and would catch up on the day's goings on during that half-hour trip. I still cherish the memory of those times together, with each of them. Unfortunately during that year of my life dad and I started to drift apart quite noticeably. I had no idea what was going on for him and it was years later that I discovered that he had actually had a type of nervous breakdown. He would prowl around the house at night unsure of what he was doing and eventually he told me that one night when he had gotten off the last train from work to come home he nearly chose to step in front of it rather than keep living. When he was explaining it to me he said that he was still unsure as to why he didn't do it. Only now, years later, do I understand what, or Who, stopped him.

During the September holidays my dad got me a job working at Hoyts 8 in the Myer Centre. I was one of the floor staff; tearing tickets and cleaning cinemas became my life for those two weeks. I loved my job and took great pride in what I did there, which may sound crazy; after all, it was just a cinema job. But it gave me a chance to prove to myself that I could do anything that I put my heart and mind into, even clean cinemas! The manager obviously liked what I did as well because I was then offered a part-time job for the Christmas holidays. I loved having the extra money also. It meant that I could buy my own clothes and buy nice gifts for my parents and friends.

During those Christmas holidays of 1990 something really changed inside of me. It was difficult to understand at the time. I had always had a great love of movies and I guess working at the cinema really cemented that as the desire of my heart. I decided that I not only wanted to clean cinemas but I wanted my movies to be shown on the screens in the cinemas. I wanted to be a scriptwriter and director. I decided that I wasn't going back to Girls' Grammar on the grounds that they didn't have film and television as a subject. I told my parents, who have always been really supportive of me creating my own destiny, and they told me if I could find a school that gave it as a subject that they would allow me to go there. They didn't agree with my decision to leave Grammar because they thought that staying there would help my future, but I truly believed that my future was in the movies. So I called around and found out that the school best known for its film and television department was Indooroopilly State High School. From that moment my life would never be the same again.

The school was on the other side of town and my mum took me there for my interview. I will never forget that day, and I'm sure that my mum won't either. When we pulled up at the front of the school my mum nearly started crying. There were a whole lot of very "different" looking people. People known as hippies, swampies and homeboys to name a few. She looked at me and said, "Bron what are you doing? You don't belong here." My response to her was, "Trust me mum, have a little faith in me." We had an interview with the principal who told me I was out of the school's catchment area due to living at Ferny Hills (45 minutes away by train), but that they would accept me anyway and I could start the next day. We were given a tour of the school and the minute that we walked into the edit suite I knew I had made the right decision. On the way home in the car my mum cried most of the way and later on when we were telling my dad about the day he just shook his head and told me that the final decision was mine. I started school there two days later.

I will never forget my first day at Indooroopilly High. To start with I had to get up at 6:15 a.m. to make the 7:05 a.m. train to get to school on time. I have never been a morning person but I made the effort to be extra alert so my parents could see how serious I was about the changes I had made to my life. When I got to school my first discovery was that my form class was my art class; I couldn't ask for much more than that. I sat at the only table in the room that had a spare seat. I had no idea that the people at that table would influence and change my life forever. There were three guys and their names were James, Ian and Bill. They all had long 'hippy-type' hair and great big smiles on their faces. I was so naive I had no idea that these smiles were due to them being stoned on pot (marijuana). They were so friendly to me and welcomed me with open arms, something that didn't change for the entire time I was at that school.

We had all of our classes together and immediately my favourite class was, of course, film and television. I had an incredible teacher; her name was Helen Strube. She could see my passion for the subject and took me under her wing straight away. I will never forget all that she did for me, in class and out of it. Most of the people in my class put 100% effort into getting stoned before school but made very little effort at school, but they were really lovable people, real characters. I excelled in the classroom for most of my subjects; my desire to learn and gain knowledge had only increased as I had grown older. I also loved my speech and drama classes and once again had a phenomenal teacher for that subject; her name was Adrianne Jones. She also encouraged me to excel in class. Those two women will forever be imprinted in my heart and mind as two people who believed that I could achieve; and I did.

Not suprisingly, the girls that I had been friends with at Grammar cut me loose when I chose to go from the most affluent private school in Brisbane to a public high school with a doubtful reputation; though I never saw it as a loss. I thankfully stayed in contact with Juel the whole time. The other awesome thing was that Jordan decided to leave Churchie and go to Indooroopilly High also. He also wanted to focus on his art and Film and television and believed that school was the best place for him.

I had been seeing a guy called Rod, Jordan's best friend, for almost six months and he was a really sweet guy. He also happened to be the person with who I chose to lose my virginity. He made the whole occasion very special with lots of flowers and candles; I did feel very precious to him. Unfortunately, our relationship was always better as a friendship and we broke up, not long after that happened. I never realised just how important my virginity was to me until after it was gone. One thing that I have always regretted was not saving myself for the person I would spend my entire life with. At the time, though, the whole concept of 'entire life' seemed like a distant reality somewhere in the back of my mind. Rod and I did actually remain friends for a long while afterwards, which I was very glad about.

After Rod and I had broken up I started to spend most of my spare time with James and Ian. They were both such funny guys. They were incredible friends to me, willing to go out of their way for me at any time. In the past I had only really experienced that with both Rani in Melbourne and Juel at Grammar. Loyal friends are, unfortunately, very hard to come by but I had certainly found two of them in James and Ian. I would hang out with them and it was strange because they would get stoned with me in the room, but because they knew that I wasn't into pot, or drugs of any kind, they would never offer me any and I never thought to ask for some. After they had smoked pot they would get really quiet and, as they were both incredible artists, they would spend hours just sketching, doodling and sometimes painting. Those suited me fine because it meant that I could read or study and not feel like an outsider because I wanted to do that. They always respected my decisions and never tried to make me sway from who I was; which is also a very rare quality in friendship.

I will never forget the first time both James and Ian came over to our house for dinner. My parents had both heard me talking about these wonderful new friends that I had made at Indooroopilly and I guess after my friends from Grammar they wouldn't have known what to expect. However, I am sure that they didn't expect two guys whose hair was longer than mine (and mine was below my shoulders), with big dopey grins on their faces to be sharing our dinner table. As is my parents' way, they did welcome them into our home, based solely on the fact that they were friends of mine. They talked to my dad about movies and as he was a projectionist, that whole concept seemingly fascinated both James and Ian. I think mum just wanted to know more about them, who they were and where they were going. It was so very different to the many dinners that we had shared with any of the girls from Grammar, but my parents seemed to accept these two guys the way they were; which was exceptionally different and very lovable.

Grade 11 moved along quite well for me. I really enjoyed my new school and put all of my efforts into doing well academically, creatively and athletically. I joined the school's basketball team as it was a sport that I had always enjoyed watching but was never offered for playing at Grammar. I was fortunate enough to play in every game for the year, and we made it into the semi-finals but then lost that game. It was an amazing experience for me to get so far in my first season. I was also picked for the school's softball team. I had been playing since the age of about eight. The team made the finals that year but lost in the final game of the year. And that was the last year that I was in a sporting team of any kind; something that I loved to do but I knew in the next year, grade 12, my focus had to be academic as I would never be in Grade 12 again. I wanted to get it right the first time.

In the final term of Grade 11 for film and television everyone in the class had to write a script in their choice of genre. I chose social-realism and wrote a script about a troubled youth and called it "Changing Times". We then had to split the class into two groups and read all of the scripts and choose one for that group to make. My script was unanimously chosen and I was totally thrilled. How exciting that one of my dreams of making movies was becoming a small reality for me already.

It was really hard work and took up a lot of time. In fact most of my spare time, when I wasn't at school or at work, was spent working on the film. Hours and hours of writing out shooting-scripts and trying to help James with the storyboard as well as trying to organise all of the locations, props and people that would be acting in it. It was certainly a challenge, and I thrived on it. Helen was an awesome help for me at any time of need, encouraging me to keep it together at all times. Being the scriptwriter and the director as well as the only female in the group proved to be difficult at times and it was then that Helen would step in and encourage me to keep my chin up and just go for it. When the final product was finished almost two months after the assignment was started I was so proud of it. Thankfully, the film received an A grade and I received an A+ for my involvement in the production. At the end of the year we also had Film and Television Awards in which the film won "Best Original Script" and also "Best Movie". I was so amazed at what could happen when I really put my mind to it. My dreams felt as though they were slowly becoming a reality. My parents were so proud of me and I was glad for that also.

The school holidays of that year basically passed by without much happening. I was working at Hoyts at least five days a week, sometimes doing double shifts. When I wasn't working I would spend time with James and Ian, just hanging out. I made a lot of money that summer for someone who wasn't even 16 yet. I saved most of it in the bank because I was too busy or too tired to do anything with it. I was very proud of all that I achieved during those holidays. I was the only person in my circle of friends that had a job of any kind. Therefore they all spent the holidays smoking pot, drawing and just hanging out together, none of which appealed to me at all at that time of my life.

When the school year of 1992 started I entered it with a feeling of great expectancy. Starting Grade 12 was really major for me. We had new people in our grade. I had a new film and TV teacher named Martin Kenny and I was excited about the prospect of finishing school after thirteen years of learning. I was excited about my future and where I was going with my life.

I had great teachers, including Mr Kenny. Once I settled into the New Year at school it was time to meet more new people.

The place where we all sat for lunch was soon inundated with new people. Simon O'Grady, who was a really special friend of James and Ian's and a guy that I had sort known the previous year had two new girls in his form class whose names were Sara and Sophie. Their look was different to mine but they turned out to be really great people. I often think about them; that if I judged people because of the way they looked that I would've missed out on some really special memories and friendships.

There was also a new guy in the grade below me who seemed to be kind of a loner. I wasn't sure where he lived but he was one of the few people from the school that caught the train going in my direction towards the city. I watched him for quite a while during the afternoons at the train station. I had seen him sitting under the tree opposite school and wondered who he was. After asking around some of my friends in Grade 11, my friend Libby told me that his name was Will and that he was a real 'groovy' guy. She encouraged me to talk to him one day at the train station – my life would never be the same again after I took those steps towards him.

Will was the type of guy that most people would classify as 'grungy' with his dark sunglasses, flannelette shirts and long messy sandy blond hair. He was everything that I had never been attracted to before, and the epitome of everything that I was attracted to after meeting him. He was kind and tender and spoke so softly. I am still not sure why I liked him but from that moment on I knew that we would somehow end up together. Very soon, after boldly introducing myself to him one day at the train station, he started to sit where we all sat at lunch times and started walking to the train station with us all in the afternoons. When we would get off the train at central train station in the city I would always try to drag out saying good-bye to him until one day I suggested that we go downtown and have a coffee and some cake. We did that and it very soon became a ritual for us, something that we would do together at any given opportunity. Sometimes other people would join us, but it never seemed the same. When we were alone we would talk about anything and everything. Our dreams and goals, our pasts and our hurts. He had been hurt by a girl and his friends at his old school and was very wary about entering into any form of relationship. I remember when he told me that my heart sunk, but I still held on to the vision of us being together one day. I loved his company and we would talk on the phone at nighttime even after spending the afternoons together after school. I am sure that we both knew that it was only a matter of time before we would be in a relationship, and it was.

In April of that year we all went to the movies in town for my birthday and then went to the botanical gardens in the city for the afternoon. Everybody else was smoking joints but Will and I just sat together, talking as usual. Eventually, he suggested that I go back to his place with him to meet his mum and have a coffee on his verandah. It sounded absolutely perfect to me. He lived at Highgate Hill, which is about a half an hour walk from the city. It was such a lovely walk, just him and I for the first time all day. I remember when we were almost there we somehow ended up holding hands with each other; it was one of the most tender moments of my life, up to that point. When we got back to his place I met his mum and then we sat on the verandah for hours talking. We ended up kissing for the first time; it, too, was soft and tender. We had both known what was going to happen between us; we just had no idea when that time would be. Now was the time.

Will was one of the gentlest people that I have ever met. He was always so kind and soft, he never had anything nasty to say about anyone or anything. He was always so positive and he always made me smile. There was nothing he did that I didn't like. Every little thing about him was adorable, that was how I first knew that I was in love with him. I knew because nothing about him annoyed me, and it stayed that way for a very long time. Will truly was a very special guy; a lover and a friend that I will never forget and will always be grateful for. He helped to shape the woman that I would become just by encouraging me to be all that I could be and by never giving up on me and my dreams.

Will's mum's name was Amanda and she, too, was a very special person. A woman who never gave up on her son, a woman who was always there when he needed her; for better or for worse. That also meant that when I became his new girlfriend she took me under her wing and loved and cared for me the way that she did for Will. I loved talking with her about all different types of things; she was very knowledgable, and she loved literature and language. She would always tell me that I was the best thing that had ever happened to Will and that she knew that I was going to bring about some major changes in his life. One of those changes was helping to bring himself out emotionally, by just encouraging him to trust me. Amanda was always willing to lend her ear or her shoulder to us when we needed her and I shared many words with her over many cups of coffee. I didn't know how she put up with us constantly being there, but I would discover that she had a very high threshold for the pain that would be inflicted upon her life by other people. I will forever be grateful to her for her words of wisdom and her understanding of Will and myself; and for knowing when enough was enough.

Will and I had been together for a few months when the issue of sex was raised. The sexual part of our relationship was missing. Because we were so close it didn't really seem to matter, but it also seemed like something that was the obvious next step for us. We had talked about it and I had actually lied to him and told him that I was still a virgin. I guess I wanted him to think of me as pure and I wanted it all to be very special for us. I don't think that I understood that it would be anyway. (It turned out to be one of the first real lessons that I learned about truth and the power of my words; I really hurt him with my lies when he did find out). When we had sex for the first time it did feel really special to Will even though I hadn't thought it would and had told myself that sex didn't matter in our relationship. But I would soon learn that without the love that we had for one another our relationship would not have survived the struggles we would face. Sex was the only way that we knew how to express our love, we just didn't know any better. (I now know the real meaning of love and of sex).

Amidst all of the romancing with Will I was also working on my new friendship with Sara. She was so funny, her family had a farm at Purga which is out the back of Ipswich, and we would often spend the weekends there just talking and laughing. Her mum was an artist and we would spend time in the studio saying that we were doing stuff for school just playing around with all of the paints and bits and pieces. I loved spending time with Sara, she always had a story to tell and she never failed to put a smile on my face. I remember that she used to take me for drives around the farm in her family's 'farm bomb' as we knew it. It was such a laugh, dodging cows and fences. She only ever let me drive once as I was unwise to the farm ways and almost drove off into a ditch and the creek. Sara and I were very different but very similar; I will always have such fond memories of my times with her.

During the second half of grade 12 we were asked to prepare a theatre performance that was at least 10 minutes long, that we would then perform in the school auditorium. Sara and Simon were in a different theatre class to me but, still, James and I struggled hard to get permission to do our performance with them. After much debating we were told to write an outline of our vision for the script and it would be reviewed. As a group we decided to do 'Chaos and Oppression in Society'. This was pretty full-on, considering other groups were doing things like women's issues and racism. But our hearts were in it and we worked hard at the script outline and permission was granted. We knew that, as a group, we would have to work much harder than the others due to the fact that we didn't all share class time together, but we also knew that we could do it. Almost every afternoon for nearly a month we would go to Simon's house and try to work on the script. We decided to use bits from scripts of 'A Clockwork Orange' and 'Waiting for Godot', and the rest we wrote ourselves. We were all so passionate about it and worked really hard. Simon was an incredibly talented actor but usually struggled to do the work in class; however, for this assignment he put in more than his all. He personally wrote our introduction about the subject and performed it so well every time we practiced. We had to perform it for three nights, and when the first performance night came around we were all so excited. The entire performance went off without a problem and it was awesome. We were all so proud of ourselves and of each other. We had done it against all odds, which coincided with most of our life stories. It was the first and last time that we would work so solidly as a group and achieve such greatness. We all got A- for our scripts and performances and we were so happy. None of our lives would ever be the same again. We were on our way up!

One of the other things that became a ritual for us during the second half of the year was lunch times at Keight's house. Keight was a really special young girl who was also in the year below me. She happened to live around the corner from school and so we would all venture there during the school breaks. Lunchtime was the most popular break and there was quite often fifteen or twenty of us there. Many of them would smoke pot in one of the rooms, watch television or just hang out. Will and I would go there and just sit together; it seemed not to matter if we were talking or not, so long as we were together we were happy.

Chapter 3

Against my Grain

During these times at Keight's place one of the guys that went there as well happened to sell pot by the ounce and he offered for Will to take some now and pay for it when he had sold it off in smaller amounts. Will took him up on the offer and when we were back at his place that afternoon I asked him if he minded giving me some to smoke. It was the first time that I had ever smoked pot and Will was the only person that I trusted to be with when the effect kicked in. Some people seemed to get really talkative, others really contemplative and others creative; I guess it was different for everybody. I happened to be one who got really contemplative and it seemed as though when I was stoned I was happy to talk about anything that came to mind for me, absolutely anything; God, the universe and everything about it. It must have seemed really funny for Will who had been smoking it since he was in Grade 8, and I actually didn't mind the effects as much as I thought I would. From then on I would only ever smoke it on the weekends and only once all of my homework and assignments were complete. How strange it must have seemed to people who lit up joints often on the way to the train station on the way home from school that by choice I would wait until all the things that were more important to me were complete.

So I had officially gone against my own grain and decided that I would enter into a new, and what seemed to be exciting, realm of life experience – drugs. It didn't actually seem like that big of a deal once I had started smoking pot. I had it so built up in my mind that it would change my life forever, and, of course, it did.

Towards the end of the year we all started to think about the fact that our school formal was coming up. I had decided that I wasn't going to go because one of my favourite bands, Public Enemy, was playing at Festival Hall that night. James was going to come with me and it was only after spending time with Sara one day when she said to me that she was going to ask James to the formal that I realised it was going to be a once-in-a-lifetime opportunity. Never again would I be in the position to go to my grade 12 formal and, so, at the last minute I changed my mind and decided to go. Of course, my partner was to be Will. I went shopping for a dress the week of the formal, though funnily enough there seemed to be something more important than that on the horizon for everybody else – what drugs to organise. I wasn't going to take anything, due to the fact that I had really only just started smoking pot not long before. I soon realised just how big a night it was going to be and thought I would do drugs after all.

One of the most precious memories that I will ever have about my dad and I was the night of my formal. I had spent very little time getting ready, but I felt like a princess, nonetheless. One of the things that I really wanted to do was to go and visit my dad at work so that he could see that his little girl could be such a beautiful woman. That night I felt like the most beautiful woman in the world; the minute that my dad laid his eyes, he melted. I am still sure that tears welled up in his eyes, as his vision of me became clearer. His little girl was just around the corner from being a woman. I could see his adoration for me and when he hugged me I thought that he was never going to let me go. I think he knew that my life was taking a major change, and he didn't believe that it was for the better. Nonetheless, that night he loved and adored me and told me how beautiful I was and just how proud of me he was. That part of my night I will always cherish and hold close to my heart. That night I knew deep down that my dad was always going to love me; I had no idea of how far I would push that precious love away though, only time could tell that tale.

One of our friends was organising acid trips but all that I understood about them was that they were quite potent and hallucinogenic. I made a decision to wait until half way through the formal before I would take one. When the time was 'right' Sara and I went into the bathrooms and took half of one each. The small piece of cardboard that we chewed on and then swallowed was bright purple with a small yellow symbol on it; I honestly had no idea what it was or exactly what effect it was going to have on me. Within an hour I started to feel a bit strange and people started to seem different to me. Simon was chosen to do a speech on the night because he was someone who had attended the school from the first day of Grade 8. He was all dressed up with make up and everything – Gothic he told me. He got up to do his speech just as my acid trip started to really kick in, so I giggled my way through most of what he said. Five minutes after he finished I couldn't even remember what he had spoken about and that actually scared me a bit.

After Simon had finished his speech, and the other people that were speaking had spoken, dessert was served. I remember talking to Mr Kenny for almost five minutes about how beautiful the strawberries and cream looked. He must have thought that I was definitely on something, though he actually never spoke of the night with me once it was over. Once we had eaten what we could of dessert (I couldn't eat much as it felt horrible in my stomach) we made our way out onto the mall.

One of the guys in our group was in a band and they practised in the old Target building in the middle of the Valley Mall. He had somehow talked his way into hiring out an entire floor of the building for our post-formal party. It was to be a night that we would never forget and as time passed I realised I couldn't actually remember what was happening to me; I was quite freaked out by the whole 'tripping out' experience. I remember going to the roof of the building at one stage of the night and having, what I thought was, a full-blown conversation with a pigeon. Will and James came up and saved me from myself and talked me through most of the rest of the night. The music seemed so loud, as though my head was going to burst, and everybody seemed so animated. At one stage I remember thinking I wished it would all just hurry up and be over. I no idea at that stage what was going to become of my life, but I knew that I didn't want to 'waste' too much time in any state like that!

The remainder of the school year went so quickly, with so much assessment and studying for end of year exams, that it almost passed by unnoticed to me. I just wanted so much to achieve the best that I could and I was more than willing to put in the hard work to do so. While I was busy studying most of the other people in the group, including Will, were busy organising a week away. Not to be anything like the 'Schoolies' week that is celebrated by the majority of people finishing grade 12, this was to be something different, and special. The time finally arrived that we were all to take off to one of the guy's parent's beach house on the Northern NSW coastline. We all organised borrowing cars and whatever we might need to get there, while the guy whose place it was organised all of the drugs. I will never forget when I first walked into the house, looking down onto the table and seeing white powder, tablets, acid trips and marijuana and thinking to myself, "What am I doing here?" So much of that week is a blur to me; I do know that while I was there I shared so much with Will, including my first experience on speed (amphetamines), ecstasy and both of these together. I remember sitting on the beach for hours on end just staring; at the sky, at the water, into people's eyes, thinking about the wonder of creation. It was a pity that it took being 'high' on drugs to feel like I could enter into this realm of wonderment and peace.

When we returned to Brisbane and normality I applied for a job at the Metro cinema in Edward Street in the City. I had been working at Hoyts 8 now for over two years and, thankfully, had happened to apply for the new job the same day that somebody else had quit and was given an interview and then the job. I loved my job at the Metro, it was an arty type of cinema that showed mostly foreign films and classics on Sundays. I met some really interesting people and made some special friends with the other staff members.

That school holiday passed by without much really happening. Will and I were still very happily together and working on helping one another become everything we dreamed we could be. Sara, Simon and Bill had moved into a house on Coronation Drive in the suburb of Auchenflower and I spent a lot of my spare time there. They had a couple of really big parties during those holidays, much like our time at schoolies – drug infested zones of nothingness. We all thought that we were pretty special and grown up, making decisions that would change our lives forever.

Then one day our results arrived for the end of Grade 12. When the envelope arrived I sat down on the end of my bed and just stared at it. Will was sitting there with me, holding my hand, encouraging me that I would be fine and that I had worked hard to achieve results and so I may as well open it up and see what they were. I waited until my mum and dad were both home from work as well before I opened the envelope. Then when I did open it I didn't want to look at it. After about five minutes my dad talked me into looking. I had gotten an O.P score of 8. Which was totally amazing to me as I had thought that I would get around 11 or 12. I was so excited I started to cry; I must've been overwhelmed because I have never cried very easily.

The next important thing to wait for during those holidays was the newspaper announcing the university offers. I had applied to do Film at the Queensland College of Art or the Bachelor of Arts at Griffith University majoring in Film and Media. Mum drove me to the Courier Mail newspaper printing factory just after midnight on the day that the offers were to be released and joined all the other school leavers in a hurry to find out where their futures lay. I opened up the newspaper quickly and sighed with relief I had been accepted into the Bachelor of Arts course at the Nathan Campus of Griffith University, to start at the beginning of March. The year was 1993; a year of major changes for me.

University started without too much upheaval in my life, besides that of the 8:30 a.m. viewing of a film every Wednesday morning. This meant I had to get up around 6:30 a.m. – time that I had hoped would pass with the completion of Grade 12. I made a few new friends on the very first day. We all caught the same bus to uni and had all the same classes and tutorials. They were all really interesting people. They too all had big dreams of making movies that would be shown on the big screen, and we weren't going to be told differently by anybody. I was doing subjects that included film studies, social studies and psychology, which proved to be a very interesting mixture. It was a mixture that I was hoping would help me with the type of films that I wanted to focus on making, social-realism. Getting into the nitty-gritty of the way that people function seemed very interesting to me at the time. I had no idea how close I would get to such realism in my own life.

The group of people that I had become friends with were all into studying and doing well, which was really encouraging for me. They also enjoyed going out on the weekends and taking drugs, especially speed. We all had a few long weekends that lasted all the way from Friday afternoon until very early Monday morning. A bad habit to get into and an even harder habit to get out of. We would also go into the pub at the bottom of the Myer Centre on a Friday afternoon and drink lots of cheap alcohol. Will would often come in and join us there. I was so in love with him. He was so encouraging for me when I first started out at university. He was like a tower of strength for me at the time. I would sometimes also see James, Ian and Sara on the weekends, and soon enough Sara moved into a house with one of my new uni friends, a girl named Kristy. They were living at Petrie Terrace and I was soon spending a lot of my spare time there. We all knew how to have a good time. Drugs such as speed, ecstasy and pot were soon a normal part of my 'wind-down' time (even though in actuality they wound me up). I found that when I wasn't working at the Metro or at uni I was doing something to 'wind-down'. I was still quite happy to be living at home at the time and of course my parents had no idea what I was doing in my spare time. I spent most of my time with Will, somewhere or other. My parents loved and trusted Will to be with me and to look out for me: and he always did.

I did move out of home in the school holidays of September in that first year of uni. I moved in with some friends from Indooroopilly that also happened to be at university with me. Christine and Rod, my ex-boyfriend, were the people that I chose to live with for my first experience out of home. My parents were upset but supportive, as they were about most of my life-changing decisions, an attribute that I have always loved about them. When we found the place I thought that it was perfect. It was a falling down three-bedroom house on the main road at Highgate Hill. Between the three of us we paid $180 per week, for what we all believed was our dream house. When I moved my mum went through all of her stuff for the house and gave me anything 'spare' that she had. So I moved into the house with absolutely everything that we would ever need.

Because we were all students of some kind we all spent a lot of our time in our rooms studying. It was great for me that Christine happened to be doing the same course, so we often spent late nights comparing notes. Will lived just a ten-minute walk from the house and he spent a huge amount of his time there. He and I would often just sit in my room and listen to music or talk about the future and what we wanted to make of our lives. I was determined to be a scriptwriter/director and he was keen on being a musician with an interest in film also. I used to love those times just lying on my bed talking our dreams out loud.

One of the things that Rod had brought into the house was a Nintendo 64 and I soon became an expert at Sonic the Hedgehog. Many a late night that should've been spent studying was spent playing that game until I 'beat' different levels. It is amazing what we can achieve when we really set our minds to it. It is also amazing to think just how much time I would have wasted playing that silly game. I would sometimes get home from work at around 10p.m and play until midnight then study until 2 or 3 am, only to get up at 7a.m for uni. What a crazy life that uni students lead. Then on the weekends when I wasn't working I would go out, take drugs and not sleep, and still be able to function on a Monday morning. I cringe at the thought of what I put my body and mind through at the time, let alone my soul.

The Christmas holidays of that year were very different for me. I was working almost 40 hours most weeks and when I wasn't working I was taking drugs, going out to parties or just hanging out with friends. I still saw Sara and James quite a lot. We had all changed quite significantly to when we had been at school, but I think that I was making really deep changes. I was seeing even less and less of Will and I didn't really know why I was choosing to do that. It was partly my work schedule choosing for me, but when it came down to it I was more inclined to not want to see him much. It was strange for me because I was so used to wanting to be with him in every spare waking moment. One of the other reasons for my disinterest was because he had caught up with his old friends from State High and was spending a lot of time with them. They seemed to be really nice people and I guess I wanted for Will to work out his friendships with them before I came into the picture too much. At the time I knew my life was taking some turns – I just didn't know exactly how much they would affect the rest of my life.

The second year of university started without too much stress or trauma. I met some new people and caught up with the people from the previous year. I started to feel a little bit bored with university life around the first break of the year, the Easter holidays. It was around this time that I broke up with Will. I was a real coward about it. I called him up on the phone and told him, after talking to him for almost an hour, that I didn't think things were working out for

us and it was time for me to take some time out, time for me. It came
out of nowhere; there was no obvious distress in our relationship.
For some reason I just felt as though it was time to move on. Will
was very upset about my decision and so was I, but I knew that it
was the right thing to do at the time (for me, anyhow).

The other change that took place during those holidays was that
the lease on the house that I was living in ran out. By this time Rod
and Christine had started seeing each other and were quite happily
in love. I decided that with everything that was going on in my life
at the time to find a place just for me. Of all the people to help me,
trusty Will was the person who stepped up and offered his
assistance. He was so good and loyal to me, way beyond the call of
friendship. We found a small but cute two-bedroom flat down near
the river at Hill End. It was $110 per week, which was a lot for just
me. But I was working and could afford it at the time. Anyhow, I
thought that I needed the space for myself. Little did I know what
would happen, being the giving person that I was and having a 'spare'
bedroom.

I was basically working and studying and going out on weekends.
During this time I was still actually spending quite a lot of my spare
time with Will, and I happened to meet a lot of his friends. People
that he had known for years suddenly became friends, or
acquaintances, of mine. Life was a little strange and definitely getting
stranger. I suddenly had a new circle of friends that all happened
to be my ex-boyfriend's old friends. It must have all been very weird
for Will at the time. Some of the people that I met at the time would
become real friends and others were just passing through life and
happened to venture into mine.

The place where I lived was around the corner from a squat that
a lot of these people were living in. I would spend some of my time
there and take them food and cigarettes when I could afford it. They
would also come around to my place any other time that they needed
a feed, a cigarette or some pot. I would give to them all continuously
and was quite happy to do that. At the time I started to like one of
the guys there, his name was James. He was six foot four, blond mohawks
on each side of his head, tattoos on his arms and chest; and I thought
that he was just beautiful. James was totally unlike anybody that I
had ever known before and something about me must have intrigued
him as well because we seemed to spend a lot of our time together.

Within a couple of weeks we were sleeping together regularly and he was spending most of his time at my place. Some of his friends would often be there when I got home from work or uni and they would eat nearly all of my food and then want to sleep in the spare room. I knew that this wasn't any sort of healthy relationship that we were in, but for some reason I didn't stop it.

It took me another couple of weeks before I just came home one day and exploded and told him and his mate to get out, I needed my space back. That was the end of my short lived relationship with James. I got my space for a short while until the next person in need of a bed came to me – I had no boundaries. I soon realised that the spare bedroom was more of a hindrance than a blessing and started to look for somewhere else to live, as my lease was almost up anyway. Unfortunately, it was the first of many broken leases. I spread the word around the people that I had met through Will, as I really wanted to stay in the area.

At the time Will was living in a beautiful large house on the top of Dornoch Terrace at Highgate Hill, 'Rodmaun'. This was, and probably always will be, one of the most special places that I would ever live in. It was huge, two-levels with separate households on each level, a magnificent backyard and incredible people; a dream home for me at the time. No description that I could give would ever possibly do that house justice. All I needed was for one of the rooms, preferably downstairs, to become available, and it did. It all came about when one of the guys that lived in the downstairs section of the house invited me around to smoke some pot one afternoon. We both got really stoned and listened to some old Nina Simone albums and realised how well we got along. He then just asked me if I wanted to move in and I said yes straight away; I had already thought about it so much. So I gave two weeks notice at the flat and started to think about moving into my new home. I hadn't even asked which of the rooms I had. As it was, it was one of the smaller but really long rooms; it had sky blue painted walls and black floorboards. All this for only $60 per week – I thought that it was a dream come true.

All of this was taking place amidst me going to work and studying. The cinema that I was still working at had moved to George Street in the city and was now known as the Dendy Cinema. One of the special guys that I worked with there, Stephen, worked at the street newspaper called Time Off and was starting up a fashion page and asked me to be the very first model. No doubt I was flattered. At the time I had just shaved my head for the first time and wasn't really what I considered to be conventional model material, but for the experience of it all I said yes.

I had an absolute blast doing the photo shoot. I remember the day so clearly. Stephen picked me up early and we went to his friend's place for breakfast who was the creative director. A very special lady named Anna was the photographer and she was there as well. We all drank lots of coffee and ate pastries and I just sat there listening to them all discussing what they wanted to do for the shoot. They wanted to focus on my head; they all commented on how beautiful the shape of it was and how great it looked shaved. So off we went. Many of the photos from the shoot had me with things on my head. One of them was of me sitting on a malibu-style skateboard in the middle of the road with no shoes on, a hat on the ground and a half-eaten apple on my head. This strange photo happened to also be the one they chose as the most effective. I was very excited to get my first copy of the paper with my photo in it. Another new and vivid experience under my belt, and life felt so exciting for me at the time.

Chapter 4

Altered Existence

Everybody that I knew had copies of the skateboard photo in their houses. One of the new guys in my life, a really wonderful guy named Troy, invited me over for a smoke and I noticed that the photo was cut out and stuck on the wall in his living room. I didn't comment, I must've been too embarrassed. Anyhow, we were there to kick back and get stoned while listening to some of Troy's incredible music. The photo seemed to have no relevance at the time. He was doing some DJ work and to me his vinyl collection was just amazing. So there we were, quite comfortably listening to the music that he had so finely selected for our listening pleasure, when there was a very loud knock on the front door. Troy suggested that it might be his younger brother, Jack; someone who I had heard a lot about from people but never met. Troy didn't answer the door so Jack just went around to the back door and let himself in. As soon as he walked into the room we made direct eye contact – he had the bluest eyes that I had ever seen. I was fixated on him when Troy interrupted my train of thought to introduce us to one another. Jack said that he had heard a lot about me; I was the girl that had broken Will's heart, the new girl at Rodmaun and the beautiful girl on the skateboard. A perfect explanation of who I was at the time; they were all correct. And in that short two-minute conversation I knew that I had just met the guy that I was going to fall for next. I had absolutely no idea at the time what a profound effect he would have on my life.

When I was back at home, after sitting with Jack and Troy for a few hours smoking, talking and listening to music, I proceeded to talk to one of my friends, Kent, who was visiting at the time about my afternoon. I told him that I had finally met the Jack guy that everybody talked about and how beautiful and amazing that I thought he was. I will never forget Kent's response to me; he told me, very plainly, that Jack was a junkie, a heroin addict, and that if I ever got involved with him that is exactly what would happen to me too. At the time I had no idea what heroin really was. I knew that most of the guys had experimented with it and I knew that Will had been using it quite a bit since we had broken up, but I had no idea how powerful it was and had absolutely no desire to find out. I did, however, have a desire to find out a lot more about Jack; and I would.

I started to spend more of my time with Jack, we would just sit around and smoke pot and talk about whatever we wanted to talk about, which seemed to be absolutely everything. Within a couple of weeks we started seeing each other everyday and were very soon sleeping together (that happened to be the only way that I knew we were 'going out' so to speak, as we never actually went anywhere). I didn't understand at the time that the reason we didn't go out anywhere was that because of Jack's heroin habit he only ever had money for his next score of heroin. I did soon discover that the only reason I saw him everyday at home was because his dealers lived around the corner from 'Rodmaun', and he was either getting on for himself or for one of the many people that were constantly at our place. I wasn't very impressed, but neither did I change things.

Around this time Kent moved into our place as well. So there were five very different people all under our roof, and then the upstairs household consisted of another seven very different people. How we all survived each other I'll never truly understand, though I am sure the drugs we all shared had a lot to do with it. In our household there was Matthew; he had lived there the longest and was a gay uni student who loved smoking pot and listening to really good music all the time. There was Tania, the second longest resident, who happened to be a student by day and a sex-worker by night. She also happened to be the household drug dealer – she sold everything except heroin, which she was totally against. Then there was Will. At the time he was 'experimenting' with heroin, working casually and trying hard to hide the fact that I had broken his heart and then jumped up and down on it by moving into 'Rodmaun'. Then there was Kent; he loved to smoke heaps of pot, listen to really awesome music and just lounge around the house all day waiting for the many visitors to stream through. Then, of course, there was me; at the time I was a full-time student, part-time cinema worker, a heroin-addict's girlfriend and I thought that I couldn't have been happier. Life for me was pleasantly strange.

Jack had an incredibly intriguing character. I use the word character because he was so unusual, so unlike anyone that I had ever met before. As already mentioned, he had the bluest eyes that I had ever seen, regardless of the state that he was in at anytime, and they were always very inviting. He had a strangely crooked smile and from years of drug abuse many of his teeth had started to rot, but that was a fact that I looked beyond every time he smiled or we kissed; it seemed irrelevant to me. He had a long skinny face which was also accentuated from years of drug abuse, beautiful soft lips and skin which was perfect – except for when he would take drugs and pick at the imaginary spots on his face after which he would end up with great big scabs on his face. Jack also seemed to be a wealth of all different types of knowledge; he knew about the realities of life and was also well read, as his dad sold second hand books. All of this and I thought that I had found the love of my life, I truly adored him.

One of the things about Jack that intrigued me most was his life stories; every time he would talk of his life or his upbringing I would want to just hold him and comfort him and tell him now that I was there everything was going to be okay. I thought that I could rescue him from himself; unfortunately, I would give away much of myself trying to save him. Jack was the middle of three brothers. Up until his mum died, from infections relating to the treatment of Hepatitis C brought on from her younger years of heroin abuse, he had always been her favourite child. Losing her at thirteen was the beginning of the downward spiral for him. He often spent hours talking about his beloved mum and would tell me stories about growing up like 'gypsies', taking off at the whim of his parents: he loved his life and I loved his stories, regardless of how tall they often seemed; his life was poles apart from my own and I was so interested in hearing more. It was unfortunate that I only seemed to see him when he was really stoned on heroin and pot and, so, wasn't always able to stay awake to finish his stories; however, I would always be there when he was ready.

One of the things that I found really different about Jack's family compared to mine or anyone else's was that with Jack's dad it was quite normal to just sit around and smoke joints all day long; for them it would have been strange if they didn't do that together. Whereas my family smoked cigarettes, but didn't drink alcohol nor do any drugs at all; especially not in the middle of the lounge room floor! So to me it was really strange getting used to this new way of family living. Not only did I share my pot with Jack and his dad, I also used to help them with their hydroponic marijuana set up in the downstairs section of their house. They had two concrete rooms underneath the house and they had a heap of pot plants growing down there. I used to help them by changing the water over and putting the chemicals in. One day I turned to walk down their street from the main road and all I could smell was pot, but I couldn't work out where it was coming from; and because their house was halfway down the street I definitely didn't think that was where it was coming from. So I couldn't believe it when I got to the footpath out the front of the house and realised that it was indeed their house that was stinking out the whole street. We had all become so used to the smell that it was normal to us. When I told Jack and Alan about it they just laughed and said that I was too stoned and that I was imagining it. I couldn't believe how much my life had changed from the close knit upbringing that I'd had to living in a house full of stoners who did nothing but laugh about everything. I started to wonder where it all was headed.

I was still at uni and also working at the Dendy cinema three or four nights a week. I loved my work and the freedom that I received from earning my own money. Almost everyone else that I knew at the time was on a payment of one type or another from the government. I was still living at 'Rodmaun' and spending a lot of my time there but it seemed that if I wanted to spend the night with Jack I had to go to his place at Annerley; he needed to stay there in case people came over early for him to score for them. Regardless of how messed up his priorities were, most of the time I was happy to fit in with him. He was living with his dad, Alan and his younger brother, Rick, at the time. They were all big pot smokers and so as soon as I would walk in the door after work they would offer me a smoke and I would then smoke until I crashed out and needed to go to bed.

Every now and then there would be no-one coming over in the morning to score with Jack and so he would start to get sick and 'hang out' as he called it. He would get the sweats and sometimes start vomiting or having diarrhoea; it all seemed very unpleasant. The worst thing about it was his moods; he would be so grumpy and angry; and as I was the person closest to him he would unknowingly direct it at me. I just wanted to help him get better and to live a happier life, but seeing him 'hanging out' really frightened me. It was like he was another person, like the Jack I thought I knew and loved wasn't there and when he was like this it was horrible. Because I was working so much and had saved a lot of money he would sometimes ask if he could borrow money from me for drugs. I would tell him that if there was anything else I could do I would do it, but that I would never give him money to support his bad habits. This would only make him angrier. I would leave and go home and every now and then once he had 'scored' his shot of heroin he would come over and apologise and tell me how much he loved me and needed me in his life and how he would never do that to me again. I always forgave him. I loved him too much not to; at least I thought it was love.

Around this time I started to get sick, feeling tired all the time and not eating much. I was generally unwell and I wasn't sure why. I went to the doctors and no matter how many or what type of tests they would do they could never find anything wrong with me. I was still at uni at the time, but with all of this going on; and my life seeming to take a new and exciting path of sorts, I decided that I would defer. I told myself and everybody else that I would be returning the following year, but in the back of my mind I knew that time would come and go without me returning there. My parents were very upset and disappointed with my decision, but once again allowed me the freedom to make my own choices; after all, I was now nineteen and a half – a true 'adult'. Anyhow, the doctors continued testing and my boss at the Dendy was very understanding and allowed me to take time off when I needed it. During those times I would generally lie around at home at 'Rodmaun' and feel sorry for myself. I would smoke heaps of pot and write or listen to music until someone would come into my room to talk to me.

As it was, Kent also wasn't working at the time so he and I would spend most of our days lying around talking, we were (and are) very similar in so many ways. I sometimes would wonder if I was with the wrong person being with Jack because Kent respected me and genuinely liked me for who I was; he would go out of his way for me all the time and I liked him. But whenever Jack would pop in for a visit I would once again lose all concept of reality and melt into his arms. He would tell me, in his stoned slurry voice, how he loved me and hated being apart from me; and I would believe his every word.

I wasn't sure myself how much of my sickness was real and how much of it was in my head, but whenever the doctors would mention that it might by psychosomatic and something that I was imagining becoming real in my body I would get very defensive and upset. I would then be back the following week to the doctor for another check-up, only to be told the same thing week in and week out. My mum came with me once as she had seen how upset I was about the doctors not being able to tell what was wrong. She also argued with the doctors about it, backing me up as she always did. We sat there as the doctor told me that she thought I needed to see a psychologist and that she thought that there was an issue going all the way back to my father when I was a child. This really upset my mum no matter how adamant I was about it not being true. We left the office and were both crying about it. My mum was always there when I needed her to be and I will never forget her face when all of this was happening. It only seemed to make me sicker when the doctors would carry on like that. I would smoke more pot and want to lie around even more. Mum returned home much more upset than she was when she arrived. I wanted to make things better for her; I hated that she was hurting because of me.

Life continued on like that for me for a long time. I would work when I felt like I could survive the week and when I didn't feel like it I would get a doctor's certificate and be paid a sickness allowance. My boss at the Dendy's name was Peter and he was an awesome guy as well as a great boss. One day he showed up at 'Rodmaun' and Kent came to get me. It was so sweet; when I got to the door Peter was standing there was a bunch of flowers from their garden at home and a great big smile. He was there to let me know that they were there for me and that they would do anything that they could to support me. By this stage I had worked for the company for over two years and had always been a very hard worker and loyal employee. I loved my job and that my boss came to show his support. It was almost 4 o'clock in the afternoon when he got there; I was still in my pyjamas and had been lying in bed all day, again.

One of my other co-workers, a guy named Steven, would also come and visit me or he would call me to see how I was going. When I was working he would drop me home, even though it was quite out of his way. He was such a sweet guy. One of the things that he did to try and get me motivated, was to organise a fashion shoot for me to model at. He had been appointed as the new fashion guy at Time Off, the street mag that did the skateboard shoot, and he wanted me to be his first model. I was quite sick on the morning of the shoot and was so skinny and dark around the eyes I actually looked a lot like Jack when he was 'hanging out'. The photo shoot was at a bowling alley and he had arranged some dance party type clothes. It was a lot of fun and Steven made it all the more fun. He was such a funny guy to be around. Always trying very hard to make me smile and laugh. We would sing along to dodgy songs in his car and I would always leave his company feeling better than what I had previously. He was such a gem to me, and always would be; I no idea at the time how I would come to treat him and take him for granted, and neither did he.

One of the things that I was still yet to try and wasn't actually that keen on doing at all, until I met Jack, was injecting drugs. I had seen it in movies where it is all quite glamorous but had never thought about doing it myself. One night I got back to Jack's from work and I could tell that he was on ecstasy. He was extra lovey-dovey and all he wanted to do was kiss and cuddle me, which is probably quite normal in most relationships but not in ours. When I asked him if he had any for me he told me that he did have but that he really wanted me to try shooting it up. The guy that had sold it to him said it was much more effective intravenously. I thought I might as well give it a go as I knew that it wasn't addictive and there seemed no harm in trying it. I sat down on the floor with my legs crossed and watched as Jack mixed it all up and sucked it up into the syringe. It seemed like such an operation, the entire scenario from start to finish was so clinical. He asked me to give him my arm so that he could find a vein and it was when I did this that I realised what I was doing. I was about to enter into a whole new realm of my drug taking life, and there was absolutely no fear inside of me, only excitement. He found the vein and then he told me that it would hurt for a second as he put the needle into my arm and then it would pass as the drugs kicked in. I had only ever swallowed drugs and so I wasn't ready for them to kick in straight away. When he took the needle from my arm I closed my eyes because my head started to spin. When I opened them again it was almost 45 minutes later. I had been in a trance like state where I was in another world, and I liked it. I enjoyed not being in my own frame of mind because that way I didn't have to think too much about anything. That night would change so much about my existence as I knew it. I had no idea at the time just how changed it would become; but I was about to find out the real 'power' behind the drugs that I was consuming.

It was around this time that I started to ask Jack if he would give me some heroin one day. He was always very adamant that he wouldn't and never would. He would ask me if watching him and the way his life was wasn't enough to make me never want to touch it. I would go on and on about being sick and how I had money for it, but he would always say no. I used to see that as a way of him showing me how much he loved and cared for me. I would think to myself that if he really loved heroin more than he loved me, the way people told me he did, then he would jump at the chance to give me some and get me hooked so that then we could use it together. This didn't seem to be the case and after a little while of hassling him I gave up on it. I would still smoke heaps of pot and if something heavier was going I would use it. Things like speed and ecstasy seemed to be around whenever there was a party or a big dance party on funnily enough I was always more than well enough to attend these parties, and sometimes even organise them! But I could never see beyond my 'sickness' at any other time. It seems so strange now to realise how overcome I was; all of my thoughts about being unwell had truly manifested themselves into my body, and seemingly, my soul.

In late 1994 when the Livid music festival was on we all had one of the biggest weekends imaginable. It started on the Friday night with lots of pot and acid and very loud music at our friends' house. The name of that house was 'Flamingo House'; there was even a sign on the front of the house stating so. We all called it 'Flaming House'. And that was where the festivities began that night. We all had a very big night and then after a few short hours sleep we wandered up to 'Rodmaun' where we all proceeded to have pot cookies with our cereal and then acid tabs after breakfast. By the time we started our walk towards Davies Park, where the festival was, we were all totally losing the plot. We were all babbling. I was walking arm in arm with Jack most of the way and with another special friend of mine named Tammy the rest of the way. Tammy and I had gotten dressed up together. My aim of the day, as I had been telling everyone for months, was to meet Ad-Rock from the Beastie Boys. I thought that he was the most handsome guy that I had ever seen, and even Jack was encouraging me to try it. Everyone actually thought that I was crazy and that I had no chance, but I was going into it with 100% determination. Anyhow, I was wearing a blue halter neck top that showed off my skinny belly, red cord pants that also showed off how skinny I had become, and black Doc Marten boots. My hair was short and blond and spiky, and everyone kept telling me how spunky I looked. I knew I had a chance to meet him and I also knew that I was going to try very hard!

By around lunchtime I had taken some speed and an ecstasy tablet and was definitely losing it. I had bumped into James and Simon from school and they were in much the same state. When I told them about my grand idea to meet Ad-Rock they laughed and gave me great big hugs and told me to go get him. I was enjoying watching the bands and sitting on the hill when Jack and Will came and asked me if they could borrow some money from me. Because of all the 'upper' drugs they had taken they were starting to feel sick and needed some heroin. For the first time ever I gave in to them and I am sure that it was due to not being in the right state of mind myself. I gave them $150, more than they needed; what a foolish, clouded decision I had just made.

By the time they got back I was in the front row waiting for DJ Hurricane, who was the Beastie Boys DJ who was doing a solo set in the middle of the afternoon. I had been standing there for nearly half an hour waiting for him when I looked over behind the security fence and there was Ad-Rock, plain as day, sitting on the hill behind the stage. I knew this was going to be my one and only chance to meet him, so I made my way over to the security guard behind the fence and told him that my name was Bronwen and that I needed to speak to Adam (Ad-Rock's real name). He went and spoke to Ad-Rock who looked over and waved me in. I couldn't believe it. I was inside the gate by the time it hit me, I was about to meet and sit down with Ad-Rock to watch Hurricane play. What an amazing experience I was having. He was such a nice guy and he was very gentle also, touching my hand and telling me that I was an angel. I asked him to write his autograph on my shoulder, I knew that I had worn a halter neck top for a reason! By this stage friends of mine had spotted me behind the fence sitting with him, and they were all coming up to the fence asking me to let them through as well, but Adam was adamant that he wanted to sit with me alone.

When I looked up Jack was beaming a huge smile at me; kind of like a 'that's my girl' type smile. Then it seemed like everyone that I knew came up to me. Nobody could believe it, especially me. Everyone was asking to look at the autograph on my shoulder, like they needed to see it to believe it. I had done it. I had met Ad-Rock just like I said I would. I knew then that I could do whatever I put my mind to, and from then on in I would always attempt to do just that.

That night we had one of the biggest parties that I have ever been too. By this stage word had gotten around that the Beastie Boys had been invited. We all had a great night; unbelievably, Jack and I took more ecstasy later that night and then were dancing all over each other and anybody else that would come near us. We were basically in pretty much the same state. It seemed totally normal for me to be so out of it that I didn't have a very coherent comprehension of reality. Regardless of how much I liked to be in control of my life, I was very quickly losing it.

Not long after the Livid festival I got a phone call one day from James and I knew as soon as I heard his voice that he was upset about something. I immediately asked him what was wrong and he told me he needed to see me in person, that he had something to tell me. He came straight over to my place and when he got there he hugged me and then burst into tears. He told me that our friend Simon had died of a heroin overdose the night before. I couldn't believe it and I asked him to repeat it. He told me again that he had died. I sat down and started to weep tears, tears from really deep down within me. He had been such a special person, such a creative inspiration to me. Such a waste. I guess it was also very upsetting because for the first time I realised that the same thing could happen to Jack at any time. It made me glad that the last time I had seen Simon had been at the festival where we were all off our heads and very happy to see each other. Simon had always had the ability to make me smile, regardless of how I was feeling. He had been such a special guy. James and I just sat there holding each other, saying good-bye to him through the tears that we shed for him. He was the first of many people that I knew to die from heroin; the drug that was eating away at the soul of so many friends of mine, so destructive yet also so very inviting.

Early the following year, 1995, two friends of mine started up a special tradition at one of the clubs in town – every Tuesday night we would all get out of our heads and go dancing. The night was called 'Buggered', not standing for anything in particular but describing perfectly how we all felt after a night there! Anyhow, Troy and Scott were the friends and they were also the DJ's there. I always had an absolutely awesome time. When the night first started up there were only a few people that went and so Kent and myself, and Jack if he was stoned enough to come, would take up the dance floor and have so much fun just dancing and laughing. The nights very quickly got more popular and one night Scott asked me to be the guest DJ. I had never done this before but was very keen to have a go. So I planned out what I wanted to play and the following week just went for it. It all went off perfectly. After that I had people asking me to DJ at parties but I never really felt into it enough; I actually preferred dancing than playing the music that others could dance to!

It was always a treat for me if Jack happened to be stoned enough to join me there. I loved to spend time with him even though the only time that I did spend with him was when he was stoned on heroin, and then he would only come out dancing if he could take speed or ecstasy as well. At the time I promised myself to never end up so dependent on anything that I felt as though I couldn't leave the house with out it but I had no idea at the time what my life choices would lead me to in the future.

During the hey-day of 'Buggered' it happened to be my nineteenth birthday and so I decided to have a huge party at 'Rodmaun'. I spoke to all of my housemates and all of them told me to go for it. So I told everybody that I knew and told them to tell everybody that they knew. The word went around for nearly two weeks before the night. I had asked Troy and another friend of mine to DJ at the party and they had both agreed. Kent and I spent all day organising the house. We were going to have the turntables set up in the hallway and the rooms were to be for dancing. We made the lounge room into a chill-out area with big cushions and lots of fluff everywhere. We wanted people to have a place to relax amidst the madness that we knew the night was going to entail. We were expecting around 150 people, and were all really looking forward to it. After all the house was huge, the backyard was also huge and we all wanted a huge night!

Someone gave me two ecstasy tablets for my birthday which I took one and a half of and gave the rest to Jack. He had already taken enough speed to keep me up for an entire week, but was complaining. As the night progressed and more and more people arrived I was given more drugs. It seemed that everybody was giving me something, not that I was complaining, neither was Jack. By about midnight we had nearly 300 people on the property and we were all having a blast, or so we thought. Some people were roller-skating up and down the hallway with watermelon and others were getting naked and writhing around on the floor; it was a modern day Sodom and Gomorrah, and we were loving it. I never wanted the night to stop, but it did when the police were called at 5am because the music was still blaring. We all must have seemed like lunatics to the neighbours, and even though they had been warned about the party nobody had any idea how huge it was going to be; especially us.

The clean up the following day was also huge; one of the things that I never stopped to think about, consequences for my actions. There was watermelon all over the entire house; you couldn't take two steps without your feet sticking to the floor. It was such a mission to clean it all up. Kent and I must have mopped the floor almost twenty times before we decided to just hose it out; after all it was floorboards. We had no comprehension of how much water comes from the end of a hose and we almost flooded the house, but we just kept laughing. It is amazing just how stupid you can be when you lack control of your mental co-ordination. We just thought that it was really funny and because all of our housemates were in similar mental states they all thought that it was hilarious as well. This being just one of the many parties that we had at the special house called 'Rodmaun'.

About a month later I was starting to feel really sick again, and even though that seemed to be part of my normal existence in those days, I felt even stranger than normal. I would wake in the middle of the night just to throw up, which was something that I had never experienced before. I spoke to Jack about it as it seemed that he and I were spending almost all of our time together at that stage and, after all, he was my boyfriend. He told me to go and see the doctor because the vomiting and lethargy was starting to freak him out. He actually came with me to the doctor. The doctor took one look at me after I told her how I felt and told me to take a pregnancy test. I hadn't even thought about that as a possibility to explain the strange feelings I was having. I did the test and as we sat there, waiting for the line to either appear or not appear, Jack just squeezed my hand. For the first time in a long time I got comfort from knowing that he was there for me; thankfully so, because two minutes later the doctor announced that I was definitely pregnant.

My heart skipped a few beats and the doctor must have sensed that because then she asked what we were going to do. Jack just kept squeezing my hand. I understood that no matter how much I knew I loved Jack, I was in no state to be a mother of any description. I was still happy to party and take drugs and that was a lifestyle that I wasn't ready to give up just yet. We told the doctor that we would go home and discuss it and get back to her very soon. I cried all the way home on the bus and as soon as we got back to Jack's place he called Will and they organised to score some heroin so that Jack could numb out his reality. That was what I felt like doing at the time, but I couldn't even bring myself to ask him. I couldn't believe that I was pregnant. Jack and I had never used contraception of any form, but I still never expected to fall pregnant, not then anyhow. My life was starting to seem very messy, and that was exactly how my mind felt also.

Jack and I did eventually discuss it the next day when he was stoned on heroin and I was stoned on pot, and we both agreed that there was no way that I could keep the baby and that the only option was an abortion. I didn't even think of what was growing inside of me as a life; that was how deceived I was. It all just seemed like a huge mistake that needed fixing and the easiest way to do that was to remove it. The doctor made all of the arrangements for me. I had told Will what was happening and he agreed to take me to the clinic the following week. For an entire week I dwelled on the fact that I was pregnant and what a hassle it all was for me. I never once stopped to think about what a miracle it all was; I was so blinded.

That week was one of the longest of my entire life. Will and Jack were with me when I arrived at the clinic. I was using $180 of my savings for the termination and they asked me to borrow that much again to give to them. I was so out of sorts that I agreed. I had no idea or comprehension that the moment I went into the operating theatre they left in a hurry to go and score heroin. So there I was aborting the growing life inside of me and there was the father of the baby getting stoned and with someone who I though was my friend. When I came to after the operation they weren't even back there to pick me up. I had to get out of my bed, very groggily, to walk to the pay-phone to call them to pick me up. When they did get there I just sat in the back seat and cried the whole way home. Neither of them even bothered to turn around to ask me if I was okay, which I obviously wasn't; I felt so alone, so very alone.

I spent the following week at Jack's place, just lying downstairs feeling sorry for myself. His dad, Alan, got really worried about me one day and came down to ask if I was okay. I was a blithering mess, and so he rolled up a big joint and we sat there and smoked it. Afterwards I told him what had happened and why I was feeling the way that I was. He was very understanding and told me that he had thought that was the issue anyhow. He said that he had been giving Jack and me some room to work through it. The problem was that Jack was now using more heroin than before and I was all alone, crying and feeling so guilty for what I had done. The reality got worse for me everyday that passed; I was smoking much more pot than before; not realising, or caring, that pot was actually a depressant. Which I definitely didn't need, I was depressed enough by myself.

I returned back to 'Rodmaun' because I couldn't handle watching Jack and his friends so numb and out of it when that was what I was wanting to feel at the time; nothingness. Life at home seemed to be relatively normal, even though I felt far from normal. Kent and I were spending heaps of time together again and that seemed to be the nicest thing about my life at the time. We were constantly talking about music, television, movies; whatever we could think about we would discuss it. It was so good to have a friend like Kent at the time – he knew nothing and I could pretend like nothing was wrong when I was with him and that suited me just fine. If I didn't have to think about anything I didn't have to face anything either.

One night Kent and I were sitting in my room on the bed playing game upon game of backgammon and smoking cone upon cone of pot. We were pretty smashed when one of the girls that we were currently living with came home. She was younger that us at age 17, and acted it. She smoked a lot of pot and seemed to take a lot of speed now that she was at uni; quite familiar really. About half an hour after she got home we heard her talking on the phone in the kitchen at the end of the hallway. She was always very loud and animated so we didn't think much of it until we heard her scream for help. She was screaming something like, "Help guys, quick, help. Fire, I need your help!" Kent and I ran to help her; I unknowingly pulled my bedroom door closed behind me. As soon as I got into the hallway I could see smoke billowing out of her bedroom doorway. She was standing there just screaming something about her cat and the money hidden under the bed. All I could think about was our precious home, and getting the fire put out anyway possible.

We started by getting blankets from the lounge room to throw over the flames but each time we would arrive back to her room the fire was getting bigger and bigger. It was becoming uncontrollable. I picked up the phone and in the state that I was in forgot the emergency phone number. I screamed to Kent to ask what it was, and in his state he yelled back that it was 911; proving just how influenced we were by American television and music. I dialled 000 and still panting from running gave them every detail that I could think of. I still can't believe just how detailed the information was and how quickly I spat it all out. All I could think of was the house being our home and all of the memories of the place started flooding before my eyes. The woman on the phone told me to wait outside. But Kent and I wanted to do something. We ran to get the hose to try and put the fire out, but by this stage the hallway was ablaze and the kitchen was starting to go up too. We ran upstairs to warn the household up there about what was going on and then we ran for the front yard. We stood there together arm in arm, watching our home burn down. It was all so quick. Waiting for the fire engine seemed like forever as the fire took control of the house. I was in total disbelief. Minutes later Matthew and Andrew, another new housemate, pulled up and came running to us. We all just stood there. A part of us all disappeared that night in that fire, a young and innocent part of me seemed to fade into nothingness. I had no idea at the time just how much that fire would change the whole course of my life; but it did so, very rapidly.

The following day we all returned to walk through the rubble and collect what we could out of what was left. But we all knew that no matter what we took with us, our lives were never going to be the same. It was a very sad day; it had all been so sudden. I guess that is how change tended to be for me, sudden and painful. I had decided to go and stay at Jack's house, his household all agreed that was okay. After all, I was still working irregularly and had money to spare for things such as pot and food. Matthew and Kent decided to move in together, and even though I was now officially living at Jack's I was spending an awful lot of time with Kent at his place. Jack never commented, probably because it gave him the freedom to take heroin without me bothering him. Sooner, rather than later, Kent and I ended up sleeping together. It was all a part of the grief after losing the house and everything else and we were a stable part of each other's lives. I knew that I had to stop it as soon as it got started. After all, I did love Jack and I didn't want to hurt him, or lose him. Unsure why, I gave up what could have been a real, loving relationship with Kent to go back to live with Jack full-time. It is strange how 'love' can get a hold of you and control your every thought and action, no matter how destructive it all is.

Chapter 5

Foolish Games

Very soon after the situation with Kent I moved in to a one bedroom flat on the other side of town; in New Farm. I saw it as a completely fresh start; after the fire and everything else I just wanted something new that I could call my own. I had been living at 'Rodmaun' for over 18 months, which seemed like a long time to me then. The place that I moved to was very old and funky, not unlike the feel that 'Rodmaun' had had. The block had young and creative-types living in it. There was a fashion designer, a DJ, a photographer, an artist; and there was me – a semi-depressed, part-time cinema worker, part-time model, whose boyfriend was a junkie, who had just had an abortion, whose house had just burned down and who had just had a mini-affair with her best friend. My life seemed to be so disastrous. I was unsure of where I was going or what I was doing. I spent most of my life stoned on pot trying very hard for my reality to blur into some kind of non-existence. I found what I thought to be the perfect answer in Jack; the answer for me was heroin.

Now all I had to do was convince Jack that he needed to give me some. He kept refusing. As it was, he and I had been together for almost a year and a half and Jack had been using heroin everyday but I was still yet to use any; therefore, as I saw it, I had already beaten the odds. At the time nothing that anybody said to me would have made me change my mind, I was determined to try some heroin. I had seen most of my current friends, and friends that had disappeared from my life, using it and thought that the numbness they all seemed to experience was exactly what I needed at the time. I gave no thought to the fact that everybody that I had seen try it was now addicted to it; that thought never even entered my mind. It is so plain to see now just how deceived I was at the time.

My so-called "break" finally came one Saturday after Jack had been to the stall at the Valley markets with his dad, which happened to be just down the road from where I was living. He and Will came over to my place and asked me if they could borrow some money. Jack had already spent the money that he had earned that day at the stall and they needed more money to 'get on' to more heroin. They both knew that I had been bugging Jack to get some for me, and even that night he kept saying that he never wanted me to have any. I ended up telling them that they could have $200 so long as they gave me some heroin. They, and their addictions, eventually gave into me and my money. Little did I know that I would only need a small amount. Even $10 worth would have been enough. As it was, because they had been able to buy so much with the money that I had given them, they ended up giving me almost $50 worth.

I had already shot up speed and ecstasy so the actual experience of shooting up directly into my bloodstream wasn't strange for me. But the tingling sensation that I got immediately as the liquid entered my vein was all consuming. By giving me $50 worth of the drug, Jack had given me enough to make me very 'stoned' and also very sick. Heroin in large amounts makes people vomit; a lot. In time I would come to know that either too much or not enough of the drug gives your body the same reaction. As it was I spent most of the night feeling very nauseated, lying on the couch trying to watch videos between "nodding off" (the desired effect from taking heroin being a semi sleep state) and vomiting. Not a pleasurable experience to say the least. Unfortunately for me I saw it as 'the best vomit' that I had ever had; I had no idea at the time just how deceived I was. Jack and Will had been hoping that by giving me such a large amount and me being so sick that it would put me off it heroin but it had the opposite effect. A week later I wanted to try more. Jack gave in, and soon gave in to me every few days. After all, every time he got some for me he got some himself; how foolish I was not to be able to see what was going on. I was so blinded by my deep (and unhealthy) love for Jack and my newfound love for this drug called heroin.

It wasn't long before my entire life was turned upside down by this substance. The beautiful flat that I had been so glad to call my own was 'suddenly' way too expensive and when I became three weeks behind in the rent I decided to move out and let my bond pay any money owing; it had all become too much for me to deal with. The work that I had been doing three or four days a week became one day and then no days within a month or so; it seemed like too much of a hassle to get up to go there every second day. My relationship with my parents, which had still been existent, became almost nothing. I just stopped contacting them. I no longer saw much of anybody except Jack and anybody else that happened to stop around to get him to buy drugs for them; which meant that I saw Will nearly everyday. When I moved out of the flat I moved into the house that Jack shared with his dad and his brother in Annerley. I shared everything with Jack from that time on; including my savings from all of my years at work. Unfortunately, just a couple of months of using heroin everyday and that was all gone; what was next?

Jack and I were using heroin sometimes two or three times a day. So we were, or I was, spending anywhere from $25 to $150 per day. Like I said, my savings became null and void within a couple of months of living like this. So I started to go back to work a couple of days a week. I needed to have used heroin before I could go to work because otherwise I would be sick due to 'hanging out'. I had become exactly the person I had promised myself I never would be. I was a heroin addict, but worse than that, I was a heroin addict in denial about the problem that I had created in my own life. It would take me years to come to any type of realisation of what I had become and what I was doing to my life; destroying it quite rapidly.

One of the most ridiculous things that Jack and I used to do after scoring in Highgate Hill but living in Annerley, which was 10 minutes away on the bus, was to go to a high rise apartment block on Highgate Hill and sneak underneath it to shoot up there. It got to the point where we were so desperate for a shot that we even had a sharps (syringes) kit stashed away there. We carried our own spoon around with us and we would shoot up there and then walk out from underneath there like nothing was any different. A few times people would look at us strangely, as though to ask where we had come from, but we didn't care. At this point in my life all I cared about was that I got the shot, it didn't really bother me about the hygiene behind it all or where I had to go to have it; so long as I got it.

Soon I came to know the guy that ran the local pawn (second hand) shop on a first name basis – I was there nearly every day pawning my stuff of any value; even things that were worth not much ended up in there. He knew Jack and I very well and I'm sure that he knew that we were drug addicts. We must've looked so pathetic going in there in the mornings looking really sick and haggard; dark bags under our eyes and very pale. I had no idea just how bad I looked and I actually didn't think that I looked as bad as Jack did; I was so deceived. Anyhow, the guy at the pawn shop would give us 'loans' on things like boxes full of board games or paints that had already been used. I did actually always have the intention of paying off my loans every fortnight and would always add up the value of the interest due. By this stage I had nearly $2000 worth of loans so the interest was phenomenally high and totally unrealistic to any junkie; including me. It seemed as though all of my good intentions flew out of the window very quickly. I wonder still how much of that came from having an already fully fledged junkie for a boyfriend and using partner; though I will never blame Jack for any of the choices I would make. Even though as the male partner in the relationship he should have discouraged me from certain things (and did), I was such a strong-willed female partner that I probably would've stood up to him anyway. We were in a no-win situation and were too blinded by our sick love for each other, and for heroin, that we couldn't even see it.

One of the other things that we used to do for money to score drugs was to work at Jack's dad's bookstall at the Valley Markets on a Saturday morning. We used to have to get there at 5:30 am, so if we hadn't saved any heroin for the morning we would be trying to set up but both feeling very sick and not much help to Alan at all. It was so ridiculous because as soon as we had made the first $50 we would call Will to drive Jack to go and score for us. The first money wasn't meant to be our wage, it was meant to cover Alan's costs, but we would always spend it anyhow. Jack would leave me there to go with Will and I would wait there and work. Sometimes I would get so sick that I would need to vomit but because I was at the stall by myself I couldn't and instead I would curl up into a ball on the pavement and just lie there waiting for a customer to come and spend more money. When someone spent money I could almost taste the rush in the back of my throat from the heroin going into my arm. My existence was a very sick one but I couldn't see it; I couldn't see beyond getting my next shot. Sometimes I would wait for Jack and Will for a couple of hours and not understanding why because to score was just a 10-minute drive. When they would return I would be furious with both of them and so sick I was nearly keeling over. At the time, I still never injected myself so I would have to get Jack to come with me, sneak into the bathrooms and do it for me. Sometimes, when I was unable to walk in case I went to the toilet in my pants, we would just hide under the tablecloth and do it there. At the time I had no understanding of what I was doing, and sadly enough, I didn't want to know.

I had no realistic view of the amount of money that we would spend on heroin in any one week. All I knew was that no matter how much we did spend it was never enough. We were both getting a payment from Centrelink; they had eventually put me onto a Disability Support Pension because I had been on and off sickness payments for almost two years. That meant that I didn't even have to go to the office any more. At the time I was getting paid over $400 a fortnight and paying Alan only $100 which was for rent and food. The other three hundred dollars would be spent within the first day. It was the one day of the fortnight, other than Jack's payday, when we would actually get 'properly' stoned on the heroin that we would buy. We would buy a pouch of tobacco and some papers and the rest would go on heroin. I always looked forward to pay day. The day after payday I would start to look forward to the next one; my life had become something that I never expected – a drudgery of trying very hard just to get by. I still couldn't see beyond my love for Jack and the drug enough to want to change

Sometime during the beginning of that year Kent's parents offered me a job at their bakery in Highgate Hill. I was to work on Saturday mornings, five hours for $60. I was still a hard worker and so I accepted the job. I loved his parents; they had always treated me like a very special young woman, especially his mum Elizabeth. The biggest problem was that their bakery was directly across the road from our dealers' house. I could actually see people walking towards their door from the counter that I worked at, people who included Jack. This was only a problem if I hadn't saved any heroin and I was a bit sick. Jack would somehow come over to me and give me some so it was at this time that I learned very quickly how to inject myself; otherwise I would have had to go without. I would sneak down to the toilets out the back and have it and then have to go back to work and face Elizabeth. Facing her was the hardest part because she was such a lovely lady, and I knew that she trusted me. She knew that I had been sick and that that was why I wasn't working at the cinema at the time, but she had no idea what was going on for me and I definitely couldn't tell her. One morning I got to work and hadn't had a shot yet so I lied to her and told her that I had my period and she allowed me to lie down in between busy times. Jack had told me that he would bring me some over as soon as he could but I had seen him go into the dealers' house and not come over to me. By the time four hours had passed I had severe diarrhoea and didn't know how to explain that as part of my supposed period pains. The shop was so busy and I had to just tell Elizabeth that I was leaving. She paid me and I walked out, never to work for her again. Unfortunately, I didn't see her for many years after that morning. As it was, Kent had to explain to her the whole heroin problem and tell her that I was a lost cause; I know now that she continued to pray for me, she knew that there was more to my life than that.

Not long after my stint at the bakery Jack and I moved into a house right around the corner from our dealers' house. It was one of the biggest and most beautiful houses that I have ever lived in. I still don't know how we afforded to do it, but I do know that the government paid for most of it. We stated irreconcilable differences with Jack's dad and so they helped us out. Although Jack's dad was a very open man he could no longer live with two very active heroin addicts and support them most of the time when it came to food, cigarettes and pot. It was sad when we had to move out, but also understandable. Alan explained to both of us that he couldn't sit back and watch Jack and I killing ourselves slowly but surely with every shot of heroin that we had. The numbers of shots were also increasing. Jack would score for lots of other people and get bits from them and share them with me some of the time.

Anyhow, the house was literally a one-minute walk to the dealers' front door. We actually would spend time with them just sitting around. They had two young boys and the youngest one really liked me and loved it when I popped in; so did I because it meant that I was about to have a shot. I had no real idea how sick and sad the whole situation was. This little boy only knew me because I would go to his house to score heroin. I would often do the deals with his parents right in front of his face. He loved me so much, he would ask me to stay and read books to him; but once the heroin was in my hand it was as though it was burning a hole in it and I would leave immediately. How sad for that little boy, and for me. I really liked little kids. I liked him so much that I offered to babysit him if they ever needed me to. Very rarely they would both go out together but when they did I got to look after him. They would give me drugs to look after their children, which at the time I thought was a great deal. Sometimes they would even let them sleep over the night, which meant I got to read lots of books to them. I always loved this time with them. I had absolutely no idea of how destructive the whole situation was for those kids; I could only think about me and my drugs. That had become the way my life was and I had gotten to the point where I couldn't see beyond it.

One of the other things about the location of our house was that all of our drug using friends would come and lie around the place almost every day. That was fine with me so long as Jack was scoring for them and I was getting little bits here and there. It always amazed me that Jack would never introduce any of our friends to the dealers. They all thought that it was ridiculous, but he would tell them that if they wanted to go elsewhere to score they could. Sometimes they would, only to return to Jack because he got bigger deals, stronger drugs and quicker service; especially now with the location of our new house. So most of our days were spent lying around the house, just being on drugs.

During this time of just being a drug addict and not doing anything with my life something happened that would change me forever. I got pregnant again, and this time I decided to keep the baby. I didn't know how difficult it would be, but I was determined to do it. My doctor advised me against it because of the heroin abuse but I was determined, after the last pregnancy, not to destroy this chance at motherhood. Jack was also very excited about the pregnancy, and talked about being a daddy all the time. I had no idea how difficult it would be for me to stop using, but I was going to put 100% effort into it, for the baby's sake. I started off by cutting back on the amounts that I was having daily and then, within about a month or so, I was down to only one shot in the morning; and more than anything that was to help me with the morning sickness. I obviously had no comprehension of the fact that everything that went into my body entered the baby as well, regardless of the size. It was around this time that I decided to just stop using it all together. I did it for almost two weeks. Then I went for a check up at the doctors and she suggested that I go and have an ultrasound as I was now approximately 14 weeks pregnant. I was so excited, and so was Jack. He too had been making an effort to cut back on his drug intake and looking forward to being a family.

We went in for the test and I knew straight away that something was wrong; the nurse's face looked distraught. She went out and got a doctor who came back and pushed the cold, wet, probe thing around on my abdomen. He also looked concerned. It was then that they asked me to get dressed and meet the doctor in the room down the hall. I started to cry straight away; I knew something bad had happened; I just had no idea what it was. When we sat down the doctor looked me straight in the eye and told me that the foetus had no heartbeat, the foetus had died inside of me and needed to be surgically removed before it caused any damage to my reproductive system. I was absolutely shattered, I couldn't stop shaking and crying. I didn't know what I was going to do. I looked across to Jack, who was squeezing my hand, and he was bawling his eyes out. We were so alone; all I could think about was heroin. I told myself that I needed it to numb the pain of the loss that I was feeling. I had the biggest shot I had ever had that night and still felt pain and heartache. The aching continued for weeks regardless of how much heroin I used. Nothing that I did or anyone else did eased the pain for me. I felt so much grief, I felt empty on the inside. I was so alone and so lost; nothing mattered to me anymore. It was then that I realised I was quite content to just give myself over to heroin and let it control me. I had told myself that I had nothing good left inside me; I just didn't care about anything. I had officially given up on myself and my thoughts for the future. I felt like I was in a valley of death with nowhere else to go.

Every now and then I would go to work at the cinema until, eventually; I decided to go back on a part-time permanent basis. My boss was very understanding and so long as I had a shot of heroin before I went to work I thought that nobody would be any the wiser. Eventually I even started to think of ways to scam money from the cinema to support my lifestyle. Because of the experience that I had with cinema work my boss put me on during the day by myself, so

I had free reign with the money. Peter, my boss, was such a nice guy that he would often come over just to ask me how I was feeling and to make sure that I wasn't doing too much. Every now and then Jack would bring me in a shot of heroin to have at work. I would do what we had done at the bookstall and either run to the toilets or just have it under the ticket counter. I nearly got caught a few times. One time I was sure that Peter had seen blood trickling down my arm five minutes after Jack had 'popped in', but he never said anything to me.

They didn't keep a very good inventory of their stock for the candy bar and the ticketing system was the old tear off one; and neither system had a register. So I started my theft by taking small amounts of money from the candy bar and when I thought that nobody knew I took a bit more. I was the one in charge and had to count all of the money, so I would write in a respectable amount and pocket the rest. It got out of control and I was just taking so much that I realised I had to think of something new. That was when I started taking money from the ticketing system by using a different roll of the same colour tickets that were being used and keeping whatever money my tickets made. I would always make sure that I sold more real tickets than my own but no matter what I did nobody seemed to notice anyway. This went on for a few months and I was taking up to $150 some days. What I was doing was so ridiculous and nobody seemed to notice.

I knew that I was doing the wrong thing but my addiction meant that I kept on going. By this stage, as a result of me stealing from work, my habit had increased to almost $100 per day. Things were out of control; something had to give, and one day it did. I was doing my usual ticket scam when all of a sudden Peter came out of the office and started tearing tickets as people went into the cinema. He had never done that before, but because now I needed a certain amount of money every day I kept going with my ticket scam. My addiction was working overtime and my conscience wasn't working at all. Peter said nothing to me and I left work that day with just as much money in my stash as usual.

When I got into work the next day there was another staff member behind the counter and Peter called me over to the office. He told me that he knew what I had been doing and that he had been hoping it would stop, he said that he also thought he knew why it was happening and that he really wanted me to get some help. I started crying and trying to defend myself but there was nothing I could do; I had been busted. He told me that I no longer had a job with him and that he really wanted me to get better and get back to the beautiful young girl that I had been when he first met me. He said he had spoken to the owners and that they weren't going to press charges against me. I thanked him for everything and walked out bowing my head in shame. Five minutes later I realised that this meant that I wasn't going to get any extra money that day, and that meant that I was going to be very sick. I needed a plan and I needed one that was going produce lots of money for me, and for Jack. The whole concept of stopping using or cutting back was just not realistic for me at the time. I had no idea what I was going to do, so my brain started ticking over ideas as my body started to realise that it was going to get very sick; I needed to think fast.

My mum called that afternoon just to see how I was going. She knew that I had been using drugs but had no idea which drugs or to what extent. When I answered the phone and sounded so upset she asked me what was wrong so I told her that I had left my job at the cinema. I didn't tell her that I had been fired because even though she knew that I was no longer in control of my life, I wanted her to still believe in me. She asked me what I was going to do for money and I asked to borrow $50 from her. We then got into a huge fight and she hung up on me. That was the last contact that I would have with my parents for a very long time. The family love that had once surrounded me I had now pushed very far away and all I could feel was loneliness.

Chapter 6

Little Girl Lost

I will never forget the events that followed me being fired from the cinema. I caught the bus home and started to think about what I was going to do to get money from now on. I couldn't think of anything. I had ripped off every family member or friend that I had; I had sold everything that I had ever owned. I had nothing left, nothing except myself; my body was all I had left. Then I had to consider if I could deal with selling myself: my body, my soul and my self-worth. Unfortunately, where I was at with my addiction meant that I had left myself with no other option. I knew that I could never get into crime that affected anybody else's life, so selling myself seemed like the least harmful option at the time. I hadn't even considered what it would be like or how I would feel about it all; all that I could think about was the money and the drugs that would follow the money. By the time the bus pulled up to my stop, a short 15 minutes later, I had decided to discuss with Jack the prospect and the reality of prostitution. I had decided on prostitution because the thought of stripping in front of lots of men at any one time revolted me. I had obviously already numbed my mind enough to tell myself that I could sell my body to strangers so that they could have sex with me. My life was no longer my own, I had officially handed it over to my heroin addiction to control. At the time I had no idea of the wiles of the devil; but he had ensnared me body, mind and soul. I no longer recognised myself, nor did I want to.

When I got home I explained to Jack that I had been fired from my job. He told me that it was bound to happen and that things would be okay. It seemed to me that he had obviously used more heroin since I had left for work because I was now starting to feel a little bit sick but Jack seemed fine. I told Jack that I needed to talk to him. He came and sat down with me straight away; he must've known that I was serious. I explained to him my theory about going to work, about how it was going to be the only way that I could think of that we would be able to support our growing habits. I suppose I half expected him to try and talk me out of it; after all I was still his girlfriend. But as it was he too was starting to feel a bit sick and he basically said he would stand by me whatever I decided. He asked me if I thought it would be easy and I told him that it would be disgusting but to think about and focus on the money.

Five minutes later we were flicking through the phone book under 'Introduction Agencies'. I found a few but one stood out; it was called 'Companions'. I liked the sound of the name, as it didn't sound too dirty, and so they were the first ones that I decided to call. The woman that I spoke to asked me my age, weight, dress size and what I looked like: I told her 21 years old, 40 kilograms, size 6-8 and shoulder length reddish blonde hair with blue eyes. She sounded impressed and asked to meet me that night at 7pm. I said yes without even thinking about it. When I got off the phone I very quickly realised that we had no money; no money to score to make sure that I could survive the interview, not even enough money for a bus trip to Spring Hill. We rang every person we could think of, but as we had already burned everybody, nobody was willing to help us, understandable, but at the time I thought they were all being totally irrational. We decided to ask for enough gear on credit that I would at least survive the interview and if we could get that then I would just walk in to Spring Hill, which was about an hour's walk. For some strange reason our dealers agreed to give us enough for the both of us not to be sick. Jack walked me in to meet the woman and within 10 minutes of talking to her she asked me if I could start immediately. I couldn't believe how 'easy' it had all been, or so I thought at the time. I am sure now that it was all merely another plan of the enemy coming to pass in my life.

The woman then took me to the brothel that was to become my place of work; how strange that in the morning I had left for my respectable job as a cinema worker and now I was about to become a working prostitute; my life was definitely no longer my own. Before I could go any further with her she asked me what my working name was. I have no idea why but I just said, "Anna". I was then introduced to the other girls, one of whom gave me a 'guided tour' of the place. While she was doing that she gave me all of the work 'rules' and told me that best way to 'sell yourself' is to just be yourself, always make eye contact and always smile at the clients. It all seemed so normal for her and the others. I had no idea how I was going to cope but I knew that I would if only for the sake of the drugs that I knew were to follow the work. It was also explained to me that the girl takes home 50% of what she makes which sounded like a lot at the time. I had no idea that not only was I being ripped off by the brothel owner but I was also ripping myself off by willingly giving myself over to the enemies camp; as far as I was concerned there was now no turning back for me, but, thankfully, God had other ideas for me.

After the first time that I was chosen as 'the one' by a client I stood under the shower, as I had been told to do, but I had the water on so hot that it was basically burning my skin. I was trying to wash away the filth that I felt; I was trying to clean myself internally. Wondering the whole time if I could ever scrub away the memories, asking myself what I was doing there and knowing that I was not really this person that I had allowed myself to become – this 'Anna' that was now a part of me and my existence.

By the time the night had ended it was all a blur for me, all I could think about was getting paid and getting stoned; I intended to get so out of it that I couldn't open my eyes to look at anyone, especially myself. I had no idea of the work that I had done but when I left I was paid $325, plus the two $50 tips I had received from clients, probably just for being a new girl. In the cab on the way home it hit me that I was actually quite sick. I had made it through the night without thinking about it but now I could hardly sit still from hanging out. I ran inside to be sick, quietly waking Jack up to tell him how I felt. I told him that I felt so dirty and disgusted in myself but that all I could think about was scoring. We had the biggest shots we had ever had at any one time that morning and for the first time in a long time I felt totally pain and thought free; I was absolutely numb – and I loved it.

From that night on I worked seven nights a week, sometimes making up to $700 a night, including tips. I thought that all of my heroin dreams had all come true at once. I had no real concern for the cost to my life because I was so out of it all of the time. Within a couple of weeks I was so out of it that I stopped paying rent and we were evicted. Jack and I were so stoned that we just didn't care less. We moved into a backpackers just down the road from the dealers place and a short walk to the train station for me every night. It was expensive to live there but we felt like we had the world in our hands and with the amount of money I was making we just didn't care. All I was doing was using, sleeping, showering, working, using, sleeping, showering and working. By this stage I had also started using speed to stay up to go to work at night. My life had become one very vicious cycle and I wasn't even looking for a way off it.

One night just after New Years Eve the brothel that I was working in was raided. Thankfully I was not with a client at the time and the boss lady told the police that I was just a friend of hers. I was able to go home but I had no money except for what was left from the day before, which was not much. So the next day, when I was feeling quite sick, I rang one of the girls that I had met working on the street outside the strip club. I asked her if I could start working for her. At the time I had no idea of the so-called "work ethics" of the street girls and I presumed that it would be just like the brothel. I was very wrong. The first night that I was there the other girls repeatedly threatened me, mainly because I was young and attractive and they considered me a threat. I promised not to 'steal' regular clients and they left me alone. However, a week later I took a regular without knowing and when I returned I got thrown to the ground and kicked and punched until I couldn't see out of my eyes. They were trying to teach me a lesson that I needed to learn to survive the streets. I learned very quickly.

A couple of weeks after that incident the woman that I had been working for originally also paid me a visit on the street. Even though I had now made 'friends' with the other girls they all thought that I needed to learn a lesson about respecting the boss lady and so they stood back while she threw me into the gutter and picked me up only to smash my head into the car door repeatedly. It was just the way things were on the street. I returned home bloodied and bruised and told Jack that something had to give. In return he gave me a bigger shot than usual to take away my pain. It worked and I returned to work two nights later, looking a little worse for wear but I still got work – and to me that was all that mattered.

The woman that I had started working for on the streets, Tina, wanted me to start working in the daytime as well. Tina also happened to sell some really strong speed which Jack and I were soon using every night too. She said that we could live in the unit that we worked from for 'free' so long as I worked when a call came in. I didn't mind because to me it all meant money and money meant drugs. Very soon after we moved to a bigger house in Newmarket to work from and Jack and I moved to a cute little workers cottage in Petrie Terrace; a place to call our own. Unfortunately, we never properly unpacked because I was either sleeping or working, so it never really felt like home to me.

The house at Newmarket was quite flashy and things worked out well there for a couple of months until one day Jack and I were there doing some house cleaning when I heard a huge bang at the front door. By the time I got to the door all I could see were guys wearing black balaclavas holding guns – they were demanding money and drugs. They locked Jack and I in a room while they searched the house, turning the place upside down, smashing everything they could touch. One of the guys came into the room where we were telling us that we were useless junkies. He held a gun to our heads while asking us if we knew where there was any money or drugs. Until this stage we had no idea just how big a speed dealer Tina had been, but they were there for big money and once they had found it they left. The house was a mess; all smashed up and totally unworkable. I told Tina that I needed to work that night and she punched me in the mouth, for being so disrespectful, and told me to get out and that I was a filthy junkie. Sadly nothing that anybody did to me hurt me anymore because I was so numb all of the time.

My only dilemma now was where I was going to work or who could I work for so that the girls on the street wouldn't kill me for working for myself. My only answer was the woman who was the unspoken one in charge of watching the girls on the street. She was a very hard woman named Sam who was in her early-30's but looked older and much more worn, and she had worked the streets from the age of 16 but was now just the girls' minder. She lived with her girlfriend who was a worker and they just lay around all day using copious amounts of heroin and speed at night. Their lives were amplified versions of how my life was and I knew that if I wasn't careful I would end up like them; and that soon became my greatest nightmare. Anyhow, I called her up to tell her what had happened with Tina and to ask her if I could work for her. She agreed straight away. Sam and her girlfriend, Peta, came to pick us up from our place with a gram of heroin for us. We thought it was really sweet of her and I had no idea at the time that she just wanted to make sure that I was in debt to her from the very beginning. I should have known by then that nobody in the business did anything kind for anybody else; everybody was out for themselves. I started working for her that night.

Two weeks later Jack and I were evicted by the police from our house and so we moved into Sam and Peta's place with them. It just made everything easier for all of us. We were all just using, sleeping and working; all of us except for Jack. He was quite happy to just sit back and let me go to work to make all of the money that paid for the drugs we both used; and who wouldn't have been happy. I did love him in some strange and sick type of way. I believed that I wouldn't have survived doing what I was doing without him there to support me. I was blinded by love, and drugs, to the fact that I was supporting him in everyway possible; physically, mentally, emotionally and habitually.

Very soon after we moved in with Sam and Peta they decided to get a bigger house. It was in the street opposite where we worked, so it seemed so much easier. We soon settled in and things started to become 'normal' again. Sleeping, using, working, showering; my life was now definitely going nowhere fast. I felt tied to Sam and Peta in a very unhealthy way. They provided my home and my drugs. They also provided a safety net for me if I felt unable to go to work at any given time; they would just give me gear on credit knowing that I would be back at work the following night anyway.

My life had fallen into a cycle there seemed no need to get out of. I worked for our drugs and the drugs kept me at work. Everything seemed so 'normal' to me at the time. Within a few months of working with them I started to fool myself into feeling so comfortable with the whole working scenario that I started to wonder why Jack was still around. After all I was the one working to feed two peoples habits, habits that continued to grow with the money that I made. So I started to put away my tips so that Jack didn't know anything about them. Very soon I had saved up almost $800 and I called Jacks dad, Alan, out of the blue. He hadn't heard from us for over a year and so he was a little shocked. I asked him to meet me for coffee one day. I waited until Jack was out to it and met Alan at a café near our place. I told him all about what we had been doing in the time that we had been 'missing'. He was very upset. I then told him that I had saved some money up for Jack to fly home to England but that he had no idea about it. I told him that I needed to get Jack out of my life before we destroyed each other. He agreed to help me, and Jack.

About a month later I told Jack what was happening. Alan had organised the trip and Jack was going to be staying with his grandmother for three months once he got to England; he just needed a new English passport if he wanted to stay longer than three months. He couldn't believe that I had done this to him behind his back. He had become so dependent on me for the money for the drugs that we took that he couldn't imagine not being there with me, trapped in a lifestyle that was slowly but surely destroying us both. He said that he would go but that he would return within a couple of weeks. He thought that he would go for just long enough to hang out and get over his withdrawals and then he would come back. I already knew in my heart that he wasn't going to be back. I'm sure that he did too. I also knew that even if he did come back that I couldn't, and wouldn't, willingly accept him back into my life the way that he was in it now.

Jack left and things did change quite rapidly for me from that moment on. The night that he left I was able to buy enough gear for myself to get very wasted and was also able to pay out my debt to Sam. I had achieved something that hadn't been possible while I had been supporting both Jack and myself. From that moment on I felt a strange sense of release. Almost as though I had been released from some type of bondage; even though I didn't fully understand the extent of that reality it still felt amazing. Just letting go of Jack I felt like a new woman. I was still quite sad about it for a couple of weeks – that was until something happened that rocked my newfound world to its foundations.

One night while I was getting ready for work I heard a very quiet knocking on the front door. I had no idea who it could be; nobody was expecting anybody and I knew that the police basically banged the door down so I knew that it wasn't them. I quickly finished getting dressed and ran to the door. I didn't know who I was expecting but I do know that I wasn't expecting my mum, but there she was with my Uncle Peter and Aunt Robbie. They had found me via a contact with the government and had come to take me away. Because Sam and Peta didn't want them calling the police they just acted like my housemates; they also didn't want my mum to know that Sam was not only my drug dealer, but also my madam. My mum was shattered when she saw me and just started crying. Up until that point I had avoided looking in mirrors; since I had started working I had just stayed away from them. She made me look in the mirror and what I saw was a very sick, withdrawn and sad looking, little girl lost. I told her that I had been living in Spring Hill for about a year and that it wasn't that I didn't love her but that I knew that my drug abuse was destroying her and dad also. She was angry with me for not contacting her but more than anything she was upset that her little girl had become so sick and pathetic. I tried to pretend that my prostitution wasn't happening and when she asked me why I was dressed that way I told her that I was going out night clubbing. She knew me too well and knew that I was lying, but what else could I do. I had never even thought of the possibility of my mum showing up to the house that I did sex work from. She left about an hour later, but only after asking Sam for the phone number. She told me that she would call me soon. As soon as she left I felt a sense of grief and all of the shame that I had felt when I had first started working returned like a tidal wave, crushing all that I had become in one fell swoop. There is nothing like the real love of a mother to help a child come to a point of realisation about themselves.

It was a couple of weeks before I heard from mum; it probably took her that long to calm down after seeing me the way that I was. When she did ring me she had heard from a friend of hers that Will's dad had died and that she thought that I should make contact with him. She figured that after all Will had done for me that the least I could do was be there for him when he needed a friend. So I called his number, for the first time in almost a year and a half, and of all the people that could have answered it, he did. I started crying. For the first time in a long time I was talking to somebody, other than my mum, who knew me, the real me. Will said that he was glad to hear from me after all that time and asked me where I had been and what I had been doing. I couldn't tell him over the phone so I asked him if I could meet him the following day. He agreed and said that he would pick me up from my house and go for a drive somewhere.

The next day he came to pick me up at 9am. Will had always

been an early riser but that was about the time that I normally went to bed. No worries. That just meant that I had to have a shot of speed before he got there so that I could stay awake. I was really looking forward to catching up with him. After all that we had been through over the years, he still accepted and loved me for who I was – the real Bronwen. When I got in the car he started to cry; he told me that I looked absolutely dreadful. I went on to tell him what I had been doing and to what extent I had been doing it. I told him that I'd had three nights off in the past year and that I knew that I was slowly destroying myself but that I couldn't see anyway out of it. He told me that he had been clean, not using heroin, for almost six months until he heard that his dad had died and then he had started using again. He admitted that he had been looking for an excuse to start using again. It was then that he asked me if I had any gear on me; I did have some for myself but I happily shared it with him. I thought that by doing so I was being a 'good friend'. I had no thought of the destruction I was helping him do to himself. We happily spent the rest of the day in the park on the river near West End. We talked about everything that there was to talk about, we hugged and cried and then I asked him to take me back to the house so that I could go to work. He got very upset about it, but I explained to him that I needed to so that I wasn't sick. He eventually took me back there but told me that he was going to come and pick me up the following day, and he did.

That soon became our new ritual together. I was using so much of the drugs that I soon started to forget that I hadn't been sleeping, until one day when I was with Will and I almost collapsed. My diet was basically drugs, cigarettes and yogurt. My life was so lacking of anything healthy I was actually surprised that I was doing as well as I had fooled myself into thinking I was doing. It was around this time that I told Will that I wanted to stop working. I didn't know how I was going to do it but I somehow knew that I had to stop before I destroyed my body and killed my soul. He agreed to lock me in his room at his place for as long as it would take me to dry out from all the drugs. The main problem with this plan was that by then Will also had quite a bad habit from all of the drugs that I had been sharing with him, and probably wouldn't be able to carry out the plan. We didn't know how we were going to get clean but we were determined to try.

Chapter 7
Flirting With Death

One day Will picked me up in the morning and when I got in to his car I just blankly told him that I wasn't going to go back. I had enough gear for us to wean off over a 24 hour period and that was what I intended to do. When we did eventually run out of the drugs that I had, about 12 hours later, he took me back to his place and locked me in his room. Before he did that he took a photo of me so that I could remember what I looked like when I was 'hanging out'. At the time I was less than 40 kilograms, had big black bags under my eyes and basically looked like 'death warmed up'. I now know that at that time I was actually under the influence of a major attack in the spirit realm. Allowing the enemy to take control of me, I had no idea that what I was doing was flirting with death. But satan wanted me dead. It was only God that I survived that detox experience at all. Will actually did what he had said that he was going to do and had locked me in his room downstairs. I did everything humanly possible to him and to his possessions. I punched and kicked Will and his dog; I smashed some of his records and threw anything that I could get my hands on across the room. I screamed at the top of my lungs every time he tried to speak to me; the neighbours must've thought that someone was being killed. I was totally out of control. He had gotten me a lot of different pills from his doctor but nothing seemed to work; all I wanted, and didn't want at the same time, was a big shot of heroin. I begged him to take me back to work, and he wouldn't; he was definite about keeping his word to me. He never wanted to see me like that again and he definitely never wanted to see me go back to being a prostitute, and he was determined to do all that he could to help me. He couldn't believe that I had gotten so badly into heroin in such a relatively short time; I think he was afraid that if I kept going with it at the same rate that it might kill me – that was a revelation that I personally didn't get for quite some time. In doing everything that he had done for me Will put up with much more than any friend deserves, and was willing to put up with more. After four days the heroin and speed were somewhat out of my system. I was still screaming and writhing in pain; I didn't think that my body could take much more. Unfortunately, I came to forget the pain of withdrawal far too quickly.

Within a week of my deathly withdrawal from the drugs that were threatening to destroy me, Will and I actually tried to kill ourselves. Once the drugs were sort of out of my system I knew that my tolerance would have dropped and so I told Will that I wanted to score just one last time. Because he too was a heroin addict, he foolishly agreed with me. I called up one of the dealers that I had stayed in contact with and told him that I was going back to work, which I had no intention of doing. He knew from previous experience that I could make up to $700 in one night and so he gave me two and a half grams on credit, which was $400 worth at the price at which he gave it to me. We also had an assortment of pills from Will's doctor; enough to kill any one person. So we figured with that mix of pills swallowed with red wine and mixed with the heroin we definitely wouldn't wake up. We both had our reasons for not wanting to keep living; mine was the inability to live with the guilt and shame that I had from all that I had done for heroin. I didn't want to have to keep looking at myself in the mirror and face the reality of who I had become. We drove to the Dutton Park cemetery, which was a place where we regularly went to use drugs anyway, so we figured it was kind of appropriate. We gulped down the pills and skulled down the red wine, then we divided up the gear. When I had been working it was nothing for me to have a gram in one shot, so I had almost two full grams and Will had what was left, which was still more than he had ever had at any one time. We put on our favourite tape and kissed each other goodbye. The time was 10:40pm.

I woke up at 2:10am shattered that I had woken up at all. The tape was still playing – was this real? I felt slightly tingly but that was all I felt. I turned to look at Will; he was slumped over in the driver's seat and had turned bright pink. I tried to get him to talk to me but he wouldn't respond. All I could think of was that he was dead. What was I going to do? I tried to lift up his arm but it was wedged under the park brake and it too was bright pink. I was now terrified. Had I just tried to kill myself only to wake up and have my best friend dead next to me? What had we done? I started to slap Will on the face to try and wake him up but he wasn't moving. The only consolation was that he was still warm. While I was slapping his face I realised that I was still very stoned and I was starting to nod off. I wasn't sure what bought me back around but I came to with a start and I knew I had to wake Will up right away or he could die. I got out of the car and opened up his door; I tried to drag him out of the car into the fresh air. He fell out of the car with a thud to the ground. Was it too late for him? I still wonder if I had asked God for help at this time or not because suddenly I started to touch his face gently seeing that the slapping hadn't worked; he always was such a gentle soul. It worked. He woke up with a startled look on his face. Then he screamed. He couldn't move his arm.

Somehow we got back to his place in one piece and his mum had to take him to the hospital. The spiral just kept going downwards for me then. We had to lie to our parents and tell them that we had been beaten up, even though our stories didn't make sense at all. They must've just been so used to us not telling the truth that they seemed to let it be. Understandably, Will's mum, Amanda, didn't want me living in her house any more and so I needed somewhere to stay immediately. My trusty old friend Jordan, whom I hadn't seen for at least a couple of years, lived just around the corner from Will and they were close friends. I called him and his parents said that I could go and stay there for a very short while until I got on my feet again. The trouble was I didn't know how on earth I was going to do that or what I was even going to do. I explained everything to Jordan, he had always loved me for who I was before and he did so again. His friendship was so priceless to me at this particular point in my life; more so than at any other time. I just needed someone who would hear me out, someone who wouldn't let me score heroin, someone who was willing to protect me from myself.

It was around this time at Jordan's place, after talking things through with him, I actually started to think deeply about how I felt about everything. Without the heroin to numb my emotions I realised that I was angry with myself for becoming so pathetic. I was upset at myself for not being stronger. But no matter how I felt I still could not admit to myself that I had become a full-blown, out of control, heroin addict. Not even after everything that I had done. I wondered what it was going to take for me to get to that point; I knew from the program Alateen that the first step in recovering was admitting that I was powerless. I couldn't do that, I just wasn't willing. I still thought that I could look after myself, even though I had proven time and time again that I couldn't. It was around this time that I started to keep a journal again for the first time in years. Upon reflection it was all about how dreadful I had been to myself and that withdrawal from heroin was much worse than heroin itself. I still had so far to go. Thankfully, I still have that journal and can now see that at least I was willing to look at myself and all that I had become; I just wasn't willing to change any of it, not yet anyhow. I was just so lost.

That was when Jordan's brother had some guys from Holland that were in a band come to stay with him. I started flirting with one of them the day that they arrived and soon he returned the advances. I didn't know any other way to express myself with males than to be sensual and sexual with them. They were all going on a trip up to the Great Barrier Reef, hiring a car and just leaving. It sounded like exactly what I needed and I soon persuaded Richie to take me with them. (I hadn't been using for almost two weeks by this stage and actually felt amazingly well, all things considered). We were gone for almost two weeks. It was an awesome time for me, just enjoying being alive. They were really fun guys to be around and they were helping me forget what I was running from. The problem remained in Brisbane. It was heroin. No matter how much I was enjoying my holiday and my time away from it all, I couldn't get it out of my head. I knew that when I got back there that I would have a shot as soon as I could, so it was then that I started to encourage them to head home; and they did.

When I got back to Brisbane I was completely out of money but I had already talked myself into scoring. I called Will, but his mum didn't want me to have any contact with him for a while. I thought that she was being totally irrational and I couldn't think of what to do, so I called up one of my old regular clients; a 'family' man named Steve. By then I hadn't worked for almost 6 weeks and he said that he had missed me. I told him that I needed to borrow some money and that I also needed him to pick me up and drop me somewhere. He was madly in love with the 'Anna' in me, and so he agreed. I told him straight away that I wasn't going to sleep with him; I'm sure that he already knew that anyhow. But I was quite happy to exploit him for all that it was worth to me, he still didn't even know my real name. So that day he picked me up from Jordan's place and I didn't return there for a very long time.

I went to stay in another backpackers in Highgate Hill, while happily asking Steve for a lot more money. It was there in West End that I bumped into Jack's stepbrother Drew one day when I was scoring. He was a few years younger than me and looked very much like Jack. I started to sleep with him straight away and then moved myself into his bedroom so as to save myself some money. A couple of weeks later I decided that I needed to get out of Brisbane again; I needed to get clean...again. So Drew and I took off to Melbourne, but we only made it as far as Sydney. A whole heap of my old friends had moved there and I wanted to catch up with them now that I wasn't using. I detoxed on the bus on the way down there which was an absolutely horrible experience. But as I hadn't been using too much it was bearable. Once we arrived we went to stay with Kent. On the first day there I bumped into Juel, out of all of the people in Sydney. I'm still not sure why it was that I saw her but I do know that she was being very 'spiritual'; she had just been to India for two years and was into a whole lot of strange things. At the time I just wanted to be clean and free, so I heard her out, but it wasn't for me. We then moved on to stay with her brother for a while.

Within a couple of weeks I started to find myself wondering what I was doing there. It was then that I decided to call Will. He answered the phone and as soon as he spoke I knew that he was stoned on heroin. I immediately wanted to be there with him, in the same state as him. I longed to be back home, wherever that was. He told me that he missed me and asked when I was coming back; I said soon. I called him everyday for the next week. It was comforting for me to hear his voice; long distance and stoned, but familiar. I left Drew there in Sydney and caught a bus back to Brisbane to be with Will, and heroin. He picked me up from the transit centre and had a syringe with the gear in it for me, all ready to go. We very quickly slipped back into our very sick and sad relationship with each other, and with heroin. By this time he had received part of his inheritance from his father dying, and sadly we were feeding our heroin diet with it. Every time we would spend any of it we would write down the cost and I would swear that I would pay him back some day, both knowing all along that in junkie talk that just wasn't ever going to happen.

After what had happened in the cemetery Will's mum wasn't interested in me staying there for any extended period of time; she was still quite angry with me. So I had to try and find somewhere to live. Obviously, I had no money but I had no problem in calling Steve to ask him for more money. He agreed so long as I was happy to see him every now and then and I agreed so long as I didn't have to have sex with him. He gave in to me, again, and agreed. Will helped me to find a one bedroom flat in West End the following weekend. It was a cute little place that I could call my own. Thankfully it was furnished because I owned nothing. Steve gave me the money that I needed to get myself set up. The flat was handy because we were close enough to our dealer's house that they were willing to deliver it to me. That meant that I didn't need to do anything, all I had to do was make the initial phone call, then I could lie there and just wait. Will spent most of his days there with me, just using drugs and listening to music. My life was once again stagnant; but once again, I didn't care.

While I was living there in that flat I started to do a lot of writing – my renewed passion for it meant that I was doing it almost everyday. I would always wait until I'd had a shot of heroin and then I would begin my time of reflection. The words that I was writing at the time, upon reflection now, were so sad and so depressing. I was trying so hard to find the answers to my life, trying to work out why I was where I was and how I got there. I was searching for my redemption within myself; attempting the impossible. I was looking for a pathway to forgiveness without even knowing that was what I was doing. I was searching for the 'old' me even though that was never, realistically, going to happen. I was never going to be the same; my life had been altered. My mind was so clouded and so dark. I thought that I wanted better for myself, but I was too comfortable in the seemingly pain-free life that I was living that I wasn't willing to try and change where I was at. The enemy was having a field day with me, and my mind, because every time I would write something I would get more and more depressed and wind up much worse than before. Now I understand that those words were not from God; they were painful and dark, and I fooled myself into believing that I was 'cleansing' myself by getting them out. I was trapped, with nowhere to turn but inwards.

I was trying to write down what had happened to me with heroin, with Jack, and all that had become of my life during that time. It was difficult but I knew that I wanted to do it. Funnily enough, it is only now that I am whole that God would have me write it. But the enemy had me fooled into thinking that I was in control of the words that I wrote even though I wasn't – the devil had control of my mind and thoughts (it's funny that I am still not in control – those are God's words from my pen). Some of the titles that I had written down at the time include; 'When the Devil Comes Knocking', 'In the Service of Satan's Army', 'In the Lap of Satan', 'Self-loathing in the Devils Playground', 'Dark Soul Rising'. At the time I had absolutely no idea that there was an enemy or a God. It is only now, with a fuller understanding of the spirit realm, that when I read my old notebooks I am amazed at what was occurring in my life at the time. I thought that I was in control of my own life but, indeed, through the addiction and all that came with it, I had given myself over to the enemy for him to control me. I was deceived to the point where I had absolutely no idea what was really happening in my life, and that would continue for quite some time yet.

A couple of months after I moved into my flat things started to change for me. I was still using every day but my outlook seemed to be changing for the better. I now wanted something more from my life; I just had no idea what I was looking for. At the time my mum would always call me and tell me that my life was going nowhere and that I needed to just walk into a church and ask God to forgive me. I had absolutely no plans to do that because I didn't think that I had done anything wrong, by God or by anyone else, including myself. My mind was just so clouded and so deceived that it was actually the furthest thing from my mind, especially going into a church. I had been to church twice when I was a young girl for my neighbours' communions and it had seemed dull and boring. Besides which, I didn't think that I believed in God. I had no idea that God was making a way for me even then, at a time when I didn't believe He was real, let alone watching over me.

The next big thing that happened in my life was that my childhood friend from Melbourne, Rani, wanted to come up for a holiday. She wanted to have a holiday on the coast at my mum and dad's place, so I asked them if that would be okay. At the time they thought that I wasn't using and so they agreed. I'm still not sure how I fooled them into thinking that I wasn't using at the time one look at me and I thought that they would know for sure, but they didn't. Before Rani arrived I stopped using as much heroin so as to make it a bit easier on myself and I took a little bit with me thinking that it would help me through the five days there. When Rani arrived, at the airport, and I hugged her it was like I had just seen her the day before. It was such a warm and welcoming hug, the type of hug that you need when life seems to be too much. We spent a lot of time talking and I told her everything that there was to know about my life; the good and the bad. She too had some horrible stories to tell me about her own life. We drank a bottle of gin that first night and stayed up talking until nearly dawn. I had needed a friend to hear me out; someone who knew me and that loved me enough to be honest with me. That person was Rani. We learned a lot from one another over the next couple of days and then I ran out of heroin. I tried to think of ways to get Will to bring some up but his car had broken down. I wasn't willing to stop using and so I had to go to Brisbane. I made up some dreadful excuse and Rani agreed to come down there with me.

We caught the train down to Brisbane and Will picked us up. I had told him on the phone that I needed a shot. We drove straight to the dealer's house so in the car on the way there I told Rani that I was just running in to pick up some pot. I don't think that she knew any better, and if she did she didn't let on. We drove to Will's place and he fixed it all up downstairs then I snuck in to have it. I was quite stoned but Rani didn't say anything. We all sat around and talked and listened to music. Later in the afternoon Rani started to say that she thought we should organise getting back up the coast to my parent's place. I really wasn't into it at all. She was due to leave in two days and the whole thought of going up there for a day just to have to come straight back didn't interest me at all. I gave absolutely no consideration to the way Rani felt about the whole situation. I called my parents and told them that she was catching a train up there at lunchtime the following day by herself. My mum got very angry with me and I thought that she was a little out of control so I ended up hanging up on her. Rani left the following day and I told her that I loved her and that I still had an issue with heroin and that I would talk to her at some later stage. I didn't know when that would be, and at the time I didn't even care. She walked down the platform crying deep tears for me. I knew then that heroin was destroying my life as everything that I held dear to me no longer mattered; and I didn't care.

My life basically continued on much the same way for most of that year; I would use drugs and then look for money to use more drugs. Will and I spent over $40,000 in just a few months. We didn't really see the money as real money; it was kind of like play money. Unfortunately it was very real; it was money that his father had left him when he had died. But that just didn't seem to phase us when we rang the dealer to score drugs – we would have used money from any source. I would always tell him that I was going to pay him back, and God willing I will at some stage of our lives. It got to the stage where, on paper, I owed him $23,000. Of course that was above and beyond any reality for me; even $100 was more than I could afford. But we kept spending it. The addiction was our whole lives, much more important to us than money. Our lives were so messed up; we lived a very sick and sad existence of loving and using each other at the same time. We needed each other as much as we needed the heroin that kept our relationship alive. We were trapped in a life that we didn't know how to get of and didn't want to get out of.

It was around this time that we bumped into our old school friend, Sophie, one day in West End. She asked us what we had been doing with ourselves and we said that we had been using heroin and not much else. She laughed and told us that her and her boyfriend had been dealing heroin and not much else. She told us how much her gear was and gave us her phone number. It is only now that I realise how intensely the enemy was working at destroying my life by dropping all of these people at my feet. Her phone number even ended in 666! I would even joke to Will about calling up the devil; and I had no concept of the spirit realm. We very soon became regular customers of hers as the deals were bigger and better, so of course we became very good customers for her.

All this time I was still in contact with Steve and he would take me out for lunch every now and then and I would hit him up to loan me more money and he would always give in. It was around this time that I told him my real name. The charade was just too much to take and besides I needed him to put money into my bank account so I had to give him me real name. It was strange for me when he would call me Bronwen, because I still felt like 'Anna' to him. I was still conniving money out of him for doing very little; I didn't have sex with him, I just gave him companionship. It was around this time that I started to realise that he was really falling in love with me. Sadly, I thought that was okay because it meant that I could wrangle more money out of him, and I proved that to be true. One day over lunch I told him that I need to look for a job and I joked about what I would put on my resume; heroin addict, prostitute, good-for-nothing. He got quite upset that that was how I saw myself, but it was true. He told me to leave it with him. I totally forgot about the whole conversation half an hour after having it; he obviously didn't.

Two months later he called me up and asked me if I still wanted a job; I laughed and asked him what he meant. He came and picked me up and took me for a drive to the suburbs. I had no idea what he was doing but just went along anyway. He drove past the local cinema and told me that there was a café behind the cinema and he had just signed the lease for it that afternoon. I couldn't believe it; I truly thought that he was joking.

It was then that he asked me to work there with him. I wasn't sure how I was going to do it, but I agreed anyway. It was October 1998, my life was going nowhere – I may as well get a job. He agreed to pay me cash in hand so that I could keep getting my disability pension from Centrelink. He must have figured that at least this way I would stop asking him for so much money, which I did for a little while, until I started to need more heroin to help me with all the hours that I was working. It was then that I started to just skim little bits of money off the top of the till – nobody seemed to notice. I had done it at the cinema and I knew I could do it again. Plus, I always looked at it as Steve being an ex-client of mine, so I deserved to treat him that way. I was always able to justify my actions when it came to using drugs.

Around Christmas time Steve asked me if I knew anyone that needed some work. I suggested Will, so soon we were both working there; and because it was busy, I was skimming more and more money from the till. I gave it no thought and nobody mentioned anything to me, so I just kept doing it. Just after New Year's it was still busy and he asked me if I knew anybody else that needed a job because one of the other girls was leaving. She didn't like me but she knew that Steve would never sack me, so she left instead. That suited me fine because if anyone was going to work out that I was stealing money from the café it would have been her. I suggested Sophie to him because she had told me that she wanted to get a legitimate job as well as do the drug dealing. She was young and beautiful, and Steve hired her straight away. This made life even easier for Will and I because now we didn't even have to leave the building to score drugs; we just had to ask Sophie. We would wait until the end of the night and then tell her how much money we had skimmed and buy heroin from her accordingly. I thought that I was in heroin-heaven as things couldn't get any easier for me.

Things continued on like that for a couple of months when out of nowhere my brother, Adam, called me from Thailand. He had moved there a few months before that after he had broken up with his wife, Lynda. He offered to pay for me to get over there for a holiday and he said that he really missed me. I had never been overseas before and I thought that it would be a good opportunity to spend some time with the brother that I hardly knew, after all, I was nearly 24 years old and he was nearly 30. We weren't getting any younger or any closer. I agreed to go and got a month off work, (having power over your boss seemed to have unlimited advantages). As I had never been overseas before I didn't have a passport or any money so Steve offered to pay for it all. The day that I went to pick up my passport he sat down with me and told me that money had been going missing from the café and that he was quickly on the way to being broke. I lied and told him that I had no idea who it was but that I would keep my eyes open. At the time he thought that I was clean off drugs and so I don't actually think that he suspected me. I knew that a holiday was going to be that best thing for me and for everyone else in my life. I needed some time away from heroin, and from myself. Of all the places for me to go, I had to go to one of the heroin capitals of the world, Chiang Mai.

I was so excited about my holiday. I packed up my flat and stored it all at different people's places. I had told everyone that I was going for a month, but I wasn't sure when I would be back. The whole idea of an exotic getaway appealed to me so much I didn't know if I would ever want to come back. I had my last shot of heroin the night before

I left which meant that I would be hanging out on the plane. My parents came to see me off at the airport and they too thought that I had been clean for quite a while so they were very excited for me. The plane trip was very long and felt even longer because of the withdrawal, but the whole excitement of the holiday made my mind too excited to really think about the pain I was feeling. I must've looked a wreck because when I got off the plane and spotted my brother he looked concerned. We had a beautiful big hug and headed for our hotel. We were spending the first two days in Bangkok and then heading up north on the train, to Chiang Mai, where he lived. I was so excited to be in a new country, I took everything in. I was totally amazed at Thailand and the Thai people, they were so friendly.

That first night was one of the most memorable of the entire trip for me. My brother took me out for dinner and then we went to the red-light district, known as 'Patpong'. We sat outside a bar and as I watched all of the working girls parading around I felt very sad inside. It wasn't that long ago that it had been me, selling myself to strangers. The thought revolted me and I started to cry. It was then that I realised that not only was I sad but I was also emotional because I was hanging out. Adam wasn't fooled and he picked up on it straight away. He grabbed my arm and stared at my vein and told me that it looked like a fresh wound. I tried to tell him that I had been clean for ages but I am sure that he didn't believe me, and all I remember was him saying that instead of using heroin and killing myself slowly why not just use a gun and get it over and done with quickly. Those words have stayed with me until this day. It was my brother's way of letting me know that he cared for me because he went on to tell me that he loved me. It was a very memorable and special night for us both.

I had an amazing time in Thailand, cruising around on the back of Adam's motorbike. We would often go to visit the Buddhist temples and it was there that I realised that I needed to make some spiritual changes in my life or else I was never going to get better. I started reading some books on Buddhism and thought that I had found the answers to my questions, even though I didn't really know what my questions were. I was learning that to be at one with yourself was the answer. With all of the wounding and turmoil that I had going on inside of me, being at 'one' with myself was never going to be possible without God; but I tried to be my own god anyway. Not surprisingly it didn't work while I was in Thailand I replaced my drug intake with alcohol. Because of my dad's problem with alcohol I had never been a big fan of it, but over there it was so cheap. Adam and I would stay up late every night drinking, talking and listening to music. Our relationship was strengthened so much during the time that I was there. We shared words and experiences that we otherwise would never have had the chance to. I will always remember my time in Thailand very fondly and I will always love my brother on a totally different dimension from having been there with him.

Six weeks later I returned home to Brisbane and the life that I had left behind resumed immediately. Will and I and heroin all picked up where we had left off. I had experienced such beauty in Thailand and it was all basically forgotten as soon as I landed. I knew that my life had to change but I didn't know how to go about it. Will and I just plodded along like that for a couple of months and then Steve called me in one day to tell me that he had gone bankrupt and that he was closing down the café. My immediate thought wasn't pity for him, or guilt, but it was how I was going to support Will and my heroin habit without that extra money. It was then that Will and I decided to try and find some help.

Chapter 8
Following Through

About a week later Will and I were 'hanging out' one day (we had money but we were trying to quit using, again), when we decided to go to see a counsellor. We went to the Alcohol and Drug Foundation counsellor at Indooroopilly. The guy who saw us was called Peter. He was quite an understanding guy but because he worked for the government all he could do was recommend that we both go on methadone. We had been drug users for years and had never taken methadone for a reason – we didn't want to take one addictive substance to get off another addictive substance. We sat in his office for a couple of hours, getting sicker as the time passed. But we were determined not to use that day. The decision had been made and this time we were going to try and stick to it. It was then that Will mentioned an article his mum had showed him about naltrexone. We didn't know much about it, and seemingly neither did Peter, but he gave us the phone number of a doctor that treated heroin addicts with it. We had no idea at the time, but calling that phone number, and following through with our decision, was going to change our lives so dramatically, and so rapidly. Now all we had to do was make the call.

I had been staying at Steve's place, in the spare room, and that night my mum was coming down for a visit. Will dropped me at Steve's place. I went inside and my mum was already there. So I told them that I was going to have a shower as it was the only way that I could get to the bathroom in order to ease the pain that I was in. I had intended to just crush up some pills that I had and inject them. A couple of minutes later I heard a knock at the bathroom door but I chose to ignore it. I had all of my equipment laid out on the floor. The next minute I looked up and there was my mum; absolutely mortified. She started crying and yelling at me and walked out of the bathroom. When I went out into the lounge room my mum just looked at me, she was horrified. She told me that this was the last straw and that she couldn't do this any more. She told me that if I didn't get help that she was going to leave then and there and never enter my life again. That thought was more than I could cope with and I broke down in tears. I told her about the counsellor and Dr Reece. She asked me how serious I was about giving up heroin for good. The amount of times that I had promised that it would be the last time and then started using again were countless. I knew that I was serious this time. Something inside of me was different. I didn't want to keep using, I didn't want to die but it was now up to me.

After many more tears my mum asked me to call the doctor right away and make an appointment for as soon as possible. The receptionist said that I could go over there now and just wait for an appointment, but to only come if I was serious about giving up. Steve offered to drive mum and I over there straight away. In the car on the way there something inside of me told me that this was going to change my life forever (I just had no idea how radically). The wait in the reception seemed to take forever. My mum couldn't bear it and she went and waited outside on the verandah. The receptionist, a very special lady named Paula, went outside to pick some flowers for the desk and saw my mum out there crying. She gave my mum a white rose from the garden and told her that everything would be okay. My mum held on to that rose as though it was my life – she knew that my time was now or never, and she knew how delicate I was. My life was so precious to her and she couldn't understand why I would continually threaten it. Meanwhile I was sitting inside with my stomach churning, just waiting. Something was burning on the inside of me and I was unsure what it was. It is only now that I know that at that same moment my mum was outside praying to God to spare my life and to save me from myself.

The doctor called me in after almost an hour. He was very loud and outspoken. He asked me all about my drug taking history and started to tell me that the problem was that the drugs had created a big void inside of me that could only be filled by Jesus. At the time

I didn't care what he was saying; so long as he thought he could help me I was willing to listen to anything. He told me that because of the excess of my addiction the only way naltrexone would work for me was if I was willing to submit myself to a rehabilitation centre to go through the treatment. Naltrexone is a tablet that must be taken every day and it blocks the effects of opiates in the system, but a junkie taking it themselves daily is very unlikely. I understood that and so I agreed to find out more about the rehab. Dr Reece started to tell me that the only real option for me was a house at Mt Gravatt that was run by a big Maori guy whose name was Mr T. He said that he ran the place with his wife, Josie, and that he would call in advance to let them know that I was going to be calling. It all sounded very full on to me, but I was willing to give it a go. In the past, anytime anyone mentioned rehab to me I ran from the whole idea, but I knew this time things were going to be different. So the doctor gave me Mr T's number and encouraged me to keep calling until I got to speak to him and then he gave me all of the medication that I would need to help me through the withdrawals. I had to have a carer that would dispense the pills to me and my mum agreed to do that until I got into the rehab.

I started trying to call Mr T as soon as I got back to Steve's place and every hour after that. I just wanted to get in touch with him and let him know my predicament, so as to help him make a decision to take me in. Because I hadn't used all day I had a really rough night and when I woke up in the morning my mum told me to start trying to ring the rehab again. So I did, and I finally got to speak to Mr T at about lunchtime. He had been very busy and was happy to speak to his wife to find out if they had a spare bed for a female. He called me back a couple of hours later and told me that they had a spare bed but only if I was able to meet him the next day and then move in the day after that. It sounded perfect for me so I agreed and mum agreed to pay the money that was needed to secure my position there. So within 24 hours my life had already taken a dramatic turn. A complete turnaround was just around the corner for me, I could feel it.

The following day I went to the address in Highgate Hill that Mr T had given me. He had explained to me that the house there was only used for people that were doing a day program. When we pulled up outside the house I realised that I had scored drugs from there a few years before that, before it was a rehab. I knew then that

I was in for a hard time. As it was, the place was just around the corner from my dealers' house. I knew that I was going to go through with the whole rehab thing when I had no inclination to just run away and score. There was something deep within me that was helping me to stay where I was. When we went inside Mr T explained the house at Mt Gravatt to my mum and I and asked me if I was really serious about quitting the drug life. I told him a brief history of my drug taking and myself and told him that I knew if I didn't do something about my addiction now that it was never going to happen. He told me that I would be a welcome addition to the house there and that I was to go to the house first thing in the morning. That night was really hard for me, I was very sick and in a lot of pain but like earlier on, I knew that there was something helping me to pull through. I just had no idea of God or of the power behind the Spirit of God at the time; but I was about to find out.

My mum agreed to stay down in Brisbane until the following morning when I was to go to the rehab first thing. The house was in a suburb called Mt Gravatt, which is only 15 minutes from the city but I had never heard of it, so to me it was like travelling to the bush. I had only dwelled in the inner city areas of Brisbane, because that was where all of my dealers lived. So this trip to Mt Gravatt seemed to take forever because not only was I withdrawing from heroin, but from pills as well. My discomfort levels were starting to increase. Because of the intensity of my habit with both heroin and pills Dr Reece had placed me on a regime that meant that I would have to detox slowly for 2 weeks before he could do my naltrexone rapid detox. That was to allow my body the proper amount of time to be clean from all drugs. I knew that it wasn't going to be a pleasant two weeks, but I also knew that something inside of me was different this time; I just had no understanding of what that was.

When we pulled up at the house it looked very much like many of the junkie houses I had visited, or lived in, before. There were people sitting on the verandah smoking cigarettes and talking amongst themselves. It was the first day of July 1999, and I was bitterly cold. I had chills from the withdrawal, so I was rugged up like I had just come from the snow, yet I was still cold. As we walked up the stairs I felt a strange internal peace within my physical discomfort. We sat in the lounge room and waited for Mr T to call us down to his office. As I sat there I watched people vacuuming and wiping down furniture and felt as though I was witnessing real life. Housework had not entered my mind for years. I had no need to try and be house-proud because all the visitors that I ever had were on drugs and would never have noticed. But this place was different. These people may not have been enjoying what they were doing but they were being disciplined into doing it anyway; that was what I needed – discipline.

Mr T eventually called us downstairs and as we sat and listened to all that he had to say about the program I knew, deep inside myself, that I was in the right place. He said that the program was to help people work through more than just the actual addictions; they also worked through the issues related to the problem through intensive counselling. I had always shied away from counselling when it came to my drug abuse. Probably because I knew that it would help me to stop and up until that point in time I hadn't really wanted to stop. Something inside of me kept telling me that I was ready to face all of my problems. I had no idea at the time that it was the Spirit of God stirring deep within me, and I wouldn't know, or accept, that for quite some time. As Mr T told us about what the house was all about I could sense a peace in my mum as well – probably a knowing that so long as I stuck to the program, things were going to be different this time and not only that, but that they would stay different.

When we went upstairs to say our good-byes my mum just hugged me tightly for a really long time. She told me that she loved me and that she hoped that this was going to work for me because she could no longer handle my life the way it had been for so long. She was crying as she walked down the stairs, and inside of me I could feel her sorrow. My mum loved me so much. I had never stopped to think about how my life choices had affected her, or my dad. It was only then that it struck me that they, too, were hurting. I wanted to change for them, but more importantly, I finally wanted to change for myself.

I spent the remainder of that day just tidying up the room that I had been allocated and getting settled in. The people that lived there came in every now and then to introduce themselves to me. They all seemed like very interesting characters, each with their own painful story of addiction to share. At the time I was the only female other than Josie, Mr T's wife. There was another girl moving in that night, so I had an opportunity to settle in first. Once I had made my bed I sat down on it and thought about where I was at for the first time that day. I had decided to go to rehabilitation for my drug addiction only two days earlier, and there I was sitting on my bed. I felt lonely but not alone.

That night a young 17-year-old girl named Monique moved in to share my room with me. She was a very pretty young girl, but I could see the pain on her face. She had her own tale of heroin addiction to tell and over the coming days we would both share our tales of woe with one another. Mr T called a house meeting that night so that we could be officially introduced to the other members of the house and so that he could let us know what our roles were going to be once we had detoxed. It all seemed very surreal to me, like I was there but I wasn't there. I had never envisioned myself sitting down in a room full of people that were trying to beat their addictions and feeling as though that was where I wanted to be. I really wanted to fight my addiction and all of the problems that had stemmed from it or that had been rooted in it. I knew that I was finally in the right place to do that. I felt for Will who was going through the same experience of detoxing, but at home alone with his mum. I hoped that things were going to work out for both of us. After all, I missed having him in my life as a friend instead of a drug partner. I really wanted things to work out for both of us, as individuals, and deep inside of me I knew that at least I was going to be okay, finally.

The following day was much the same as the first. I spent more of my time talking to the other people in the house and finding out where they were at with drugs and their addictions to them. I was having a really interesting time discovering who they all were. That afternoon we were called to the lounge room for a workshop of sorts. We all had to tell our tales in just a couple of minutes. I was intrigued by some of the things that people were sharing. Everyone seemed to be so open and honest and everybody seemed to trust Mr T almost like he was their older brother. I was looking forward to having some counselling and trying to work out how I got to be where I was. I had to wait a couple more days for that.

That night I lay down on my bed and just contemplated all that was going on around me. There seemed to be so much happening but I almost felt as though I was in a different realm. My body felt very sore and I felt physically sick but inside me I had a strange peace; a peace that I had never known before. While I was lying there I decided to write down what I was feeling and thinking – something that I loved to do and hadn't done, without drugs, for such a long time.

This is the exact journal entry that followed:

*[54 hours here at the house, clean for approx. 95 hours (almost 4 days) 6:45 p.m. Saturday 2nd July 1999?] Why is it that I feel so comfortable and fulfilled and supported + cared for as I do. already I'm third degreeing everybody. All I want and feel + believe as I do is to really feel is a loving, sharing, honest household. Where people genuinely want to care and help each other in so many different ways. So special, so willingly genuine. I feel very 'safe' here. Comfortability beyond any detoxing experience I've had so far. People with similar stories of weakness, well and witnessed by all. People with such similar experiences I can't help but feel secure already. It's exceptional. In my head there is just so much going on – my truly knowledgeable brain is slowly but surely kicking in. My thoughts are clearing, my words feel easy. There's always something happening for someone. Everyone obviously with their own little nuances. But above all – I know I'm doing it for my true self because if I weren't I would not be here. Calling out for help. Reaching for a hand and it's there. So lovely, thoughtful, but busy. It's understandable they've got many living spirits under their eyes – and they need to be careful eyes for all of them. So few pairs of eyes for so many people. Everyone at some evil stage of withdrawal, over something, mainly 'the little white god' – heroin. So the level of understanding about all the different phases are covered and then after looking at the others I look at the big, beautiful Mr and Mrs T. Everyone, everywhere has their stories, you just have to want to discover a friend, if possible, out of mutual pains experienced. And this particular placing truly was divined into by a higher power. Ears are here to listen, and they shall. I have already spoken to everyone individually about me and them and it 'the power that be heroin'. I pretty much know and relate to their stories of the way the world works for a junkie. It spins all day – wake up, try to move, try + find money, try to call (sometimes depressingly engaged numbers), get on, mix up, whack up, get ****ed up. then minutes later you wonder how you're going to be able to get the cash to score again. Such a vicious ****ing cycle. It can definitely get you when your body is screaming and slap you in the face – that you are a junkie. A very difficult thing to admit to one's self – that the powder is more powerful than you.*

That journal entry was the first of a lot of writing that took place in the house. I would often go to my books for some place to be alone, just me and my thoughts. I had no idea at the time of the power of what was going on in my life, but God knew that I needed to keep writing it down. He had a bigger purpose for my gift of writing. Thankfully, I am still in possession of all of my notebooks; and I will always be grateful that I have the opportunity to share that which I am led to share.

Later that night when Josie gave me my medication before bed she told me that she would be in to wake me up around 8 a.m. if I wasn't already awake. I thought that she should leave me to sleep as long as possible, because sleep is one of the most difficult things to do during detoxification; and I told her just that. She laughed and told me that I had to get up and go to church. I honestly thought that she was joking with me, so I laughed. Then I realised that she was serious. I got my back up and started going on about that not being mentioned to me before. The reality was that it probably had been mentioned to me when I first met Mr T but I hadn't really been listening. Either way, there was no way that I was going to church. I made my opinion very clear to Josie. She came to me about an hour later and said that because I was detoxing I didn't have to go that week, but it was a Christian rehab so church was compulsory. I thought the whole thing was absolutely ridiculous, but at the time I just agreed. All I knew was that at least in the house I was getting, and staying, clean off heroin; and that was all I needed to know.

The next thing that made me question what I was doing there was on the following Tuesday night when we were asked to clean up the house after dinner, for a prayer meeting. I had no idea what all this was about and when I asked Mr T he told me that a bunch of people from the church gathered together every Tuesday night just to pray together. It sounded very silly to me but I was willing to sit in and watch; I had to anyway, as it was compulsory. The pastor from the church was David Hunt and he led the prayer meeting. He introduced himself to me and told me that I was a very welcome addition. I was still feeling quite sick and so I just lay down on one of the couches and watched the proceedings. David started by reading something out loud from the bible and then people just started to pray. I couldn't understand a lot of what was being said and I wasn't even sure if they were talking in English, but all together it sounded quite lovely.

Then they started calling people out into the middle of the circle and they all put their hands on whoever's turn it was and prayed for them. It seemed very strange to me but the people being prayed for seemed to get a lot from it. They all walked away calm and peaceful. It was a very odd experience for me. I declined when I was called out for prayer and David seemed to understand; he said that it might take some time to get used to. I wasn't interested in getting used to it; all I was interested in was staying off heroin.

The following day, after I had been at the house almost a week, I had my first counselling session with Mr T and he asked me to write down what I thought my issues were and what I thought needed to be dealt with. I had no real idea of the depth of pain some of the issues had created but I knew that I had to start somewhere. This is the list that I came up with (in no given order): drug addiction, sickness/pain, abortion, miscarriage, junk relationships/fake love (Jack/Will), PROSTITUTION – self abuse/self esteem/self punishment, loneliness, lack of emotion, childhood/parents/family, loss of 'clean' friends. This list was to become the starting block for our counselling sessions and he suggested that we tackle them by just working through whatever came up at the time. I honestly had no comprehension of the damage that I had done to my self or that had been done to my spirit but I was finally willing to face up to myself and my problems; regardless of the pain that would stem from it. At least I was in a safe place to do all of the internal surgery.

That night I had a really rough night, the doctor had started to cut back on my medication so that I could do my rapid detoxification the following week. I couldn't believe how great I felt inside considering all of the pain that my body was going through. My mum and dad had been calling every night to talk to me; which was a breakthrough in itself. I was enjoying telling them what I had been doing and how I was feeling and they genuinely sounded proud of my efforts. I know now just how hard it was for them for me to be where I was in life; but they stood by me regardless. In their very different ways they always had. My mum had always tried to stay in contact with me and talk me out of the life that I had trapped myself into with her loving words. My dad had tried to bear with me until a couple of years before when he told me that he couldn't do it any more. He told me that I was destroying him, and mum, and that he needed to cut himself off from me. I know now that during those really bad years he had walked into a bottle shop for the first time in 20 years and just stared at the bottles, honestly thinking about picking up a drink. I had no idea just how much my heroin addiction, and lifestyle, had wounded my parents. My entire life needed mending; I just had no idea how close I was to that becoming a reality in my life.

The following morning Pastor David turned up at the house with his wife, Frances, and their two children. Frances was carrying her guitar and they sat down in the lounge room. I had no idea what they were doing there, but after Tuesday night I did know that just about anything was possible. I asked Josie and she explained to me that they were there to do a bible study, something called Alpha classes. I had no idea what any of it meant, and I wasn't going to hang around to find out either. I went to hide out in my room. That was until Mr T came in there and told me that the classes were a compulsory part of the rehabilitation program. I followed him out to the lounge and decided to sit and listen; but I totally closed my heart off to any thing that David or Frances said, or so I thought. Frances started the meeting by singing some songs about Jesus. She had a really lovely and peaceful voice and I enjoyed her singing, despite my closed heart. God obviously had plans for me. I had always loved music, and it was a great way to get people into the spirit of the teaching. At the time I had no idea about the real 'power' behind the music but I know that it touched me deep within. All of the others in the house were laughing and making fun of it all, but I actually quite enjoyed it, suprising myself. Then David did a teaching about Jesus, the Son of God and Son of Man. It confused me a bit, but it also interested me enough to make me look forward to the follow up lesson. He was talking about how Jesus, the Son of God, died on the cross for the forgiveness of our sins. It was all quite intriguing, but not the thing for me.

One of the other things that happened in the house that day, and every day, was Josie playing her 'Jesus music'. She used to play the same C.D over and over again I knew that it was called 'The Stone's Been Rolled Away', but I had no idea what it was all about. But like Frances' singing, the music seemed to touch me somewhere deep down within. I had no idea at the time that God was using that music to soften my heart towards him. Josie, thankfully, was just being an obedient vessel.

Most days in the house were spent by everyone being coerced into doing their chores, which I didn't have to do yet because I was detoxing. Then we would all sit around and talk about drugs and the lives that we had, hopefully, left behind. I started to notice that most of the people there talked about drugs in a way that they felt as though they were missing out on something great by being in rehab. I felt the total opposite. I was so glad to be there and so thankful that I had been placed somewhere 'safe' to get clean. Most of the guys were missing their old lifestyles, but I was just happy that I didn't feel as though I had to use drugs any more. I knew that I was set apart from them for something bigger; I just had no idea what that meant at the time. I was very similar to a lot of them, story wise, but very different in my personality. I felt like I was stronger than most of them, and time would prove that to be true. Inside of me I knew that something very big was being stirred up, but was totally unaware of all that the Spirit of God was actually doing.

I went to Mr T at the beginning of my second week in the house and asked him if there was any way I could structure my time. I knew that if I didn't do it then that my time would be swallowed up by unimportant discussions about drugs, something that I no longer wanted to hear about. I found myself just sitting around when I felt as though I could be doing something more constructive. When I first asked him about it he appeared to be shocked and told me that he was happy for me to wait until I had at least done my detox. I wasn't happy to do that. I had spent the previous years avoiding time and now I wanted my time to account for something. I needed structure in my life otherwise my mind had too much free time; and I knew that was a bad thing. So he gave me a copy of a timetable and asked me to fill it in appropriately. Mr T was very happy with it and agreed to check with me at the end of the week to make sure that I was sticking to my plan. That was exactly what I needed, someone to help me make my vision become a reality.

The next major step for me, personally, occurred early in my second week at rehab. I was still detoxing and medicated accordingly. One afternoon I went into my bedroom and found a couple of the guys in there with Monique. They had a spoon and other shooting up utensils laid out on the floor; they were about to inject themselves with heroin. When I walked in their immediate reaction was to offer me some, so that I wouldn't tell Mr T or Josie what was going on. I agreed, even though I didn't actually feel the need to have any. When they handed my syringe to me I looked down and realised that my hands were shaking. I then did the unthinkable in any drug addicts' eyes – I squirted the drug onto the carpet. I don't know why and at the time I couldn't understand myself. They all got mad at me and told me off for 'wasting' their precious drugs. But I felt comfortable with what I had done, which was very strange for me. Never before in my drug taking life had I chosen to waste any amount of heroin. But inside of my self, I knew that I had done the right thing. I left the room feeling much stronger for what I did, even though I had no real understanding of it. I knew then that my drug taking life was coming to a very sure end; and inside I was dancing. I know now that it was my spirit inside of me leaping for joy at the major breakthrough that had just taken place; but at the time I just felt amazed and thankful that I knew my life was changing before my very eyes.

The very next day two ladies came to the house that would help to change my life for the better. Their names were Arlene and Vanessa. If I had gone to church on either of the previous Sundays I would have met them, but having them come into the house the way they did made me more comfortable. I felt able to open up to them in a very different way. These two ladies had come to the house, as they did every Tuesday, just to sit with us and share their lives with us. They both had hearts for the broken-hearted; they were there to try and raise our dying spirits. They bought with them food to share and my first thought was that they actually wanted to spend time with us, with me. Not for years had any one wanted to spend time with me without wanting something from me. But these two women genuinely wanted to share their time. They never once judged me or looked at me with disgust. They willingly chose to be in my company, and that amazed me. I felt so loved and so special to them in an instant. At the time I had no idea it was the Jesus in them that loved us as people; not because of what we had done, but because of who we were. We were created by the Creator and in the eyes of these two women we were very precious people. That was exactly how I felt in their presence. Loved and wanted were two things that I hadn't felt from anybody, other than my parents, for a very long time. I opened up with them and shared some of my story with them. They in turn asked if they could pray for me, but I declined. I just wasn't ready for that step yet. They understood and when they left they hugged me and told me that they would pray for me at home and that they looked forward to seeing me in church on Sunday. I knew they were speaking the truth and when they left I realised that I felt touched in my heart by being in their company. I started to tell myself that I was special and precious, and I actually believed myself. I actually looked forward to seeing them in church the following Sunday.

The night before my rapid detox Steve had called Mr T and asked if it was okay to come and visit me, to wish me the best for the procedure. I had spoken to Mr T earlier about how I felt about Steve. To me he would always be a 'client'. The thought of being anywhere near him without drugs in my system repulsed me. I knew that I had to tell him that I no longer wanted him in my life. I knew that he had gone out of his way for me in so many ways, but I also knew that most of that was out of the guilt that he felt for ever meeting me the way he did. I told Mr T that I wasn't ready to do any of that but he allowed him to come over anyway. The moment that I saw him I knew that I couldn't bear to be around him. He had come bearing gifts, again. He gave me cigarettes and chocolate and also gave me money to help me get by. I understand now that he didn't know any better. He only ever knew me as a taker, out to get all that I could from him; and he couldn't yet change his ways. He told me that he was very proud of me, but I realised that in his company I just felt dirty. I told him that I needed to go to bed to get some rest for the following day. When he was leaving he tried to hug me and I cringed. I knew at that moment that I could no longer have him in my life. The 'relationship' was firmly planted in unhealthy ground, and that was all it had ever been. I couldn't do it to myself anymore. I ran to my room and started to cry for myself, for the life that I had led, for the choices that I had made. I cried myself to sleep.

Chapter 9

On the Road to a New Life

The following day was my big rapid detox day. I was so excited at the whole prospect of being drug free, including the medication that had helped me to detox. Despite my dreadful night of emotional upheaval and sporadic sleep, I woke up early; I was so ready to take this very major step in my life. I knew that once I had undergone the procedure that I would then need to take a tablet of naltrexone every day to help with the cravings, and I was even excited by that thought. For years before that day I could never imagine myself not taking heroin, and from that day on I would never imagine myself ever taking heroin again. My life was changing so rapidly; it felt so surreal. Little did I know, or understand, that God was protecting me every step of the way. He loved me so much that even when my heart was hard towards him, especially then, He still loved me through it.

I entered Dr Reece's surgery believing that I would leave a different person. When I got there he asked me how I was and how I had been going. I told him that even though I had done it quite hard physically that I felt very strong otherwise. I don't know if he thought I was just saying that but he told me to wait until the procedure was underway before I commented. He asked if he could pray for me beforehand and I told him that I wasn't interested. He then went on to tell me, again, about the big hole in my soul that only Jesus could fill. I just wanted him to hurry up and so I listened. I took in what he was saying but I just felt as though it wasn't the right time for me to be hearing it. The medical part of the procedure included some injections and then drinking naltrexone at hourly intervals. I took it all very well; even Dr Reece was surprised. I understood his amazement considering the state that he had first met me in just two weeks earlier. I took it all so well that I was back at the Thelma Street house just after lunch. I had gone into the surgery believing that it would not be hard, and it wasn't. At the time I had no idea of the people that had been praying for me, and even if I had of, I had no idea of the power behind prayer. All I knew was that now I was well on the road to my new life.

My mum had called the surgery just after lunch to speak to me and was surprised when they told her that I had already gone home. She had seen stories on television about rapid-detox and all she knew was the hard stuff. She then called me at the house and I told her how it had all gone for me. She started crying, she couldn't believe that I was the same person that she had walked in on just two weeks earlier. I tried to explain to her how different I felt but she just kept crying. Then she told me that she was proud of me for coming this far and to keep up with it and then I started crying. It was a very momentous occasion; I hadn't cried tears of happiness for years. But that day something broke inside of me, and my mum, and we both knew that my life was never going to be the same again.

The next major step for me happened just two days later when I woke up on the Sunday morning and knew that I had to go to church. I wasn't looking forward to it very much, but I was looking forward to seeing the two special ladies that I had met on Tuesday. The house was all abuzz with every body trying to get ready and leave the house by 9:30. Somehow it happened and when we arrived it felt very strange for me to be there. Church was held in a small hall in West End, of all places. As soon as we pulled up something clicked inside of me and I knew that I had changed. Never before had I gone to West End for any reason other than to score drugs. Not only was I not there to score drugs, but I was there to go to church. And not only was I there to go to church, but I was there with a bunch of other drug addicts. It all seemed very strange for me.

I coped with my feelings by refusing to go inside for the church service. Instead I sat outside on the footpath and smoked as many cigarettes as I possibly could. Nobody seemed to mind that much. I knew that Josie really wanted me to go inside, but she didn't push me. I guess she knew that it would happen in my own time; believing all the while that God would intervene with my personal schedule. I received big hugs from Arlene and Vanessa after the service and they left saying that they looked forward to seeing me on Tuesday. To me that was great. If church was to be like that every week, it wasn't so bad. Mr T told me that one Sunday soon I would have to go inside but for now I had grace from him to stay outside. I understood that and was comfortable with his decision. They were very understanding of where I was at, and treated me accordingly. This is something that I will always be grateful for. If they had have tried to force me inside it may have been too much pressure for me and I may have decided to leave. However they didn't; and my life just kept changing for the better.

One of the things that I did in the house to pass the time was hanging out with the boys a lot. I guess because of my background and where I was at, right then, it seemed very normal to me. The guys were nothing like the type of guy that I usually spent any time with, but they had me curious. They were all into crime of some sort and that was something that I had no understanding of. One of the guys' names was Dan – with his long blond hair and rude demeanor; I was quite attracted to him. I wasn't sure if it was more to help me pass the time in the house or actual attraction, because whenever it came down to doing anything physical with him I could never follow through with it. I think that I was just so used to having a male partner around that I figured he would do. Mr T and Josie were always telling us to sit apart and to never spend any time alone together. I think they thought that he would corrupt me. He was the known 'bad boy' of the place. He was always messing up with drugs and trying to sneak out of the house in the middle of the night. He had also been known to have sex with any girl that was willing. I knew all of these things about him; and I wasn't terribly concerned. I knew that it was a game for both of us: we were playing with each other's minds, probably just because it was convenient.

Nothing ever eventuated between Dan and I. One night he and Paul snuck into our room to see us. Paul had become very interested in Monique by this stage. They jumped straight into bed together and Dan and I were kissing, but every time he would attempt to go any further I would just stop. I am sure that this made him angry and confused but I didn't care. He wasn't my type, and all men were a game to me at that point in time. I had a lot of anger and frustration;

I was in desperate need of understanding and healing. Things that no man, or woman, could possibly give me.

One of the very interesting people that came into my life around this time was a young girl named Beth. Beth was a 14-year-old attractive girl who was very messed up in the lifestyle that I myself was so desperate to break free from. She came into the house basically just to have somewhere to stay. She and I got talking immediately. Despite our age difference we had a lot in common; including prostitution to feed our drug habits and those of our partners. Her drug partner happened to be her mother. Her mum had first given her a shot of heroin when she was just 12 years old, just one week later she was out working the streets alongside her. Beth's story really touched my heart. I wanted to reach out to her and help in a way that I knew I could only if I was stronger. She was comfortable with me, free to be herself. There were no expectations of her from me and she appreciated that. She confided in me that she didn't actually want to get off drugs and that she was just there for a few days to get her habit back down and then she was going to go straight back out to work. I wanted so much to just hold her and tell her how special she was but every time I tried she pulled away. She had always been hurt by people that she let close to her so she decided to not let me anywhere near her heart.

I tried so hard, with Beth, to get near to her. One of the ways that I attempted this was to share my story with her and try to get her to see that she didn't want to be my age and trying to get clean off drugs. I wanted her to see that she had her whole life in front of her if only she would decide to make a go of it. Nothing that I could say was going to change her mind and so one day I just decided to sit down with her and try to get her to open up about how she felt about prostitution. I mean for me, at the tender age of 14, I hadn't even thought about sleeping with one person, let alone anyone that would offer me money. She was so broken but so was I. Together she and I sat down with a piece of paper and wrote down how we felt about what we had done with our bodies. This is some of what we wrote down: easy way for women on the road to hell, selling your soul, selling your body to the 'BIG' white god-the endless battle, the devil from within will eat you inside out until slowly there's nothing, you'll bleed or burn forever for selling your body!!, fake name and false pretences, as if it's about the sex, money for a day or complete sanity for a life time.

All the while we had no comprehension of God or what he could do for us. All we did know was that inside we were hurting and as long as we could talk to each other that hurt wasn't so bad. I loved the fact that I knew that she trusted me. Beth and I had a special bond; I was like her big sister. Someone that would love her no matter what, through all things; and that was all that she needed – love that would help her to heal. However, she kept running from it, and me, and two days later she took off. I looked forward to the next time that I would see her and hug her and tell her that I was there for her. I had no idea that the next time I would see her I would have a totally different love to share with her – the precious love of Jesus.

The following day almost everyone at the house decided to use drugs together, and once again I was totally uninterested. The only things that I was still interested in were cigarettes and pot. I would sneak down to the park on my way to the shops to smoke joints and then come back to the house stoned. I didn't get into trouble for it but I am sure that Mr T and Josie knew. They probably figured that even though it wasn't good, a little bit of pot every now and again was better than a constant heroin habit. They did search my room a couple of times but I always stashed my pot outside in a tin so it was never found. They did find Monique's stash a couple of times but that never bothered me. One of the other things that I would do every now and then was buy a couple of drinks down at the bottle shop and skull them on my way back to the house. I had never been very big on alcohol, but I did it then just because I could. It wasn't an every day thing, just now and then; which is really no justification for doing it at all.

As a result of the house using drugs together on that very day a few of them were told to leave. It was a major shock to everyone because normally they would have just been given a warning. Mr T had obviously had enough of them abusing the grace that he continually gave them. Monique however wasn't asked to leave; she was just given a warning. But in her very strange way of declaring her 'love' for Paul, she packed her bags and left with him. I was then left basically alone in the house with nobody else there. I spent a lot of the following few days talking with Mr T and Josie on a deeper level. I was now free and able to open up to them about the real inner me. The seemed genuinely interested and always went out of their way to listen to me. However, I am sure that they were also concerned about how they were going to fill the house up with paying clients. This was the next step in my rehabilitation adventure; new housemates; or playmates, as I saw them then.

Other than the house being basically empty while we awaited the arrival of new house members, life there continued to remain stable, which was a major culture shock for me. I was used to my life being a shambles and coping with it the best that I could. Now, however, my life was starting to become relatively normal. The prayer meetings and Alpha classes continued that week and on the Saturday night the first of the new people arrived; his name was Ben. When he first got there his dad had to carry him up the stairs. He was obviously detoxing and very sick. I offered to help Mr T with him in any way that I could so he told me to just talk to him and let him know that I was there and that I understood. I did that and even though he wasn't very together he seemed to understand where I was coming from. I knew that because the next day he thanked me for talking him through what was happening to him. I was so excited to have someone new in the house that I could try to encourage not to use drugs, unlike the others that were left. I immediately knew that there was something different about Ben; I just had no understanding of what that was.

My parents came to visit me on the third Sunday that I was in the house. That day was another church day and again I didn't go inside. I just didn't feel like sitting still. There was a change going on inside of me that I couldn't understand. When my parents got out of the car I went down to meet them. They hadn't seen me since before my detox and they thought that I looked like a different person. I was so glad to see them and they were genuinely happy to see me; something that they hadn't been for such a long time. We all hugged and my mum and I cried. They were tears of absolute happiness. They saw how comfortable I was in the house and they knew that I was in the right place. They both said that they could hear the changes in my voice over the phone but now that they could see them as well, they were just so happy. They decided to take me out for dinner, which I was really looking forward to. Since my detox on the previous Friday I had eaten so much food, probably making up for the years of not eating very well at all.

I had been looking forward to seeing them; since I first went to rehab they had been in Darwin for an A.A round-up. The first thing that I felt when we sat down at the restaurant was their unconditional love for me. No matter how bad my life had become, they continued to love me through it. In their own ways they had handed me over to God for Him to watch over me, but they had never stopped loving me, no matter how hard I made it for them. That was my first real glimpse of the love of a parent; totally unconditional and forgiving. I loved them so much and they understood that nothing that I had ever done had been to intentionally hurt them; that had just happened along the way. They told me all about their holiday and I told them about my life in the house so far. They couldn't believe that I was so happy, in a Christian rehab of all places. Mum told me that she remembered Mr T telling her about church and the other Christian activities but my mind at the time had obviously just not wanted to hear it or I probably would have talked myself out of going there. They told me that they were very proud of me and my dad told me to just stick at it, that every day clean was another day to be grateful for. I will never forget those words of wisdom that he shared with me. The other major step that my parents took with me that night was to give me some money to help me buy luxuries for the following week; things like cigarettes and chocolates. They hadn't given me money for years because they always knew where I would spend it – up my arm. They both agreed that they now knew that wouldn't happen and that by giving me money they were expressing a deep desire to start trusting me again. Money wasn't important to me any more, but the gesture of them giving it to me was absolutely priceless. That night was so special to me, and to them; one that we will never forget. When they dropped me back at the house they left smiling, knowing that I was in good hands and that, finally, I had decided to get my life right. I fell asleep with a smile on my face and tears in my eyes; such reconciliation had taken place and I knew that my life was slowly falling into place.

That same afternoon Paul and Monique had returned; they had run out of money and needed to come back. For whatever reason, Mr T agreed to let them come back but he told them that one more mistake and they were gone, for good. I spent most of the afternoon talking to Ben and explaining to him where I had come from and just encouraging him to keep going, that getting clean was definitely worth it. A couple of days later another new guy, Grant, came to stay at the house. He was older than I was and seemed to think that he knew all there was to know about life and recovery. I wasn't very comfortable with him; I wasn't sure why but we just didn't click. He told us that he was a Christian and was looking forward to staying in a Christian rehab. He then proceeded to show us his bible, called a Recovery Devotional Bible; whatever that meant. At the time I wasn't at all interested in finding out. That was how our introduction began and how our relationship, or lack thereof, continued.

A couple of days after that a young couple came for counselling with Mr T, and they had what looked like their entire families with them. Grant said that he had met them before. He spoke of them as very nice people and he said that he hoped we all got to meet them. After their counselling session we did all get to meet them; their names were Mark and Vanessa and they were a young married couple struggling with their own personal addictions. They both did seem to be quite nice and the guy, Mark, was also quite attractive. The whole reality of them being married just didn't occur to me at the time, and I am sure that I started to flirt with him almost immediately. He told us that he was going to be coming to the house during the day while Vanessa continued on at work – that suited me just fine.

Whilst all of these changes were taking place around me something inside me remained the same; I was still hurting. I had chosen not to take drugs to numb my feelings, so I was still feeling them deeply. No matter how much I talked about them with anyone, it seemed that no one was quite able to help me. One of the things that did help me was Mr T asking me to write down a list of what was important to me. He figured that we would be able to work out where I was going once I had started to really sort through my own issues. This is the exact list that followed. IMPORTANT TO ME not in total order (but almost): 1. Life – talking about with others 2. Family support 3. Other people's lives – support 4. True love (not a junk relationship) 5. Cleanliness 6. Sharing/Give and Take (you get what you give) 7. Importance of time and life (age 24 and 3 months) 8. BELIEF – astrology/Buddhist thought=keep life clean, be strong, together, the being-the real and true deep inner being. 9. Finding myself again- the real me time management, reality, freedom true me. 10. Truth as your reality – being true to yourself and others 11. TRUST.

Doing the list for myself had helped me to sit down, alone, and actually think about exactly what was important to me. For years I had fooled myself into believing that things such as drugs, money and men were important to me but in reality none of those things mattered to me at all. The list also helped me to realise how much I had changed in such a short period of time. I had only been at the house for just under three weeks and already I was seeing the world from a different, clearer angle. I was living on a different level and really looking forward to all that was to follow.

One of the things that doing the list had helped me to do was to pull out all of my Buddhist stuff from Thailand. I had heaps of photos that I had taken while I was over there, of temples and sacred sights. So I sorted through them all and made a little 'shrine' on my wall. They were photos that were significant to me at the time. There was one of me releasing the three birds from a cage, which in Thailand symbolised body/soul/spirit. There was me standing with different buddha statues. There was me and my brother. At the time they were all very meaningful to me. The next time that Josie came into my room I, very proudly, showed her my photo collage. She smiled and said that she wasn't into all of that stuff and that she prayed they would come down soon, when I was ready to take them down. I didn't understand what she meant. I had no idea that I had offended the Holy Spirit that dwelled inside of her, and I wouldn't understand for quite some time. What I did know was that I was glad that she hadn't forced me to take them down because of her beliefs; it had been pushy people with closed minds that had kept me from religion my entire life. I was very into making my own decisions, even though being in rehab for my drug addiction wasn't enough to make me realise how bad my 'free choice' was. I would soon come into a much greater understanding.

Mark started coming to the house every day. Vanessa would drop him off and immediately he and I would start talking. He would even offer to help me with my chores. I was comfortable with him in a way that I hadn't really felt since coming into the house, and I didn't know why. One day he and I were sitting on the couch and we got to talking about his marriage. He explained to me that they had been married while they were both on drugs, hoping that getting married would help them to get their acts together. It hadn't. He then started to tell me about his background, and Vanessa's, as well. She had come from a similar background to me, with drugs and prostitution, which helped me to understand why I felt so comfortable with him. I felt as though he understood me, and that he even went out of his way to do so. I had no real idea at the time, but upon reflection I now know that I started flirting with him the moment Vanessa walked out the door and down the stairs. I didn't mean to, I just did it. I also understand now that it was a part of me that I had chosen not to address; from the work that I had done I knew how to 'play' men to get from them what I wanted. From Mark I wanted a friend, a confidante; or so I thought.

I also connected with Vanessa on a different level. It helped me to have someone who was a little bit older than me to talk to about where I had come from; someone that understood the pain that I felt inside of me. She and I would spend hours talking about our lives and how we felt about what we had done. I trusted her and she trusted me; even though when she wasn't around I gave her no reason to. I just didn't know any better. The whole concept of her and Mark being married – the commitment, the vows – never really entered my mind. I guess from the work that I had done, I just thought that being married was irrelevant. But they were two confused young people that had made a commitment to one another, and I chose to ignore those sacred vows. I thought only of myself and how I felt, instead of thinking of them.

Within the first week of Mark coming to the house during the day they had moved into the spare room in the house. They needed more support and comfort than what they were getting and giving each other at home. They came to stay one night and basically never went home. I enjoyed my time with both of them, but especially liked my time with Mark when Vanessa was at work. I don't think she knew that we were flirting with each other, although everyday when she got home Mark and I would always be together, somewhere in the house, talking and laughing. I am sure that she would have to think something was wrong when Mark would make excuses to come and talk to me, whether she was home or not. They had been through some really rough times together and seemingly survived.

One of the things that Vanessa and I did together was to celebrate my 4-weeks-clean anniversary. We celebrated by going into the city and doing some shopping, spending time together and by me getting my belly button pierced. I had always wanted to get it done, but when I was using drugs I never had a spare $80 to do it. I wanted to celebrate being clean that long, because to me it felt like an eternity. I wanted to do something that I would remember and I couldn't think of any better way. So she and I went together. While we were in the city she actually asked me what I thought and how I felt about Mark. She said that she thought that he was interested in more than friendship from me. I laughed and just reminded her that he was her husband. She kept asking me what we talked about when she was at work and I kept just telling her "whatever". To be honest, I couldn't really remember what we talked about because when we were together time just passed us by, and before we knew it she was home again. She told me that she had been watching him watching me but I told her that it must've been in her imagination and she seemingly let it go, for then.

I had now officially been clean for a month and Mr T had given me permission to get in contact with Will again. I called him up and, thankfully, he answered. I told him everything that had been happening for me since I had been in rehab and he was amazed even at the change in the sound of my voice. He said that now I sounded as though there was actually life inside of me. He went on to tell me that he had also done a rapid detox with Dr Reece and he, too, was clean off heroin. I was so excited to hear that, for his sake and mine. I was only allowed visitors who were not drug takers, and that now included Will. He and I had been through so much together and I wanted him to come and meet all of my new house mates. Mr T said that he would have to meet him and talk to him first before Will was able to come over to visit, which Mr T did and said that it was fine for him to spend the day at the house. At one stage he took me for a drive, and we smoked a joint and he gave me some more pot for later. I hadn't actually been smoking much and so I was looking forward to a nice quiet joint by myself at some stage. He told me that a friend of ours was having a party and had asked Will to invite me along. I wasn't sure if I would be allowed to go but I asked anyway and Mr T said yes, so long as I didn't take any heavy drugs while I was there. I agreed.

The party was the following night and as it was my first time out of the house alone with a friend and not my parents, I was very excited. Will and I spent the early evening drinking and smoking joints. Will asked me if I was interested in taking any ecstasy that night and I said that I wasn't allowed to and that I didn't actually want to. There was no desire in me to take any drugs and lose all of the privileges that I had worked so hard to get or relinquish the freedom that I had been granted by Mr T and Josie. He said that he respected my decision and I was glad. Once we got to the party I realised that I was practically the only person there not on ecstasy but I wasn't going to let that spoil my night out. The party, and the music, was great and I had a really good time without hard drugs. I was happy to smoke a little bit of pot whenever a joint passed me by. The people there couldn't believe the change in me. They said that I even looked like a different person. I definitely felt like one.

Having been at the party and being strong enough to say no to the drugs on offer made me realise how far I had come in such a short time. I felt so much stronger in myself; stronger than I had ever felt before, but I still had no real understanding of why that was. When I returned home the following day I was very hungover from all the joints and alcohol, but I still felt great within myself. Mr T came out to talk to me and I told him immediately what I had done and also what I hadn't done. He told me that the freedom to go to the party had been a test to see what I would do in the real world and that he was very proud of me being strong enough to say no. I explained to him how strange it had been for me to not even have the desire to use any drugs; he said that a lot of people had been praying for that to happen to me. I just laughed and chose not to think about that. I had to do a urine sample to prove that I hadn't taken any drugs, which I happily did. None of the others could believe that I had gone to an ecstasy party and not taken any drugs. I was so happy with myself and my decisions, and there was so much more to look forward to.

Very soon after this another interesting girl came into the house. Her name was Ainsley. I had never met anyone quite like her. Because Monique had gone she was to share my room and we immediately hit it off. We were very different, but both in need of a friend. She was a couple of years older than I was and she was in rehab to deal with her addiction to amphetamines. She was very loud and talked a lot – she was a hairdresser so she was used to talking all the time. She was so interesting; I loved listening to her; which was great considering she very rarely stopped talking. The first day that she was in there I asked if she would cut my hair. I was in dire need of a change, at the time my hair was shoulder length and felt very boring to me. Over the years I had had every length of hair and almost every colour of hair too. So Ainsley had come just in time. She cut it short and spiky at the back and longer at the front, and I loved it. She and I spent a lot of time singing and dancing around our bedroom, she was such a welcome addition to our home.

The house had started to feel like a home, not a house, to me. The people there had started to become very much like family. After all, we were with each other all day every day and we had to put up with each other even when we didn't feel like it. They were all very special people and we were all getting closer the longer we were there together. Every now and then a new person would come and spend the day at the house, for workshops and friendship. After they had gone Mr T would ask me if I thought that they would be a welcome long term, addition to the house. Sometimes the people would be really dodgy, like coming into the place and asking people if they wanted to score any drugs. I had become very protective of the people in the house and my dream was to see them all clean and well, so those particular people would not be invited back into the place. Otherwise everyone in the house was enjoying spending all of our time together – much like a family; enjoying our time together, and our time apart.

One night when everyone had gone to bed Mark and I stayed up to play backgammon. I think that we both knew that we were interested in each other by then, but we had never actually admitted it to one another. Mr T had given us permission to stay up late that night because we had all been behaving ourselves drugwise. Vanessa went to bed early because she had to get up and go to work the following morning and one by one everyone else drifted off to bed. Mark and I just kept looking at one another, and we knew that neither of us was going to go to bed just yet. About half an hour after the last person had gone to bed I asked him for a hug. He willingly obliged but while we were hugging we were discussing the fact that his wife was asleep in a room in the same house. We agreed to stop what we had been doing and to stop flirting with each other because he had chosen to make a go of his marriage, perhaps for the last time. Within minutes we were involved in a passionate kiss. Neither of us had actually expected that to happen and I think we shocked ourselves when we realised the extent of our interest in each other. I don't remember who was the first to pull away, but I do know that it was the beginning of something very major in both of our lives; a big change was just around the corner, only I had no idea how big my change was going to be.

Chapter 10
Never Be the Same Again

Two days later it was Sunday and that meant church day. It started out just like all of the other Sundays had since I had been in the house. Josie came in and woke me and told me to start to think about getting ready for church. I put off getting out of bed for as long as I could, until she got really firm with me and I knew that if I didn't get up I would soon be in trouble. She always laughed with me once I was actually out of bed, which helped me to understand that she believed it was in my best interest to get up and get ready. The entire house seemed to be extra slow and sluggish that day. I don't really think anyone was interested in spending the morning in church; it was a cold August morning, much better spent in bed, (or so I thought). Once I'd had my shower and was fully dressed in my winter wear I sat down to have my breakfast and the next thing I heard was Josie's 'Jesus music' blaring in the lounge room. I had grown used to the music being played, almost constantly, but this particular day it seemed to bother me more than usual. I moved back to my room to eat my breakfast and the next minute Mr T came in and told me to go down to the car and leave with the first car load. I couldn't believe it; not only was I going to church, but I was going to be there early. My plan was to get there and grab a cup of coffee and say hello to a few people and then move outside to my position and smoke some cigarettes while I waited for the service to be over; God, however, had very different plans for me that day.

When we were half way there, it started spitting with rain and by the time we arrived it was pouring. I knew then that I would have to go inside and sit through all that was going on. I sat next to Josie during the music, which she told me was called 'praise and worship time'. I had never sat through that time in its entirety before and at first I felt uncomfortable, there were people with their eyes closed and hands raised and I didn't understand what they were doing. Then I just sat down and gave in to the fact that I was stuck there. I rested my head down on the chair in front of me and listened to the music; the people singing with their beautiful voices, and I closed my eyes. I don't remember what the song was about; something about softening my heart, opening my eyes and surrender. I do remember Josie tapping me on the shoulder, after the music had been finished for a while, and telling me that I had been singing along. I laughed and told her that wasn't possible because I didn't know the words. She told me that the song that had been playing was from the CD that she played at the house all the time. I laughed and thought that she had been joking. But inside of me something had changed, there was a stirring in my spirit. Something major was going on and I had absolutely no idea what was happening.

For the first time I sat and listened to the message that Pastor David was preaching and I actually found myself being interested in what he had to say. He was talking about God and something called the 'anointing'. I had no idea what he meant, I had never even heard of the word. But I do know that he was saying that the anointing was "the burden removing, yoke destroying, power of God". I didn't really comprehend what he was going on about but something inside of me understood exactly what he meant, and that it was exactly what I needed. I needed to have my burden's removed, my many yoke's destroyed and I definitely needed the power of God; I just wasn't willing to admit that to anyone. Thankfully I didn't have to admit it to anyone except God Himself. The next thing that I knew David was calling people to the front for prayer and before he had even finished, my feet had lifted me up and I was walking down the centre of the church, right to the front, where immediately God met me. I don't remember anything other than David asking me if I wanted to receive Jesus Christ as my Lord and Saviour. The moment that I said "yes" God touched me in a way that I never knew was possible. I felt as though God was holding me; I felt warm, almost hot, and I started to sweat. God had been waiting for me to tell Him that I needed Him in my life before He would meet me. He had found me just where I was and He had made the way for me to give Him my life. I don't know how long I was standing up the front, with God holding me, before people started to come and congratulate me. My mind felt so clear and so light. My body felt as though it was gliding across the room, I felt so strange. My hands were burning and sweat was pouring out from the palms of them. I had no idea what was happening, so I just sat down. One thing that I did know was that with that one decision, a decision that I couldn't even remember making, my life had changed and I was never going to be the same again; thankfully.

The next thing that I remember was Josie coming to me and just resting her hand on my shoulder. She stood there for a few minutes; we were both just silent. I had no idea that she was praying for me and had been since she met me, for this very day. Then she asked me if I was okay. I felt okay, I felt great actually; it was just the strange burning and sweating in my hands that had started in my head also. She said that it might sound strange but all she could describe it as was 'Holy Spirit fire'. She tried to explain to me that God was beginning to change me, starting from when I had spoken "yes" to Him; and that He had been waiting patiently for me since before I was conceived. It was all very full-on for me and I just remember sitting there unsure of when it would stop. As it turned out it didn't stop for almost 48 hours: God had a lot of work to do in me and now I had given Him permission to do it by accepting Jesus, His Son, as the Lord of my life; and I was so willing for it to be done.

When we got back to the house everybody started asking questions like: what was it like? what made you go up the front of the church? do you feel different? did God touch you? They were questions that I too would have been asking had it been somebody else, but at the time they just sounded so strange. I tried to answer them as best I could. My responses were: It was strange, and wonderful. I don't know what made me go up, but before I knew it I was up the front saying "yes". Yes, I felt different, very different. Yes, God had touched me, like He was holding me, like I could see Him standing right there with me. It had been a totally amazing experience, and I was more than willing to share it with anybody that would listen. I couldn't wait to tell my parents.

I called my mum and dad as soon as I could to tell them what had happened to me that morning at church. They were both very excited; my mum started crying as soon as I told her. She said that she had been waiting for something like that to happen ever since that day that I had first told her I was a heroin addict. I tried to explain what had occurred and how I felt so different. She told me that she thought that I actually sounded different, even more alive than usual. I was; I was more alive than I had ever been in my whole life and I wasn't afraid to show it. I am sure that the smile didn't leave my face the entire day. I'd had experiences like that before – that had made me feel alive – but they had always been false, brought on by substances. I knew then and there that that would never be the case again. I knew deep down inside of me that God was changing me from the inside out, only I had no idea just how much He would change it, and how quickly He would do it.

That night I prayed; possibly for the first time in my life. I asked God to reveal Himself to me and to show me who He was. I asked Him to remove from me anything that He didn't want there. Then I told Him that I loved Him and I thanked Him for coming into my life. I could almost see Him smiling; I could definitely feel it. I fell asleep that night with my hands and head still burning up, but with a huge smile on my face. For the first time in a very long time I felt peace; the peace that can only be found in the presence of God. He was there with me, smiling down on me; His lost child that had returned to Him.

I woke up the next morning after the best sleep that I could ever remember, wondering if it had all been a dream. Then I went to brush the hair out of my face and realised that my head and hands were still wet with sweat. I went outside to tell someone, preferably Josie, but nobody was awake yet. It was very early and I looked at the clock, only to find out that it wasn't even six o'clock yet. I had never been an early riser; in fact, I was usually a dreadful person in the mornings, but for some reason I felt very awake. I rugged up and went to sit on the verandah to watch what was left of the sunrise. I hadn't watched the sunrise without the aid of drugs ever. It was the most beautiful experience. Everything seemed to have so much colour in it. The sky, the trees, the flowers; they all looked amazing to me, almost like I was seeing them for the first time. My eyes had been opened, just like the song said. I realised then that all of the music that Josie had been playing in the house had been softening me on the inside, just waiting for the right time for me to give my heart to Jesus. I had done that now and all things seemed new to me. I felt like a new person.

I wanted to understand why I felt that way and, thankfully, the first person to get up was Josie. I told her what had been happening and she explained to me that I was now a new creation in Christ. She told me that when I accepted Jesus into my heart that He had washed me in His blood and that meant that He had washed away all of my past and all of my sins and given me a clean slate, a fresh start. I told her that I didn't feel worthy of that and she explained to me that nobody was worthy, but that God had chosen to send Jesus to die for me when I was still a sinner. It sounded strange, but strange enough to make sense to me. I was so excited by what God had done for me that I felt like I wanted to dance or something. I told Josie and she put on a CD for me to dance to. Some guy was singing to Jesus and just saying thank you Lord. That was how I felt, thankful.

Later that day I asked Josie more questions and one of those was about the bible. After all, I had given my life to God and so I felt as though I should try and understand Him more. I told her that I thought that the bible was too big for me to read and she explained to me that I shouldn't try to attempt to read it from start to finish but that I should start somewhere in the New Testament and take it from there. I had no idea what the New Testament was or where to find it and she happily showed me. She then told me that when she had been a brand new Christian someone had led her to the book of Romans; that it was all about new life in Christ, and redemption for my sins. That sounded good to me and so she showed me where that was and I went to my room to read it. I did as she had suggested and asked God to reveal Himself to me through the pages of the book. I just simply said "Show me you Lord", and He did. I read the entire book of Romans that afternoon, but one part stood out for me more than any other one did. That was Romans 12:2 (NIV), it says; Do not conform any longer to the pattern of this world, but be transformed by the renewing of your mind. Then you will be able to test and approve what God's will is – His good, pleasing and perfect will. I knew as soon as I read it that that was what I needed to do. I needed to renew my mind, because it had been so messed up on drugs and the entire drug lifestyle for so long it basically needed to be reprogrammed. What better way than by asking God to change it, to transform it, to renew it? I asked Him to do that for me right then, and also every time that I woke up and every time that I went to sleep. For God to do that I needed to decide not to conform to the world, which I did the day that I decided to enter rehab. Thankfully, I was now coming into the understanding that the strength that I had thought to be my own since arriving there was actually His strength all along. He had met me where I was at, and subtly given me the grace to get to the point of deciding to give my life over to Him. That was the first revelation that I ever, knowingly, received from God and a perfect one for me at that point in time.

That week, for the first time since being in the house, I looked forward to Vanessa and Arlene coming to visit us. I was looking forward to them offering to pray for me because for the first time I was going to accept. They arrived and immediately congratulated me for giving my heart to Jesus. They asked me what had been happening to me since Sunday and I told them all of the experiences that I had been having with God. They were so happy for me and both said they had been praying for my salvation since the very first time they had met me. I believed that to be true; I had felt a closeness to both of them during that first meeting – a closeness that had been missing from my life for as long as I could remember. A love that was real and different to any love that I had ever known; a holy love – the love of Jesus. They spoke and shared from the bible for the first time and I soaked up everything they had to say. I now know that was because I had a holy hunger inside of me that the Holy Spirit had placed there; a hunger to know God more intimately. God had placed these two special ladies in my life to love me and for me to learn love; I understood that now. They offered to pray for me and the moment that Arlene laid her hands on my back I again felt the burning sensation that I had first felt on Sunday. She spoke life into me and love and a godly destiny. She prayed that the Lord would reveal Himself to me in a way that I would know Him intimately, that I would choose to walk in His light and that I would be forever changed so that I could then share His love with other people. I don't think that she knew just how much that prayer helped me then, and continues to now. She was the first person that had spoken life into my dying spirit in a way that I understood. God had opened my eyes and I now understood that He had loved me all along and that He had protected me even when I didn't know that He was there. My life was no longer my own, I had happily given it over to Him so that His will could be done in my life. I will never forget that visit from those two ladies, and neither will God. He will forever bless them for their obedience to Him and for loving me with His love; for being open vessels for Him to shine through.

That night we also had the prayer meeting at the house so I spent the afternoon looking forward to that. I knew that God was going to meet me there too. And he did. I stood up for prayer and people spoke a hedge of protection around me, that I would love God with all of my heart and that He would carry me through all things. I felt such emotion welling up inside of me. I had no real understanding of what was happening, but I had a sensation that it was all good. I knew that God loved me and I knew that my life was now in His hands. I had willingly chosen to give myself to Him and He was so glad with that decision. I had known that there were major changes just around the corner for me; I just no idea how major those changes were going to be. But God knew all along.

It was around this time that I started to search the Scriptures for something that would help me, and others, to know that God had understood my pain and suffering during my time as an addict. I was led to the Psalms and in particular Psalm 38 (NIV).

O Lord, do not rebuke me in your anger
or discipline me in your wrath.
For your arrows have pierced me,
and your hand has come down upon me.
Because of your wrath there is no health in my body;
my bones have no soundness
because of my sin.
My guilt has overwhelmed me
like a burden too heavy to bear.

My wounds fester and are loathsome
because of my sinful folly.
I am bowed down and brought very low;
all day long I go about mourning.
My back is filled with searing pain;
there is no health in my body.

I am feeble and utterly crushed;
I groan in anguish of heart.

All my longings lie open before you, O Lord;
my sighing is not hidden from you.
My heart pounds, my strength fails me;
even the light has gone from my eyes.
My friends and companions avoid me
because of my wounds;
my neighbours stay far away.
Those who seek my life set their traps,
those who would harm me talk of my ruin;
all day long they plot my deception.

I am like a deaf man, who cannot hear,
like a mute, who cannot open his mouth;
I have become like a man who does not hear,
whose mouth can offer no reply.
I wait for you, O Lord;
you will answer, O Lord my God.
For I said, "Do not let them gloat
or exalt themselves over me when my foot slips."

For I am about to fall,
and my pain is ever with me.
I confess my iniquity;
I am troubled by my sin.
Many are those who are my vigorous enemies;
those who hate me without reason
are numerous.
Those who repay my good with evil
slander me when I pursue what is good.

O Lord, do not forsake me;
be not far from me, O God.
Come quickly to help me,
O Lord my Saviour.

That particular psalm helped me to realise that even when I had been in the midst of my struggle with addiction that God had been right there with me just waiting for me to call out to Him. It helped me to understand His love for me on a whole new level. I knew then that I would later use that psalm to show others that God was with them; especially during the hard times.

Aside from my experience with God, other major changes were also taking place in my life at that time. The most major change was one that was going on around me but that also affected me. Mr T had scheduled a counselling session with Mark and Vanessa to discuss the future of their relationship and, unfortunately, Vanessa had decided not to attend. When the session was over they were in their room, fighting, and it ended with her storming out and leaving. The first thing that Mark did was come to talk to me. I know now that I did the wrong thing by hugging and comforting him, but at the time I thought that it was the right thing to do. He told me that they had discussed their marriage and decided to have a trial separation. She had left the house and was coming back in the morning to pack her things. I didn't even think to ask if I'd had anything to do with it, I just hugged him and told him that everything would work out for the best. She did come back the next day and pack all of her things and without a word to anyone, she left. Mark and I then had more time to spend together, and we did. Slowly our friendship got closer, and despite my new found relationship with God it grew into a romantic relationship.

I had not gone to rehab with love on my mind, but it had happened and now I had to deal with it. Mr T spoke to both of us very sternly about giving our old wounds time to heal before jumping into anything together. We agreed to do that; and we did try. However, we found ourselves spending all of our time together, and our relationship was growing right under our noses. Our friendship had blossomed into something more and it seemed to us as though we had very little control over it. In actual fact, we had all of the control, but we were both choosing not to exercise it. We were happy to share our time with each other and we were more than happy to be there for one another. It felt strange for me to be in a 'relationship' and not feel like having sex with my partner; but that was one thing that I knew was out of bounds, at least for the time being. We were both in rehab to work on our addiction issues; our relationship was more of a side issue. Only time would tell how it would grow and what would happen to us, and we were both happy to wait it out and find out together.

While all of this was happening I was still working on my new relationship with God. Every day I was reading the bible and trying to pray to God about my life. I had heard someone at a prayer meeting pray for wisdom and revelation knowledge and I thought that sounded like something that I would like to have. So I started to pray that prayer too. Little did I know that God was already doing that work in my life. Every time I opened up the bible or listened to praise and worship music, God was revealing Himself to me in a new and deeper way. The intimacy that I had been believing for was happening for me and it was great. I always prayed "Show me you Lord" every time I read the bible and He did. I was growing in my relationship with the Lord everyday, and my life was undertaking a very rapid change.

A couple of Sundays after I had given my heart to Jesus, my housemate Ben, had gone up to do the same thing and so he, too, was on fire for God. We would often spend time just sitting together talking about what was happening to us. I loved our time together. Ben was like a brother to me. He loved me in a godly way, and he wanted to protect me. We shared time just listening to music about Jesus and discussing where we were at with God. One of the other guys in the house had brought a bible in with him and it was called a Recovery Devotional Bible. It was for people in recovery that wanted to work through their issues with God's help. That was us. Ben and I would spend hours just flicking through the pages looking for more of God with each and every page. We were both so hungry for all that He wanted for us. I am sure that I will never forget those times together. This bible had devotions that included a small lesson and a prayer. We would read them out aloud to each other and then discuss them. Before we knew it we had started to really study the Word of God. We both have student hearts and God is the great Teacher. We were learning more, directly from God, during those times than we could have in years otherwise. We were so open to the work of the Holy Spirit. We both figured that if we could give our lives over to the enemy 100% the way that we had for years, then we could definitely give it to Jesus in the same way; and we did.

The days seemed to go by so quickly. We started to do a series of workshops with Mr T called 'I live by what I believe not what I feel'. I thought that sounded great and I did want to do that, but first of all I needed to understand the real difference between 'believing' and 'feeling', and to do that I needed to get a greater understanding of what I actually believed, so that I could then live by it. I knew that I believed in Jesus and I was learning more about Him through reading and studying the bible. I also knew that if I allowed Him to, that God would continue to change and renew my mind so that I could come into a deeper understanding about what I believed. Mr T taught me that what I believed would determine what I felt, but what I felt could not determine what I believed. I then started to study God's word about what I believed so that my feelings could be in line with the Word of God. I learnt about the joy of the Lord and got a greater grip on all that He had done for me. I realised that what I believed did control how I felt, because since I had received Jesus into my life I had known real peace and joy. These indescribable emotions had become a new part of my life; God was trying to bring my messed up soul in line with Him.

The most obvious way that He did that for me was through music. He had used music to soften my heart to Him in the first place, now He was using music to reveal His love for me. I knew that Jesus loved me; even when I would sit and just think about all that I had done and wonder how could He love me; I just knew that He did. I knew it because of what people had told me, what they had prayed over me and because that was what His word said; but even though I knew it in my head I still needed to receive it in my heart. This happened one day when I was in my room alone just reading the bible and listening to Josie's CD. There was a song on there that I had heard so many times before but it had never sunk deep into my spirit. That song was called 'Jesus Lover of my Soul'. It was the words "My Saviour, my closest friend; I will worship you until the very end" that changed my life forever. I felt a change inside of me as I lay there and listened to the words. I had known already; but this was different. It was as though Jesus was right there with me, holding me, being my closest friend. It was then that I cried for the first time in a long time, but not once did I feel alone. I felt such comfort in shedding those tears with Jesus. I knew that He was there for me and I knew, in my heart, that He loved me. That song on that day forever changed the way I was with Jesus – I now loved Him even more. I had a deep desire to worship Him and to just love Him for all that He had done for me and all that He was to me. That breakthrough had come even without me praying for it; after all, the Father God knows our heart's desires.

One night in my sleep God showed me that He knew the desire of my heart was to be set free. I woke in the middle of the night after having had a nightmare, only to feel as though the Lord was right there with me just holding me. I must've gone back to sleep because the next thing that I knew I was waking up in the morning. When I woke I felt something sharp poking into my back. I had no idea what it was so I pulled down the sheets and found my necklace from Thailand. That leather necklace had been a gift from my brother living over there and I had loved it; it was a carving of something but I had never known exactly what it meant. The leather band had somehow "snapped" in my sleep and the necklace had come off from around my neck. Then I looked up, only to see that photos I had on the wall from my time in Thailand had also fallen down. They hadn't all fallen; the only two left were of me with my brother. However, all of the ones of Buddha were on the floor and some were even shrivelled up. I knew that the weather had been cold, but not that cold. I had to ask Josie what had happened to me. She asked me to consider what I had been praying to God about. I had been asking Him to "Please change me!!" He had changed me alright; He had removed from me the things that would have held me back spiritually. God had released me without my knowledge, but with my consent. Later that day I thanked Him for what He had done and I felt as though I had to throw them out. I did one better than that and I burned them, never to return again. I then prayed for God to fill any gaps in my life that I had chosen to fill with things not of Him. He had started a work in me, but I had to choose to ask Him to continue. I gladly did so.

Chapter 11

Filled to Overflowing

One of the major things that I needed to remove from my life was a person – Steve. I had met him under circumstances that had been replaced in my life by the precious blood of Jesus; I now needed to do the same with him, replace this relationship with the love of Jesus. I spoke to Mr T about it and he agreed that now was the right time to do just that. Even though I had met Steve when I had been a prostitute he had been good to me when no one else was; although I knew that being nice to me had always stemmed from his guilt. I needed to forgive Steve and ask for his forgiveness, for all that had ever taken place between us. I prayed that the right opportunity would arise for me to do just that. He called up a couple of days later asking if he could come and visit. I had been avoiding him for quite some time, but this time I agreed.

When Steve arrived he had cigarettes and chocolate for me, but the first thing that I felt led to do was not to take them from him. I told him I couldn't accept them and he seemed very confused. I had always taken as much as I could from him, so his confusion was understandable. That opened up the way for me to talk to him about where I was at. I chose not to tell him about my salvation, as I felt that he wouldn't understand right then. I did, however, tell him that my life was taking a different course now and that I was choosing not to have any thing, or anyone, from my past that would hold me back from where I was headed in my life. Steve knew that I meant him and immediately he started to talk about all that he had done for me, and that now that I was getting better I was kicking him out of me life; I understand now that he was reacting out of offence. I told him that I just couldn't have him in my life because every time I saw him it reminded me of the life that I had left behind and I just didn't need that at this stage of my recovery. Steve didn't understand and got quite angry and upset with me. I ended up just telling him to leave, and eventually he did. As soon as he was gone I felt great relief, and I knew that I had done the right thing. I needed to grow and change and I felt as though having him in my life was holding me back. I had asked him to leave my life so that I could move on, and with the help of the Holy Spirit, had found the words to say to express why I felt that way. I had hurt him, but I decided the best thing that I could do for him was to pray for him; and I did.

The following weekend something happened in the house that I had no real understanding of at the time. The joy of the Lord came upon the entire house and we were all changed. It started on the Saturday morning. When we were doing our chores we had praise and worship music blaring (I am sure that it could've been heard down the street). After we had all finished we kept the music playing and ended up sitting on the front verandah. All of a sudden someone said something and we just started laughing. I can't remember what they had said, but I do remember that it was nothing particularly funny. Anyhow, we started laughing and basically didn't stop laughing all day. Throughout the day you were able to hear at least one person laughing at any given time. It was so hilarious to hear that it made the people listening laugh as well. That night there was a few of us in the kitchen, attempting to make hot drinks. I say attempting because every time the kettle would boil someone would start laughing and then we would all start. This continued for hours; at different stages there were people rolling around on the floor and even that was making us laugh. None of us had any real idea why we were laughing, or what we were laughing about, but it continued well into the early hours of the morning. Those people that weren't in the kitchen would come to the door to find out what was so funny and they too would end up laughing. It must've seemed so outrageous. I am sure that none of us had had any experience quite like it, besides being on drugs and just laughing at anything. Eventually we all decided that it was time for bed; as we had to get up for church the next morning; but even that made us laugh.

The following day in church we all tried to be quiet but we also wanted to laugh. I am sure that Pastor David, and the rest of the congregation, must have thought that we were on drugs of some kind. But we definitely were not and we still had no understanding of what was going on. It continued for most of that day as well. I had been laughing so much that my face was aching from it. We were all just so happy; or as I later found out, full of joy. That night when Mr T and Josie returned to the house I told them what had been happening and they just looked at each other and smiled. I kept asking them what was happening to me, because they always were able to explain things about God to me in a way that I would understand. They then just told me that we had all received the joy of the Lord; that we had been drunk in the Spirit. I had no idea what they meant, so I decided to try and find out from the bible. I found a Scripture that described exactly what they had said to me. It was Ephesians 5:18(NIV), and it said, Do not get drunk on wine, which leads to debauchery. Instead, be filled with the Spirit. I understood then that the total joy, freedom and peace that we had spent years looking for through drugs was now ours. We had all been filled, to overflowing, with the Spirit of God. The Lord had answered our prayers and the prayers of those praying for us, and changed our lives in a radical way; just what we had all needed.

After that weekend, anyone that had been living in the house that hadn't been saved soon was. There had been a few people there that had struggled with giving their hearts to Jesus, but once they had seen what He was doing in our lives they, too, wanted what we had; love, grace, peace and joy. From that time on none of us would ever be the same.

The first thing that noticeably changed after that weekend was my language. My mouth had been full of foul language and dirty words; which had been the language I had been surrounded with and, so, had become a part of my normal vocabulary. On reflection, almost every third or fourth word had been a dirty word of some variety. I had been asking God to help me to watch my mouth and to help me guard what I spoke. I had read in the recovery bible in the book of James about taming our tongue because our mouths would either speak life or death. The small prayer in that bible reads, "Lord, set a watch at my mouth and help me guard what I say". I had read that, prayed it and believed it; and God had done it. He had used the 'drunk in the Spirit' weekend, as I called it, to transform my mouth into a place of worship. I wanted to only speak words that lifted people up, that spoke life into their spirits. It is something that I continue to pray to this very day.

One day not long after, Will called me and said that he wanted to come and visit me. I hadn't seen him for a while and I really looked forward to catching up. Despite all that we had been through together, Will would always remain a very special person to me and I would always consider him my friend. When he arrived I was glad to see him, but something was different. I wasn't sure what it was. We talked about how we both were and what we had been up to. It was then that Will asked what was wrong with me; he said I seemed to be very different. I didn't know what he meant, until I remembered that he hadn't seen me since I had been saved; of course I was going to seem different to him; I was different. I explained to him that I was a Christian now and I started to tell him about some of the things that had been happening to me. He was glad for me, but didn't seem very interested; however, we knew that something major had happened in my life when he offered me some pot in the car as he was leaving and I refused it. I just wasn't interested. That was a big step for Will and I. For the few years before that we had spent most of our time together either looking for drugs or taking them; so we both knew that I was changing. When he left he told me not to change too much, but deep inside myself I knew that I was and I was glad to continue doing so.

We were still having people come to the house; some would stay and others would just come for the day – others just couldn't cope there at all. I started to pray for every person that was in my life, including those that didn't stay. Those that did got saved within a few weeks of being there! We had a couple of young 16-17 year-olds there at the time and I remember thinking that if only they didn't have to go through what I had gone through that they could make it clean now instead of in their 20's. One of the young guys, named Dane, I had met the very first day that I had met Mr T at Highgate Hill. He had been in and out of the house since then; he would get to a certain point of being clean but just didn't seem able to stay there. I prayed for him often, he had a very special place in my heart; then and now. I thought of him as a little brother and he accepted that role in my life quite happily. I prayed that he would get saved and that he would come into a greater understanding of how much God loved him and wanted to protect him. Not long after he came back to the house my prayers were answered – he was touched by the Power of God. He immediately had a hunger for prayer and the bible, and I was really encouraged. Unfortunately, within a few weeks of this remarkable change he decided to go on a speed binge for a week or so. I felt shattered, even though I knew that God was watching out for him. I couldn't understand why he would choose to do that after discovering God's love for him. It was then that I first discovered, and understood, that it was still up to the person to want to be in a continual relationship with the Lord; God still gives us free choice. When he did come back and I told him how I felt he told me that even though he had been out there taking drugs that he still knew that God was with him. He also said that he knew that I had been praying for him, almost as though he could feel it at the times I would speak a hedge of protection over his life. It was then that I realised my deep desire was for a prayer life that touched God and reached people.

A new guy started coming to the house, Jason, who was a couple of years older than me and had been a Christian for many years. He had a similar drug taking background, but he also had a lot of wisdom about God and His ways. I would sit and talk to him and take in most of what he said. Ben and I would sometimes question him about things that we had read in the bible; things that we wanted to know more about. He would always be able to give us an answer or he would look one up in his bible; he would carry his bible around with him all of the time, (I often wondered if he was serious or if it was just for the 'spiritual' effect). He had started coming to the house during the day for support and within a couple of weeks we were having a house meeting to discuss him moving in. We all wanted someone a little bit older than us, someone that we could learn from and someone that would help us to remain grounded. Even though I was learning a lot from Jason there was also something about him that I didn't like much. He spoke the truth to me at all times, but sometimes his words would hurt me. I don't think it was intentional, as he knew my background and I am sure that he just wanted to help me grow as a Christian and as a woman; but with that growth came some pain.

One day after he had moved in, he came into my room and handed me a booklet called 'Steps to Freedom in Christ' by Neil T.Anderson.

He said that he had been going through his stuff and he had felt led to give this to me to read through. It was so incredible, such Godly timing. I had been asking the Lord to reveal to me anything that was not of Him, past and present, so that He could remove them. Then Jason had come in with this booklet that was all about being delivered from those things that were holding me back from a righteous walk with Christ. When I started to read through what he had given me it said that I should read his book, 'Victory Over the Darkness' before proceeding.

The next day I asked someone to take me to a Christian bookstore for the first time. I had not been spending much money and so I had some spare to go shopping. I had been intending to buy some clothes, but God obviously had other ideas for me. Before I went into the shop I asked the Holy Spirit to show me the books that I should buy. Immediately, I found the Anderson section and picked up 'Victory Over the Darkness'. I saw many other books of his that I would've loved to have bought; however, the Holy Spirit only had me pick up and buy the one that I needed to read before doing the steps. He knew that otherwise I would just keep reading and never actually get to do the steps to freedom in Christ; and that was exactly what I needed at that point in time. As soon as I got home I started to read it, and I don't remember doing much else for the following week.

After I had finished reading the book I had a deeper understanding of who I was in Christ; that is, all that I was created to be. I now saw myself as a true child of God and I understood exactly what that meant for me. It had been the perfect book for that time in my walk with God. I then went back to the booklet that Jason had given to me and felt prepared to work through it. I knew that I would need assistance from the Holy Spirit to be able to work through it correctly, so before I even started to read through it I prayed. I prayed that the Holy Spirit would reveal to me anything that was not of God; anything that needed to be removed from my life. Praise God, that is exactly what happened.

The first part of the process involved working through events of my life that needed to be addressed. This opened up my eyes in a big way. I soon realised just how major this was going to be, and I understood that the impact it was going to have was huge. The preparation stage worked through the history of my family and myself and revealed to me areas I needed to be aware of. Then it was time to take the steps to freedom in Christ. I worked through one step a day; any more than that would have been too much for me to handle at the time. God revealed to me that I was not spiritually mature enough to cope with any more than one at a time.

Doing the steps revealed to me that things that I had considered not very important were actually holding me back from true freedom; activities that I had taken part in as a teenager were actually very harmful to me, spiritually. While I was participating in these things I had thought them just good fun and harmless, I had no idea that I was grieving the heart of God; I had no comprehension for the things of God at the time. Thankfully, now that I was aware of them, God was making a way for me to start afresh with Him. Some of these seemingly innocent, but dangerous activities were: fortune telling, tarot cards, palm reading, horoscopes, New age medicine, crystals, yoga and music. They were considered dangerous because they were false in the eyes of God. I had to confess and renounce each one by name; and thank Jesus Christ that I was now forgiven and cleansed by His precious blood.

Some of the other steps to freedom involved me making a list of all of the people that had hurt me and then choosing to forgive them. That step was difficult for me, and I remember calling upon Josie to pray with me for the strength to work through it completely. Another step was based upon me confessing and repenting of all of my sins, all of the lusts of the flesh. I knew that one was going to be big for me also. Things that had just been a 'normal' part of my existence were, in actual fact, biblical sin. Things such as; lying, outbursts of anger, lusting, swearing, complaining and controlling. Once again I'd had no idea that these things were wrong when I had been doing them, but now that it had been revealed to me I was making the choice to be set free from the bondage that they had created in my life. The steps were completed in a prayer to Jesus Christ; thanking Him for His love for me and thanking Him for setting me free. I felt so different once I had completed them, but I also understood that in order to stay free I needed to keep walking in right relationship with the Lord. I needed to stay aware of the sin in my life and continually keep a heart of repentance.

One of the things in my life that was hindering my walk with Christ was my relationship with Mark. Mr T had taken us aside one day and explained to us that romantic relationships were not allowed in the house, but that he was willing to help us further ours as long as we agreed to take things very slowly. He also asked that we be open to counselling sessions together with him, to assure him that our relationship progressed positively. We agreed, and not long after that we went our 'first' official date together. We both made a big deal of it and got dressed up for the occasion. We had a great night out together, doing normal date things, like going out for dinner and going to the movies. At the end of the night we kissed and agreed that we would take things slowly and see how things worked out. After all, he was still getting over the fact that he and his wife had come into the house as a married couple and they were now getting a divorce. Our lives were changing rapidly before our eyes and I think that we both thought that it was nice just to have someone with whom we could relax and feel comfortable with. I know for myself that it seemed easier to have Mark in my life than to go through all that I was going through alone.

With all that was going on for me at the house I did what I had always done when I got comfortable; I wanted to leave. There was no particular reason for it other than I just felt as though it was time to move on. Most of the people that I had ever known at the house had wanted to leave just so that they could use drugs, but I just wanted something different to do. I spoke to Mr T about how I felt and he told me to seriously consider my options. After all, I had only been clean for a few months, and even with Jesus in my life, I was still vulnerable. I didn't feel vulnerable, but I didn't feel indestructible either. I knew that the best decision would be for me to stay, but I couldn't the way things had been. No matter how much I loved (my roommate) Ainsley, waking me up at all hours to talk to her and counsel her through whatever issue she was working on was becoming more and more difficult. I spoke to her honestly about it and she agreed that something needed to change she felt as though she was becoming too dependent on me. I explained all of this to Mr T who told me to leave it with him. He told me that I was a great asset to him and they really wanted me to stay on so that he could train me to help other people. I agreed to wait for a week and see how things panned out. Within that week one of the guys choose to leave the house which meant that there was now a spare room and so that I was able to have a room to myself. Mr T knew that helping others was a dream of mine and so I agreed to stay.

Chapter 12

A New Creation

Having my own room opened up a whole new realm in my relationship with Christ. I was now able to read the bible at anytime and I spent hours in prayer. I loved my time with God so much; I needed it. I enjoyed telling Him how much I loved Him and just how grateful I was that He loved me. The first weekend that I was into my own room I decided to pray and welcome the Holy Spirit to my new room; and I also prayed the precious blood of Jesus over my doorway. I didn't really understand why, but I felt compelled to do it. I now understand that it was God's way of protecting me from evil entering the room and into my life. God is so amazing.

After I had prayed in there I decided to lie down on my bed and read the bible. I had read bits and pieces of the Gospels but I had never read any one book straight through. That weekend I started at the book of Matthew and kept reading until I completed the book of John. God used that time to reveal to me the mighty ways of Jesus that had occurred in bible times; and that I knew to still occur today. After all, He had found me, saved me and delivered me from many things; including my drug addiction. I knew that He was a mighty, miracle-working God, but that weekend I received a whole new revelation about how awesome He truly was. I will never forget the presence of God in my room that weekend. It was the presence of the Lord that surpassed all understanding. I almost felt as though Jesus was sitting on my bed beside me, just being with me. It was an amazing experience and something that I continue to pray to experience now in my life.

The training to help other people happened sooner than I had expected. Mr T always went to Dr Reece's surgery on Tuesdays and Thursdays to counsel people and that Tuesday he asked me to go with him so that I could sit in on his sessions. I felt honoured; I really wanted to help other people fight their addictions and now that I knew Jesus I knew that it was going to be possible. I took notes while I was there about the questions that he asked and the way that he addressed certain issues. Those people needed to know Jesus, but we had to wait for them to show an interest in Him before we could discuss the wonderful things that He could do for them. One of the best things about me being there was that people felt as though they could trust me because I had been where they had been and come through the other side of it. It was then that I was able to talk to them about Jesus. I often did this with people that were actually waiting to speak to Mr T. That way it wasn't during a session time; but, rather, merely a chat that I was having at a coffee table. I loved my time there talking to people and soon I was going every week with him. I looked forward to my days there and I knew that I was making a difference. That was all that I wanted; to make a difference in peoples' lives. I was helping to change lives that otherwise had no hope; giving them a glimmer of hope simply by sharing my story. Being the me that God had called me to be.

One of the things that going to the surgery encouraged me to do was write up a work sheet on drug addiction and how to work your way out of the struggle that it is. I started out by simply stating what I thought drug addiction was: *"DRUG ADDICTION is a way of coping with a painful reality that is self destructive despite consequences"*. I then added: *"No drug user starts out with the intent to get addicted, the addiction develops from an unhealthy choice of drugs as pleasure producer or coping mechanism"*. I then stated: *"Admitting to oneself that the powder is more powerful than you is only the 1st step – one must want to face the consequences of their actions coming from or leading to their addictions"*. I showed what I had written to Mr T and he encouraged me to continue with it. Every time I would sit down to add to it I would always pray that the Holy Spirit would assist me, because without God's assistance I knew that nothing could be achieved. The work sheet included ways to look at yourself in a different light, ways to discover what issues needed to be worked through and then moving beyond the drug mentality. I printed it up on the computer and knew that it would come in handy at some time. I had no idea when God was going to use them to help others, but I knew that was exactly what they were for.

At about the same time that I was working on those sheets I started to read more in the bible about putting off the old me and putting on the new one. I asked Josie what it meant and she explained to me about water baptism. It was when you get completely submerged in the water and it is basically the old man going down and staying in the water and the new man coming up, out of the water. It sounded great to me and I talked to the others in the house about it. Ben was particularly interested and so we decided to talk to pastor David about it. He told us that he was happy to have a baptism day and that we just had to let him know who was going to do it. We encouraged everybody and most people wanted to. The whole concept of putting off the old self appealed to us all greatly and we waited patiently for the day to arrive.

I invited my parents and when I explained to them what it was all about my mum started to cry. She told me that she had thought, just months before, that the next ceremony she would attend for me would be my funeral. That was difficult to hear and it reminded me again of all of the pain and destruction that my drug taking had caused. It also made a way for me to ask her for forgiveness. That also made her cry. She had already forgiven me in her heart but was glad to finally speak the words. She told me that she was glad to have the old me back and I told her that the new me was even better than the old one, because now I had Jesus as well. She understood what I meant.

Before we were to be baptised Mr T had asked Jason, who had already been through the baptism process, to explain to us exactly what it all meant. He showed us a Scripture that he said explained it better than any human words possibly could. That Scripture was Ephesians 4:22-24 (NIV) and it says; *You were taught with regard to your former way of life, to put off your old self, which is being corrupted by its deceitful desires; to be made new in the attitude of your minds; and to put on the new self created to be like God in true righteousness and holiness.* Those words spoke volumes to me. I longed to remove the old me from my life and to be seen as a new creation in Christ. He then explained to us that water baptism was used as a way to outwardly show the people in our lives what we knew had taken place in our inner lives. That made us all look forward to it even more.

It was due to take place the first weekend of December. I had been clean for five months and saved for almost three. Amazing and wonderful changes had taken place in my life in such a short time; I knew that it was all God. And now so would the people closest to me.

The weekend of the water baptism I had stayed at my parents' place at Maroochydore. My brothers ex-wife Lynda was up from Melbourne and I had gone up there to spend some time with her. We all woke up very early and headed down to Brisbane. I had been so excited about the baptism that I am sure my excitement had rubbed off on to my parents. We were all there before anybody else. It was at the house of one of the church members. The others soon arrived and excitement was in the air. It was going to be a very big day for all of us. At the time it was going to be Ben, Mark, Jaiden and myself who were to be baptised. We had spent the week trying to talk Dane into it as well, but we knew that the final decision had to be his own. When it was my turn to go into the pool all I could think of was the Scripture that Jason had explained to us. I knew that I was a new creation and now was my opportunity for that to become real; in the natural realm as well as the spiritual. I entered the pool and David and Mr T both laid their hands on my shoulders. They asked me if I understood what I was doing and I emphatically said yes. They then proceeded to pray for me immersed me in the water. When I came up I felt as though I was going to burst with joy. I had a verse of Scripture going around in my head and that was 2 Corinthians 5:17(NIV), which says: *Therefore, if anyone is in Christ, he is a new creation; the old has gone, the new has come!* When I got out of the water my mum ran up to me to give me a great big hug. She was crying real tears of joy. She whispered to me that she was proud of me and happy for me; and so was the Lord. I had now shown people in the natural what I had received in the spiritual: a new life.

The remainder of the day was very special also; Dane decided to get baptised and was glad that he did. We were all very excited about the day and what it meant to us spiritually – we had officially declared to the enemy that we were no longer his territory; we belonged to God. It would take some time for us to all come back down to reality. Thankfully, the joy remained with us and glory was all given to God.

The following week Mr T took me for a drive and told me that he had someone special that he needed me to counsel on my own. He said that she was a young woman who had suffered a lot of abuse as a child and had chosen to turn to drugs to numb the pain. He told me that she needed a female counsellor to help her work through her issues and that he believed that I would be the best person to help her. I prayerfully accepted. Even though I had not suffered abuse as a child, I had not had a dream childhood either and I knew that with the Lord's guidance I would definitely be able to help her.

Her name was Kylie and I first met her the following day. At first we just sat around and talked about where I had come from and the mistakes that I had made in life. I am sure that this made her feel more comfortable with me. Even though we didn't share the same backgrounds, she now knew that I had come from a very desperate place to the wonderful place I was at. She saw the peace and the joy that I had inside me and knew that I could help her. We took things very slowly, as I knew that it would be painful for her. She was open to sharing her story with me and that first session ended with me just giving her a great big hug. I knew that there was something special about my hugs; people had always told me that. But Kylie said to me that she had felt a real comfort in my arms, something that she had been longing for. Mr T was seeing her partner, Michael, at the same time as Kylie was seeing me. When the guys had finished they shook hands and went their separate ways, revealing to me the difference between men and women; and I then understood why Mr T had felt led to ask me to help Kylie.

Kylie and I continued to see each other every week, sometimes twice a week. She was very keen to work through her issues, and I was just as keen to help her do that. Slowly we tackled some of the harder issues, but I knew that with the Holy Spirit on my side we would never go further than Kylie could handle. I loved my time with her; I felt a real sense of peace every time we met. Eventually, I started to share with her little bits and pieces about what Jesus had done for me and Kylie said that she knew there had been some special quality about me that she had been drawn to. I continued to pray for her during the weeks that passed and always prayed before I saw her that God would guide me, and my words; and He always did. I knew that there was something very special about Kylie, and I knew that once the counselling was over that we would remain friends. Time would prove that to be very true.

While all of this was going on Mark and I were having troubles of our own. He had decided to use heroin again. As far as I knew it had only happened once, but that was enough for me to realise that maybe he and I weren't headed in the same direction. I found it very difficult to understand why he would choose to do that, after all of the hard work that he had done with himself. He couldn't explain it to me in any other way than to say he just felt like trying it again. It was just before Christmas and he said that he had always spent that time of the year off his face. So had I, but my life was not like that any more. I struggled to deal with the thought that he had chosen to use drugs even though he knew that it could jeopardise all that we had together. It was Mr T that enlightened me to the fact that I needed to forgive him in the same way that Christ had forgiven me. I found that very difficult, but I did it anyway. That was one of my first real experiences of being led by the Spirit even when my natural flesh felt unable to. I knew that I had done the right thing, now I just had to believe it. It took time, but eventually Mark and I agreed to just continue on where we had been before the incident had ever happened.

Before Mark's drug taking we had slept together, and we had to deal with the spiritual and natural consequences that followed. As far as we knew nobody else knew about it. We had discussed sex often and one night we just decided that the sooner we did it the better. In hindsight, the enemy was having a field day with our minds by fooling us into believing that our relationship wouldn't change and it would all be okay. It wasn't. From that night onwards our relationship went to a on a whole new level. We were now more physical with each other than we had been before. And even though we knew that we had done the wrong thing we chose to ignore the warning from the Holy Spirit. Sex then, became something that took place, though irregularly, whenever we 'felt' like it. We had no real understanding of the spiritual mess we were creating, after all he was still officially married to another woman, but we did understand that it was wrong in God's eyes. We pitifully used a Scripture as an excuse, which was the worst possible thing we could've done. We used to say *"the spirit is willing, but the flesh is weak"*. It is only now that I realise how detrimental that was to us, both spiritually and personally. Never before had I felt convicted about sleeping with someone, but God was using my relationship with Mark to reveal to me the issues of which I still needed to confess and repent. The primary one of those was lust which I recognised, but it took me months before I would totally seek God to remove it by His Holy Spirit. During this time I knew in my heart that God loved me, and that was the most important thing to me at that point.

For the first time in years I was really looking forward to Christmas, due to the fact I had a real understanding of what Christmas was all about. It was a time to celebrate the birth of my Lord and Saviour Jesus Christ. I looked forward to celebrating His birthday in the same way that He celebrated the day that I was born.

It was a special time for all of us in the house because for the first time in a long time we all actually had the spare money to buy gifts for our loved ones. I decided to buy mainly books for people – books about Christian growth were the ones that I chose as I wanted to give people gifts that would help to build themselves up spiritually. I chose to give my parents a framed photograph of myself. The photo was of me laughing and looking very happy with my life, and I wanted to capture that for them to see every day. I knew that they would love it. I knew that for the previous years we had all had miserable Christmases, and I was determined for this one to be the first of many joyous Christmases. And it was.

On Christmas day at the house we all woke up and gathered in the lounge room to exchange gifts. It was just like being a part of a really big family. It will always hold very special memories for me. Then we all ventured off on our own family-based adventures. Mark and I spent the afternoon with his family and then headed up to my parents place at the Sunshine Coast to spend a few days with them. Mum and dad had also invited Mr T, Josie and Ben to spend a few days. I am sure that my mum wanted to celebrate that Christmas with those people that had had a major influence in the turnaround in my life. Over the years I had given my parents some really dreadful Christmas memories and I was determined to change all of those that year; and I am sure that I did. We all had a really wonderful and loving few days up the Sunshine Coast. Spending time at the beach, reading and eating a lot of wonderful food. I will treasure the memory of my first clean Christmas for two reasons; my family and Jesus. After all, they had all stood by me even when I felt undeserving.

The Sunday after Christmas the church was handing out gifts to everybody. They gave me some tapes by Joyce Meyer. The name of the tape series was, 'Breaking the Cycle of Addiction'. I knew as soon as I saw it that it was a gift from God. He was going to use those tapes not only to help me understand the transformation that had already taken place in my life, but also to help others understand. I loved it immediately and looked forward to having the opportunity to listen to it. I only knew of the name Joyce Meyer because I had heard Jason mention her as someone whose teaching would be good for me and I had also seen some of her books when I had been scouring through the bookstores. Either way, I knew that those tapes were going to really minister to me; I just had no idea how deeply.

The tapes made a difference in my life for a few reasons. The main reason was the ministry form of Joyce Meyer's. She spoke boldly and bluntly about the issue and that was exactly how I needed to be ministered to. She had a way of saying things that made the unclear very clear to me. I listened to those tapes many times over, and was always able to glean something new from them. I had heard them at a time when I needed a deeper revelation of exactly all that God had done for me. It truly was godly timing, as was so much that was occurring in my life at that point in time.

A few days after we all arrived back from our Christmas break it was time to think about what we were doing for New Years Eve. It was strange for me because for the years prior I had always pre-planned my night; the drugs, the destination, the people. But this year the night that was going to lead into the new millennium just didn't hold much importance to me at all. I knew that it was a major event, but it didn't really bother me how it was spent. Funnily enough, I had thought more about it the last new years eve, how I would welcome in the year 2000; but now none of that seemed relevant. I was just glad to be spending it drug free, with a whole new destiny ahead of me. I had spoken to Mr T about it because he was planning to take most of the household to a Christian dance party at Christian Outreach Centre, one of the larger local churches. I told him that I wasn't particularly into doing that; it just didn't seem like my thing. However, I didn't actually know what 'my thing' was any more. All that I did know was that I needed to create a new type of memory for my New Year's.

One of the young guys, Casey, had a young son and a girlfriend that he really wanted to spend the night with. But he wasn't allowed to do that unless there was somebody in the house to keep an eye on them. I knew how important his family was to him and so I decided to talk to Mark about us staying home to look after them. He had spent a lot of time talking with Casey about his family and, so, he also knew how much it would mean to him. So we spoke to Mr T and offered to stay home with them. He thought that we were joking as he had given us permission to go out that night; but we just didn't want to. Staying home and helping Casey out seemed much more important to both of us. So that was how we chose to spend our first clean New Years Eve – worlds away from all of our previous ones, and actually meaningful.

We watched as all of the others left the house to go to the Christian dance party and then we rang up and ordered pizzas. We had hired some videos, but I don't think we actually watched any of them. Casey was down stairs enjoying his family and Mark and I spent most of the night just talking and enjoying one another's company. Strangely enough, we were actually looking forward to watching the fireworks from the front verandah, but as I remember, we only just stayed awake long enough to actually see them. It was a New Year's Eve with a difference for both of us and one that had been really special for me: I mean, I actually remembered it. For years before that my New Years had always turned into at least a two-day party because of the amount of drugs that I consumed and the excitement that I thought I'd had. It was actually because the drugs I had taken didn't allow me to sleep, so I just stayed awake and partied; but I almost always forgot most of what had happened. The year of 2000 had been my first New Year clean and sober, and I had really enjoyed myself. It also helped me to realise just how different my life had become; and I was glad for the changes.

Not long after New Years Beth came back to the house, once again looking for a place to stay and asking for help. I had been praying for her and I knew that I needed to just give her my unconditional love. I needed to love her the way that Jesus loved her, and me. Beth only ended up staying for a few days, but during that time I had the opportunity to share with her all that had been happening in my life. She told me that she was glad for me but that no matter how much she hated the prostitute lifestyle, she wasn't willing to give up using drugs. I knew that Beth was young and that her life had been so tainted by drugs that it was going to have to be up to her to decide to stop, whenever that would be. I told her, again, that I loved and cared for her and would always be there to help her out. I know that she knew that and I also knew that the love that she received from me was probably the purest type of love that she had ever received from anyone. I was glad that Beth knew she could call on me. When she left I cried tears for her – if only she could stop now, she had her whole life ahead of her. I loved her like a sister and had her in my prayers every night. I asked God to guide and protect her and somehow show her His great love for her. I knew that He was using me to show Beth that godly type of love; and I knew that was all that I could do for her. I had been there; strong-willed and stubborn, and only God had broken through those barriers for me. I felt a peace knowing that he would one day do the same for her.

One night, just after Beth had left, Jason knocked on my door and asked me if he could come in and sit down. I said yes, and as soon as I looked at him I knew that he was on something. I talked to him for a while and he told me that he had broken up with his girlfriend and that he was really messed up about everything. He kept asking me to repeat a 'Jewel' CD, and when the song that he wanted would come on he would close his eyes and it seemed as though he wasn't really there. I eventually asked Jason what he was on and he denied being on anything. I told him what I thought he had been doing and he laughed and said it wasn't true. I didn't understand how he thought that he could come into my room and not have me confront him about it. But he kept denying it, until a few hours later he eventually admitted to having had quite a few pills. I didn't really believe him as I thought he seemed to be on heroin, but he told me that he had been given a script of pills for a toothache and that he had taken more than he should have. That was very obvious. I didn't really know what I could do to help him. Jason had always seemed to be the 'together' one, the strong one, and the one who didn't need other people. But that night he reached out to me in a new way. He was hurting and he needed a friend, and while I was happy to be that for him, I knew that I couldn't help him in that state. He eventually toddled off to his own bed and I told him that I would talk to him the next day. However, the following day he said that he was fine and couldn't really remember much of what we had talked about. I thought that was a pity because he had shown me a sensitive and caring side of himself, a side that I had never seen before; and I liked it. It would be quite some time before that side of him would re-emerge in my life.

Chapter 13
Power of Redemption

It was at this time when I felt led by the Holy Spirit to, prayerfully, discover the changes that had taken place inside of me since I had given my life to Jesus. It was a difficult time because I was made aware of all of the negative attributes that had contributed to make me who I had been. On the other hand, it also helped me to come into a greater love relationship with the Lord when I saw, on paper, all of the amazingly positive changes that had taken place since meeting Him. This is the list as it came to me:

BEFORE CHRIST
- guilty
- shameful
- blameful
- regretful
- misunderstood
- selfish
- weak
- stubborn
- uncomfortable
- insecure
- careless
- thoughtless
- depressed
- manipulative
- conniving
- liar
- powerless
- lonely
- unlovable
- soul-less
- isolated
- bored
- taker
- in denial
- irresponsible

AFTER CHRIST
- caring
- supportive
- understanding
- sharing
- knowledgeable
- trustworthy
- lovable
- trusting
- kind
- expressive
- believing
- strong
- patient
- graceful
- forgiveable/ forgiving
- open
- happy
- giving

Once I had completed the list, a few days after I had started on it, God revealed to me that He had totally forgiven me of all of the things on the list before Christ. I had chosen Him and in doing so He had wiped my slate clean. He had washed me in His blood and those things no longer existed in His eyes. When He looked upon me all He saw was the blood of Jesus, a pure vessel. That was so major for me because I would sometimes find myself looking back upon my life with regret and shame, but He didn't want me to live that way. He had set me free so that I could live free, not bound to my past. In Him all things had been made new.

Once I had received that revelation in my spirit I started to keep a prayer journal, so that I could see how faithful the Lord was, and had been, to me. What follows is the first prayer that I wrote in it:

Thank you dear Lord Jesus, the true lover of my soul and protector of my existence – I will never let you go. You have saved and delivered me from a life of sin and death and I praise you for the grace that you have showered over me. Thank you Lord Jesus for washing me with your blood, for the redemption that you have allowed me to have. I know that you love me dearly. Thank you and bless you for the great and mighty compassion that you have shown me through giving me great strength and courage to break through the devil's bondage of addiction in my life. For helping me to come to know you through the Word of God, for guiding me to the words that I needed most, and do need most. For the deep faith that I now have in you and your blessing over my life. For the teaching of hope, perseverance, guidance, meekness and above all else – love. For working through me to counsel others in need, through the gifts of wisdom and knowledge from you, for helping me to guide others to you in the name of Jesus and by the power of the blood. Thank you for lifting me up to be seated in the heavenly realms – for truly cleansing my heart and setting my spirit free. For filling me with the Holy Spirit daily through the power of the blood of Jesus. Lord thank you for taking my past from me and for not counting my sins against me; for the great power of redemption. Thank you Lord Jesus for the love that you wash over me at all times. You are my LORD.

I prayed that prayer every morning and every night, for as long as I could remember. I knew that there was power in the words that I had written and it was then that the Lord revealed to me, for the first time, that He had given me a great gift in my writing. He showed me that people would fall in love with Jesus because of the words that I wrote, through Him. I continued to write in that book and the many books that followed it, whenever I felt the call to do so. Here I am, almost three years, later sharing my innermost self through my words, and I do pray that they will encourage you to fall in love with Jesus; for the first time or all over again.

The same week that I started to keep my prayer journal Mark took me to Koorong, a Christian bookstore, to buy me a new bible. He said that he believed that I needed one other than the Recovery Devotional Bible, one that I could learn more from as a Christian as opposed to a recovering addict. I was so excited. I prayed that the Holy Spirit would reveal to me the exact bible that I needed and as soon as we walked into the store I picked one up and I knew that it was the right one. It was called a 'Spirit-filled Life bible'. It had sections in it that would help me to grow and to better understand all that the bible had for me. I couldn't wait to get home and start reading it; in fact, I started to skim through it while we were in the car on the way home. It was so perfect, so God.

Around the time that I had gotten my new bible something started to change in me when I realised that in God's eyes I was more than just a recovering heroin addict, I was a precious child of God; chosen for a purpose and a calling. I knew that I was never going to be the same, but I also knew that I needed to never forget where I had come from. I asked God to help me to remember in a way that my words would give hope to those who read them. With all the changes in my life I needed to remember exactly what God had saved me from. This was what followed:

When I first started out in my love affair with heroin not once did I think about the consequences of my actions, the effect they would have on me or anybody else – I was blissfully unaware. When I had my first taste of heroin I never believed that I would soon become an addict. I had seen what it had done to people that I cared about but I didn't think that it could or would happen to me. It was about two weeks after using everyday that I woke up sick – a painfully alien experience to me. But even then I didn't realise, I just had a taste and didn't feel sick any more – deceiving myself with every thought, every action. Waking up with aching bones, feeling as though my body and mind were crying tears of terror. Even that was not enough to make me realise that I was now very officially a junkie. It was a long, painful journey between that first shot and the realisation of the pathetic reality that I was living. Craving to fulfill a desire that was unfulfillable, that of feeling the way that I had that first time. Constantly searching for the unfulfillable taste – a game that I would continue to play with myself and others for almost six years. Knowing what I was doing but not comprehending that the rules to 'win' only led to complete destruction of the self; body, mind and soul. Putting everything that I could up my arm, never concerned for the worth or the ultimate cost – which could have been my life.

God was using where I had come from to help me to go to a new level. I had asked Him to remind me of all that I had been and all that He had saved me from. In doing so He had given me a vivid memory of what I had felt like when I was still using heroin. He was helping me to remember the suffering so that I could understand the joy; I knew that.

One of the other reasons that I had been asking God to help me remember what my life had been like as a heroin addict was because it felt so far away from where I was; but I knew that I needed those memories to be able to help others properly. The difference was that now they were Holy Spirit inspired memories. They weren't memories that I had drudged up to hold me back, and that was what I had always done in the past. That had been one of the reasons, or excuses, that I had given myself for going back to heroin in the past – my memories were too painful. It was so different this time. I knew that my memories were going to be a key to me helping other people; they were no longer there to make me feel ashamed, but to testify to all that the Lord had done in my life. It was then that I realised that my past and my mistakes were going to change people's lives; and that really excited me.

One of the first people that was going to be true for was Kylie. It was now the new year and I had seen her a couple of times. It was around this time that we started to get really serious about working through her deeper issues. One of the things that I felt led to encourage her to do was to write a couple of letters; one to her step-father and one to her mother. I guided her in suggesting that she work from an area of forgiveness. She needed to understand that she was forgiven in order to forgive others. They were such beautiful and encouraging letters. She had written to them years earlier and been full of anger and hatred, but now she wrote from a loving and forgiving heart. It was such a special time when she shared them with me because it helped me to understand that as long as I continued to seek God on her behalf, He would meet her where she was at; that was all that He required of me, and that was all that I was willing to do. It was a huge lesson for me, that I couldn't heal her wounds for her; but Jesus could, and would.

During one of our workshops Mr T explained to us a thing that he had first mentioned a couple of months after I had arrived at the house, it was called 'The Freedom Project'. He wanted us to take our stories and testimonies into schools to help the younger generation learn from our mistakes. He explained to us that he had a vision that he needed us to help him fulfill. We were all very excited about it, partly because we all felt as though now we had a focus. He gave us all separate jobs to do; mine was helping to write a booklet. One of the other things that I was asked to do was write out a short testimony that could be used for a pamphlet. I was happy to do it; all I wanted to do was help people. Jason was put in charge of organising the pamphlet and one of the things that he wanted to do was use two photos, an old one and a current one, to show the change in my life. The old photo that I had was one that Will had taken of me when I had left Spring Hill; it is the most hideous photo of myself that I have ever seen. In it I am really skinny, so skinny that my flesh almost looks like it is hanging off my face, with big black rings under my eyes. I am staring into the camera with a look of hatred and despise. It is a horrible image, one that I no longer recognise. I knew that it was being used for the shock value and I was just glad that I actually had it. I knew that if I could get people to see where I had come from, from the despair I had been in, that they might be more willing to listen to me. I knew, from experience, that when I had been at school and people had come in to talk to us that I hadn't really taken much notice because they didn't seem to have any real experience with what they were talking about. But the difference with 'The Freedom Project' was that we all did. The project excited us, and gave us something to do.

We all worked hard on our given tasks and it all came together really well. When the school year started again we went to Brisbane State High School to talk to a year 10 class. They were young and seemingly immature, probably like most of us had been at that age. We all had an opportunity to speak and when we each told our stories you could see the kids sit up and take notice. We knew that we were having an effect when they were given the chance to ask questions. They asked us some really deep questions about addiction and how drugs made us feel. Our aim had been not to glamourise drugs or make them appealing in any way and I think that it worked when one of them asked to see the scar on my arm where I had injected the drugs. My scar happens to be a big divot that looks like a valley in the ridge of my arm; a horrible reminder of where I have come from, but also what God has saved me from. They were all horrified at the intensity of it, considering that it hadn't been used for over six months. I am sure that it was enough to make some of them think twice before entering the seemingly glamorous world of drugs. We had achieved our mission, and we knew that God would use what we had done in the past to help those kids in the future.

I knew then that my testimony was going to be used to impact the life of anybody who was willing to hear it, and that God would give me the grace to share it in places where people would otherwise have no idea of just how awesome and amazing His love and mercy are. I felt so honoured by God and entered into a whole new understanding of just how great He had been to me. I knew that He was going to make a way where there seemed to be no way. After all that He had done for me all I wanted to do was share my testimony of His great and mighty ways; and I knew that He would make that come to pass, so long as I continued to lean only on Him. I received great comfort in His arms; there was no other place that I would rather have been.

Not long after we had done the school project one of the guys in the house decided to leave. None of us really wanted him to go, because he hadn't been clean long and we knew that in the house he had been really growing with God. His name was Jaiden and he was a young guy who needed love and direction, two things that he definitely wouldn't get if he went back out into the world. He had given his heart to Jesus and we had all watched as major changes had taken place in his life. But one day I went to the shops with him and he had stolen something while we had been there. He had done it with me before and I had told him that I wouldn't stand for it one more time, and I didn't. I spoke to Mr T about it and he decided to have a house meeting about Jaiden's future in the house. It was the first time that we had all sat down together to discuss someone's future, as Mr T wanted us to feel as though we were part of the decisions that were being made. We all had our say and then we voted. I am not sure now if that was the correct way to go about deciding someone's future in the house, but that was what we had been asked to do. We had all had our own share of trouble with Jaiden. He was young, temperamental and opinionated; but realistically, we all were. When he was doing well those were things that we loved about him, but at this point in time they had also been things that had annoyed us. The only person that had stood up and said that he should stay was Jason; he said that he needed to be nurtured and loved, not abandoned. It makes sense to me now but at the time I stood my ground, as did the others. Jaiden had been talking about leaving for a while, and now we had all made that decision for him. Time would tell if we had made the right one, or not.

It was at this time that I started to read the Scriptures for new revelation on how to treat people. I knew that I had been very 'fleshy' in my decision about Jaiden. He had started to annoy me and so I had agreed with the others that he should leave. I never once asked myself, "what would Jesus do?" God really dealt with me by showing me that I needed to treat others the same way that I would like to be treated – a basic bible principle, and I had totally missed it. One particular Scripture really spoke to me at this time, was 1 Peter 3:8,9(NIV), which says: Finally, all of you, live in harmony with one another; be sympathetic, love as brothers, be compassionate and humble. Do not repay evil with evil or insult with insult, but with blessing, because to this you were called so that you may inherit a blessing. I prayed then that God would help and guide me so that I was able to treat others with the love of Christ. I asked for the Holy Spirit to convict me when I was wrong in my dealings with other people. I also asked God to lead me to repentance whenever I strayed from His word, at any time. It was a whole new realm, with God, for me. I looked forward to being a more loving person. My deepest desire was to be more like Jesus; and still is to this day. I want to be like Jesus, I want people that meet me to see the Jesus in me and want them to know what it is that makes me different to the people of the world. That is my prayer.

The first issue in my life that the Lord dealt with, after my study on how to treat people in a godly way, was my relationship with Mark. Up until that point we had slept together a few times and even though I had known that it was wrong in God's eyes, I had done it anyway. At this point in time God convicted me in my spirit that I needed to stop it, that not only was it wrong by me, but it was wrong by Him as well. I had known that before and gone ahead with it anyway but from that point of conviction on, every time we were kissing and it would seem like we were going to go further, something would happen; someone would knock on the door or someone would need me. I knew that God was helping to make my prayer a reality. I wanted to be made whole, I wanted to be holy; but like all others, I needed God to help me do so. Mark and I would sometimes pray together for God to help us and to bless us but it was the prayer time on my own when I felt the breakthroughs come. I knew that God had given me the strength to fight the battle of the flesh but I also knew that I needed to lean on Him, and only Him, for all the love that I desired. God wanted me to give myself to Him, wholly, so that He could help me to be holy. That was such a big revelation for me; and one that I prayed would take place in my life every day. Time would be the only thing that would tell!

Pastor David called the house one day looking for Mr T and I knew there was something wrong as soon as I heard his voice. Mr T wasn't going to be back for quite some time and so I asked if I could take a message. David knew that I had Mr T's private mobile number and he asked me to please call him urgently. It was then that I asked David what was going on. The phone went very silent, and then he told me that Jaiden had died of a heroin overdose the night before. I couldn't believe it – he had seemed to be doing so well. I had spoken to him just a couple of days before that and we had cleared the air about the way that we both had felt about him leaving the house in the first place. He knew that I loved and cared for him, and he especially knew that I would continue to pray for him. I was in shock; I really couldn't believe it, even though I knew that it must be true. I did call Mr T and told him what I had been told. He asked me to tell the others one by one. I did that and they each had their own reaction. Some cried, some didn't believe me (even though they knew that I wouldn't have been joking), and some just needed a hug. One thing was for sure; Jaiden had come into our lives and affected us all in different ways. He had touched all of our lives in a very special way, and that was the Jaiden that we all chose to remember.

We were all asked to sing a couple of Jaiden's favourite praise and worship songs at the funeral service; which we were all honoured to do. Mr T had been asked to say a speech and in it he declared that Jesus had been Lord over Jaiden's life when he had died and that there was a comfort in knowing that he was in heaven. It was then that I realised that Jaiden had been the first person that I had known who had died a Christian. I knew that he was in heaven; and I found great comfort in that knowledge. I imagined him, in heaven, sharing his stories with the apostles – and loving it. It made his death seem bearable to me; just having that deep, inner knowing. It was also then that I decided that I had to share the gospel with all of my loved ones; I never again want to sit at a funeral and not have that peace inside of me, of the knowledge that the person that I care for is in heaven. I declared that to God that day, and I am sure that He smiled down on me.

Chapter 14
So Blessed

The next change that took place was us being told that we were leaving the house at Thelma Street, apparently for something bigger and better. Pastor David owned the house and had decided to sell it. So we all went about a major clean up of the house. So many different people had lived there so there was a huge mess to clean up. We knew that it was going to take a long time to do it properly and so we set up a roster and a structure to ensure that everything that needed to be done got done. We were all given set tasks – mine happened to be the person in charge of the house being cleaned, from top to bottom. We chipped away at it and slowly it got done. It was a strange sensation for me to be leaving that house. So much change had taken place in my life there; I almost felt uneasy about the move. But God showed me that as long as He was with me that I would be fine wherever I was. That was a great revelation for me to receive; and one that I pray will follow me through my entire life.

Towards the end of the clean up I started to kind of lose the plot. I felt as though I had contributed a lot and others not as much. I spoke to Mr T and told him that I needed to get away for a couple of days. I didn't know how he would react because there was still so much to do at the house, but he understood where I was coming from and agreed. He and Josie actually paid for me to stay in a hotel room just around the corner from the house. I had explained to them that I just needed some time to myself. I could have gone to my parents and I know that they would've loved to have had me there, but that wasn't the break that I needed. I needed an opportunity to recharge my batteries and to refresh my relationship with God.

I used the time to reflect on all that had happened in my life, in the eight and a half short months since my decision to go to rehab. My life had done more than a 360-degree spin. I was no longer the person that I used to be; I truly was a new creation. My old life seemed so long ago, but the memories of it seemed so close. I knew that I still had so much work to do on my issues, but I had a peace inside of me knowing that with God everything would be worked out according to His timing. I knew that He would leave no stone unturned and as it was He started to do just that during my two days in that hotel room. The only things that I knew that I would need for those days were my stereo and worship music, my bible and a notebook. My life changed in an incredible way in those two days. God had met me where I was at, again, and lavished His love and revelation knowledge over me in a new and fascinating way.

I had entered into my time with God in that hotel room with tears of absolute exhaustion. I had been through so much in the months before that time and hadn't really given myself the opportunity to stop and just take in what was going on in my life. At the time it all just seemed quite surreal. As it was, I hadn't been in a hotel room for years – since my days as a prostitute; and I knew that was weighing heavily on my emotions. God knew too. He used everything about the situation to draw me closer to Him. As I sat on the floor crying out to God, with worship music drifting into my ears, I felt the hand of God rest on my head. I experienced instant peace, and I knew that He had me exactly where I was for that precise encounter. I had allowed myself to get so tired and worn out that all I could do was cry out to God; and I did. And once again He met me where I was at.

That first night I had been so tired that all I wanted to do was rest, and hopefully sleep; but God had other ideas. I had been asleep for a couple of hours when I felt as though I had been awoken by the Holy Spirit. It was a gentle nudge. Suprisingly, for how tired I had been, I felt as though I had been asleep for hours. I was led to the Scripture of Matthew 11:28-30, which says: *"Come to me, all you who labor and are heavy laden, and I will give you rest. Take my yoke upon you and learn from Me, for I am gentle and lowly in heart, and you will find rest for your souls. For My yoke is easy and My burden is light."* I knew immediately that God didn't mean rest, as in sleep, but internal rest. I knew that it meant that He would give me a rest that was beyond any sleep I would ever physically have. He knew that I had been attempting to do His work, and now He just wanted me to understand that I couldn't do it without Him.

That night I spent most of my time just reading through the bible, and at times just resting with the music. After that first revelation I had felt as though I had achieved all that I had set out to do but, once again, the Lord had different plans for me. I had my notebook out and was waiting for the right words to come to me. Then I looked down and I had already written in it. I wasn't sure when, it must've been when I was tired, but when I re-read what was on the page I knew that it was Holy Spirit inspired writing. Three short lines that would change my life forever stared back at me. They were: the grace that God has shown me – a mighty and powerful anointing to heal the hurting souls of the world. I knew that God had, then and there, revealed my calling to me. I started crying real tears of joy. I don't know how much time passed me by when I felt a sudden urge to read some bible passages. The first one that I was led to was 1 Corinthians 15:10: *But by the grace of God I am what I am, and His grace toward me was not in vain; but I labored more abundantly than they all, yet not I, but the grace of God which was with me.* God also used my current situation to reveal that Scripture to me on an even deeper level. He showed me that just as I had been the hardest worker and the strongest house member, so would my life be like that; but I would only achieve great things for God's kingdom if I leaned only on Him, and the grace that he had poured out into my life. He revealed to me that I would have to walk hand in hand with Jesus daily, in all things that I would do; I needed to be Spirit-led, not led by my flesh.

It was then that I turned to my next bible passage, which was 2 Corinthians 12:9,10 which says: *And He said to me, "My grace is sufficient for you, for My strength is made perfect in weakness." Therefore most gladly I will rather boast in my infirmities, that the power of Christ may rest upon me. Therefore I take pleasure in infirmities, in reproaches, in needs, in persecutions, in distresses, for Christ's sake. For when I am weak, then am I strong.* Once again God showed me that the situation that I had placed myself in was a perfect illustration. I needed to be glad for the pressure that I felt, for the pain that I was experiencing; because it was those things that would show the world that it was only by God's grace and strength that I could survive. In the natural I felt so weak and pitiful, but God would use that to supernaturally reveal Himself to those around me; and to those of you reading this right now. The most powerful thing about His grace occurred to me at that very moment. No matter how weak and hopeless I had been feeling, not once had I thought about using drugs. Instead I had turned to God to fill the void in my life and that was the biggest revelation that I had received up to that point in time. I knew when I realised that, that God was crying tears of joy for me. I was His child and so long as I turned to Him, He would never let me go.

At that point of the night, or early morning, I had some more sleep, and once again, I was woken to spend time in the Word of God. I had a real sense of forgiveness in my heart and in my soul. I wrote three words in my notebook; they were – forgiven, cleansed and HOLY. I knew that was what God needed me to receive in my spirit. The first Scripture that I turned to was in the Old Testament, Jeremiah 33:8(NKJV). Which says: *'I will cleanse them from all their iniquity by which they have sinned against Me, and I will pardon all their iniquities by which they have sinned and by which they have transgressed against Me.'* It was at that very moment that I felt as though God was in the room holding me close to Him, loving me and changing me. I opened my eyes, some time later, and I felt so clean. I had known that God had forgiven me and that He loved me; but that day that understanding became a part of me. I felt as though it had been etched in to my soul. God had cleansed me and He had pardoned me. He had wiped my slate clean, and I knew then that whenever He looked upon me all He saw was the blood of Jesus, a pure clean vessel. That moment will never depart from me. That deep, inner knowing, in my spirit, that He loved me so much that He could do those things for me. How could I not offer myself up to Him as a living sacrifice? I longed to live to do His will, and I declared just that to the heavens that day.

It was then that I felt led to my next passage of Scripture, which was also from the Old Testament. It was Isaiah 61:1-3, which says: *"The Spirit of the Lord God is upon me, Because the Lord had anointed Me to preach good tidings to the poor; He has sent Me to heal the brokenhearted, To proclaim liberty to the captives, And the opening of the prison to those who are bound; To proclaim the acceptable year of the Lord, And the day of vengeance of our God; To comfort all who mourn,*

To console those who mourn in Zion, To give them beauty for ashes, The oil of joy for mourning, The garment of praise for the spirit of heaviness; That they may be called trees of righteousness, The planting of the Lord, that He may be glorified." I had read that passage so many times before, but never in the way that I was reading it then. I knew then that I had been led to that Scripture because that was what I had been called to do. Those words described the path that God had laid down before me; and I wept. I felt so amazingly blessed. To be hand chosen by God to do such incredible work for Him and His kingdom was such an honour. I knew that He had saved me from myself for such a time as this. I had a deep knowing in my spirit that He needed me to prepare myself, in Him, to be ready when He called me forward. And that was exactly what I was prepared to do.

Having had that phenomenal revelation I sat on the bed and realised that I was sharing with God in the way that He had always desired me to and still desires me to; wholly and completely. I knew that I was having an appointment with God and, once again, I had a sensation of His arms wrapped around me, holding me close to Him as I drew near to Him. I knew then it was God's unconditional love.

The Scripture from Isaiah had reminded me of something that my mum had always said to me when I was growing up. A wise lady had said to her very early during her time at Al-Anon, *"Many are called, but few are chosen"*. That was true of my mum, she had been gifted to go the extra mile with people, to go beyond the call of duty; and now I knew I had been too. I was so excited. I knew that when she had said it to me it had been true of my life; but now I had a full and deep understanding of just how real it was.

That day passed me by so quickly. Mark had dropped in to share some lunch with me and I hadn't even realised that I was hungry. I had been feeding on the Word and my natural hunger had been non-existent. I then understood what the bible meant when it said that man did not live on bread alone, but by every word that proceeded from the mouth of God. When we had been having lunch all I kept doing was talking about the amazing time that I had been having with God. I know that Mark was happy for me and he encouraged me to keep pressing into Him, but I also felt that he knew the closer that I got to the Lord the further away I would get from him. Only time would tell if that were true or not. All I knew was that during that lunch all I could think about was him leaving and me getting

* *JUST LET ME SAY Words & music Geoff Bullock. (c) 1994*
   Word Music/ Maranatha! Praise. Licensed courtesy of CopyCare Pacific Pty Ltd.

back to God; I knew then who my One True Love was, and that was Jesus.

I continued on for the rest of the day just reading the bible and listening to worship music. I had pressed repeat on the stereo and it had been playing since the moment that I had stepped into the hotel room. I sung along and felt the presence of God come upon the room in a mighty way. It was at that moment that God showed me the true power of praise. As the music was playing and as I was singing along I felt a shift in my spirit. I knew that God was using that time of worship to do a work in me; and I was excited. The song that was playing at the particular time that I felt as though a breakthrough had been achieved, was called 'Just let me say' by Geoff Bullock. The lyrics were speaking out all that I was feeling, and I feel led to share them now.

Just let me say how much I love You
Let me speak of Your mercy and grace
Just let me live in the shadow of Your beauty
Let me see You face to face
And the earth will shake as Your word goes forth
And the heavens will tremble and fall
But let me say how much I love you
O my saviour, my Lord and friend

Just let me hear Your finest whispers
As You gently call my name
And let me see Your power and Your glory
Let me feel Your spirit's flame
Let me find You in the desert
'Til this sand is holy ground
And I am found completely surrendered
To You, my Lord and friend

So let me say how much I love You
With all my heart I long for You
For I am caught in this passion of knowing
This endless love I've found in You
And the depth of grace, the forgiveness found
To be called a child of God

Just makes me say how much I love You
O my saviour, my Lord and friend
Just makes me say how much I love You
O my saviour, my Lord and friend*

That was exactly where I was at with God at the time, and the music had brought about a new level of freedom for me, and a new level in my love for God. That song helped to change my perspective, then and for always.

During the night I was again woken up by the Spirit of God; He hadn't finished the work that He wanted to do in me, and He knew, as did I, that I was leaving first thing the following morning. I woke up and started praying and felt that God was trying to show me something, but I wasn't quite sure what it was. So I did what I often did at that time and got out my notebook and a pen and I waited for the words to come to me. As I waited I prayed that God would reveal to me all that He needed for me to grasp a hold of; and He did. It was then that I wrote three short lines in my book; they were: Jesus is God's righteousness revealed and His righteousness is revealed in us, through the power of the Holy Spirit. I knew that He was trying to show me that I needed to be a light to the world; I needed to lean on Him to be all that He called me to be. It was right then that I recalled something else that my mum had said to me since I had become a Christian. She had said that I was probably the only bible that she, and others, would ever read. That was what God was trying to imprint on my spirit and it had taken those words from my mum for it to sink in for me. I spent that time in prayer, thanking Him for the revelation and thanking Him for the words from my mum. I knew that He had answered my prayer; He was going to use me as His vessel. When I had first read that I needed to offer myself to Him as a living sacrifice (Romans 12:2), I had done it in faith; and He had heeded my prayer.

I had fallen asleep praying, as I often did, and had woken up very early the next morning; God obviously hadn't finished with me yet! I started to pray and read the bible. I was drawn to the book of 1 Peter. I read it in its entirety and it was at the end of it that the revelation came. The passage was 1 Peter 5:6-11(NKJV) which says: *Therefore humble yourselves under the mighty hand of God, that He may exalt you in due time, casting all your care upon Him, for He cares for you. Be sober, be vigilant; because your adversary the devil walks about like a roaring lion, seeking whom he may devour. Resist him, steadfast in the faith, knowing that the same sufferings are experienced by your brotherhood in the world. But may the God of all grace, who called us to His eternal glory by Christ Jesus, after you have suffered a while, perfect, establish, strengthen, and settle you. To Him be the glory and the dominion forever and ever. Amen.* With those words God was revealing to me the key to all that He had been showing me with the previous revelations. That was the ultimate key to surviving the call on my life. He had shown me, now I just needed to put it into practise.

It was such an amazing time that I shared with the Lord in that hotel room; all because I had been too exhausted to carry on. He had known that and used it to capture my heart and soul in the most special way. I will never forget those two days of my life; they have forever altered my destiny, and hopefully the souls of many others. I will always seek to know Him as intimately, and more so as my time with Him grows.

When I went back to the house nobody, except Mark and Mr T, had known where I had been. But they all commented that I seemed different. I was different, I felt changed. We all continued on with our projects to get the house, and the people in it, ready for our next move. It had been decided that instead of moving straight into another house that we would go out to a property at Dayboro for a camp. The property was owned by one of the lady's that did reception work at Dr Reece's surgery and she had offered Mr T the use of the property to give us all an opportunity that living in the city didn't give us. In return we would work on their land. We were all looking forward to it; it seemed like such a big adventure. Jason was the person in charge of organising it all and he was to be the team leader while we were out there. It all seemed very exciting.

The week before we were due to go out there Beth came back to the house for help. She promised me that she was serious this time and I told her that I had said exactly that to my parents many times before I truly believed it myself; but I was willing to help her nonetheless. Within a couple of days she was clearly detoxing, and because she was so raw, emotionally, she was able, and willing, to open up to me again. We talked about everything possible; from prostitution to Jesus. She told me that the changes that she had seen in me were amazing and that she knew that there had to be something in the 'whole Jesus thing'; but she just wasn't ready. As it turned out, two days later, after a lot of hard work on both of our parts, she left again. I slept for a couple of hours early in the morning, as I had been awake either cleaning or looking after Beth for almost three days, and while I was asleep she left. I was upset and angry when I discovered that she was gone, but I knew that there was nothing that I could've done differently. Short of locking her up and forcing her to stay, she had a mind and will of her own and she was going to make her own decisions, whether I liked them or not. The more I thought about it after she had gone, the more I realised that she reminded me of myself when I had been in the midst of my addiction. I knew that all I could do was continue to pray for her. She was being watched over by her heavenly Father and there was no more that I could do for her; for the time being anyhow.

Helping Beth was one of the last memories that I will ever have of the house at Thelma Street. That house had been my home for almost 9 months, about as long as it takes to grow a baby in the womb, and that was basically what had happened to me while I had been there. I had gone there a drug addicted, hopeless case and I was leaving there a Spirit-filled Christian who was growing in the love of Christ every day. My life had taken some really dramatic turns in that time, and for a change they were all for the better. I was a new creation, a new person, a new woman; and I was ready to share my testimony with anybody that would listen. I will always remember my home in Thelma Street with very fond memories. I made friends there that I will surely know for all the days of my life. It had been such a God-appointed placing; and when I had been ready to meet Him, He was right there waiting for me.

Chapter 15

Stepping Out

My next big adventure was the camp at Dayboro. The site that we were camping on was at the bottom of the property and it could only be reached by 4-wheel-drive or on foot. The first time I went down there it was nearly dark but I still wanted to walk it. When I got there it was all set up; it looked just like a tent village. Michael and Jason had set it up so that all of the leaders (me included) had their own tents. That was so essential because when you are giving out to other people all day you need a place to wind down. I had discovered that from having my own room at the house. The tent that I had been given was on the girls' side of the property, obviously, and was the furthest away from the main campsite. I had grown to really love everyone that was going to be there; but I loved my quiet time with God even more. The first night there was only a handful of us there. It was one of the most incredible experiences for me; I hadn't been camping for years and I was really looking forward to it. I felt as though I was getting back to nature and I actually felt closer to God; it just felt so right for me to be there at that point in time.

As we started to get comfortable camping on the property I decided to ask Mr T how long we were going to be out there. He told me, honestly, that he wasn't sure and to just enjoy the time that I had. That worried me a little bit, because as far as I knew we didn't actually have a house to move back into when we returned to Brisbane, which Mr T confirmed. So I decided that instead of worrying about it, I was just going to make the most of all that was on offer to us out there. Jason had decided that we would have a prayer time and a reading from a Christian book every night; and at any other time that anyone felt led to pray, they were welcome to. It was like an opportunity for people to step out in their spiritual giftings; an opportunity that they may not have received had we not been away from the hustle and bustle of our normal lives.

I loved it at camp and sometimes dreaded the thought of having to go back to the city for counselling appointments every Tuesday and Thursday. But I knew that I had made a commitment to those people and that God would honour me for keeping my word.

Every day we all had different jobs to do and we were put into small groups to get them achieved. The group that I was placed in had to clear a pathway from the campsite to the house which was covered with lantana. So every morning we would all gather together and pick up our instruments of warfare and off we would go. Within the first few days we all realised that what we were doing was actually hard work and that we could either complain about it, or sing. The other girl in my group, Jackie, and I would start singing songs about Jesus when we started work and at any time during the day that we felt as though we needed some extra strength. In between singing and working we would also pray. We would pray for strength to complete our tasks and for all of the others to complete theirs and we would pray for God to bless the owners and their family for the blessing that they were to us. It made the days go much quicker and we soon discovered that we were actually enjoying the labour work and the sense of accomplishment that we had at the end of each day. It was only one of the character building exercises that I went through during my time at Dayboro.

I also started disciplining myself to spend an amount of quality time with the Lord every day that I was there. My quiet time with God was the most important thing to me at the time; as I knew that He was helping to strengthen me for the days ahead, and for the calling that He had on my life. Sometimes I would wake up really early, before anyone else, and just sit and watch the sun come up; and while I was doing that I would start to pray. Some of the most incredible prayer times that I have ever encountered occurred during that time. I would experience a real connection with God and a real peace about where I was at and what I was doing. I had a 'knowing' in my spirit that God was walking before me as I was laying down all of my thoughts, my dreams and my plans; it was really beautiful. If I wasn't able to spend my time with God in the morning I would always take the first opportunity that I could to go for a walk and find a quiet place so that I could be alone with Him. I read a lot of the bible that I had never read before and received so many revelations from God about who He was and all that He had promised me in His word.

One of the major revelations that I received, and felt led to write down, was this: *We have all been forgiven but above that we have been cleansed of our sins. We have been made new. Our slates have been wiped clean – but we must continually go to God with our challenges and hand them over to Him. When we give it over to God we must believe, by faith, that He has taken care of it and we must let it go. No matter how big or small we believe our challenge to be – we must feel no shame in taking it to God; He knows it anyway. But once we admit it to Him, He will work on it, no matter how uncomfortable it makes us feel. We must continually fellowship with the Father – ask Him to show us our problems and He will. He wants us to be FREE. He wants to make us WHOLE. We need to be God-inside minded. The person that we are in our hearts comes through our mouths – so we must cleanse our hearts.*

The day that I wrote that I knew that it was not just for me, but it was for me to share with others. So I asked Jason if he minded if I read it out that night. He encouraged me to go for it. After I had read it out almost everybody was silent, and then we had one of the greatest prayer meetings that we had ever had. The flow of God out there was awesome. We were all praying out loud and then laying hands on and praying for one another. Afterwards, one of the girls came up to me and just said thank you and then started to cry. After I had comforted her for a while she told me that what I had said had been exactly what she needed to hear. It was then that I realised for the first time that the revelations that the Lord had given to me were not always just for me to write down or to hold on to; but they were for me to share and to give away as freely as they had been given to me. A new sense of freedom came over me as I realised that I was stepping out and God was leading the way.

I also did a lot of reading at Dayboro. Before we had gone out to Dayboro Mark had taken me to Koorong to buy some new books. I had prayed for the Holy Spirit to guide me in my choices and I came away with some amazing books. My Christian book collection was starting to grow rapidly, as I was always spending any spare money that I had on them. I loved the thought of the books being great resources for me, and for anybody else that read them. I always saw the money that I spent on them as an investment not a cost. I figured that anything that was feeding my spirit and my soul was very good for me; and whomever I would come into contact with. One of the books that I had taken out there with me was called 'Becoming a Prayer Warrior' by a woman named Elizabeth Alves. It was an awesome book that encouraged me to step out more in my prayer time and to reach toward the promise that I had received from the Lord that my prayers were going to help people reach new freedom and new levels in Christ. It was so incredible for me to be reading that particular book while I was out at Dayboro; perhaps because I felt as though being in the open space I was much more able to experiment with my prayer time. I loved being outdoors and crying out to God; it felt so natural to me. I actually felt as though I was in His backyard while I was out there; that was how amazing my experience was. I will never forget it and I would never change any of it.

While all of this amazing stuff was taking place in my life in the country the city was, somehow, totally different. Not bad, just different. I felt strange every time I came back to Brisbane; almost as though that wasn't where I was supposed to be at the time, but God knew that I was there to keep my word. Mark was not spending much time at Dayboro at all as he was supposedly helping Mr T look for a new place for us all to live. But every time that I asked him about it he said that they hadn't found anywhere yet. Personally, I didn't think that they were looking very hard, but I was happy to be spending my time at Dayboro; even though the days were turning into weeks out there. Anyhow, Mark and I just seemed to be on two very different levels, and I almost felt uncomfortable when I did see him. I didn't know why or what it was that had changed, but something had and I needed to work out exactly what it was. The time at Dayboro had helped me to grow and to realise that it was God, not Mark, who had been my comfort and my shelter the entire time. I was glad for all that had been revealed to me through that time apart. Whenever we did see each other it was different and I knew that he felt it too. I had been shown by God just how different Mark and I really were. I now understood just how little we did have in common; except for the initial physical attraction there was very little to our relationship. I still loved talking to him; he was always so willing to hear me out and to discuss my ideas. That was something that definitely had not changed, and I was glad for that.

During one of my city visits I had a counselling appointment with Kylie. As it was, she and Michael had broken up and he had decided to come out to Dayboro with us all; using the opportunity to find out who he really was, and to spend some time with some solid Christians. He was growing, spiritually, while he was out in the country, and Kylie had been doing much the same thing in the city. She had been really growing from session to session and I was always encouraged by the positive changes whenever I saw her. During one of our counselling sessions she mentioned that she had some news for me. She told me that she was pregnant and that Michael was the baby's father. I was happy and shocked at the same time. I told her that I would pray for the baby and for her. After she had left and I had the time to think about it a bit more I realised how deeply excited I really was; for Kylie, and for Michael and, of course, for the baby. I immediately started to pray for the life of the baby, and I knew that the baby was going to hold a very special place in my heart.

Back out at Dayboro everything felt so right to me. I felt so much peace and comfort, which was strange considering that I had been sleeping on a 2-centimetre piece of foam for over a month. I knew then that the comfort wasn't physical, but spiritual. I was learning a lot about myself and about the other people that were out there, and I was loving it. I had learned that Jason was a natural leader; he had the patience and the knowledge to encourage the entire team to achieve their goals. He helped us to set achievable goals so as to help us with our sense of accomplishment and growth. And he helped me to understand that I was able to take instruction from a male and respect them for their leadership. I had not been able to do that for years, but with him I felt able to. I will always be grateful for learning this lesson as it changed my life forever; I just had no idea how much at that point in time. God knew, however, and it was only a matter of time before He let me in on it.

One of the most incredible experiences of my entire time out at Dayboro was that of Easter. Just as I had my first Christmas as a Christian, this was to be my first Easter. I now had a deeper understanding of its significance, and I had so much to be grateful for. I spent the week leading up to Easter praying for greater revelation about Jesus and about the work on the cross. I wanted to know more about all that

He had done for us. As always, God answered me with words. I wrote them in my notebook and this is what they were:

> *We all need to think about the reality of the cross. When Jesus went to the cross He died bearing the sins of the world – past, present and future. So therefore if He died for sins then He died for sinners. So He died for the so-called 'bad' people, that they could be made new. New creations in Christ. So just as Jesus died for us so we must die to ourselves – be made new. We must hand our wills over and truly pray for God's will to be done in our lives. We must hand ourselves over to Him daily. We have been forgiven, released, cleansed by the precious blood of our Lord Jesus Christ. As forgiven as we are is as thankful as we should be. As much as we are given so we are required to give.*

Those words spoke volumes to me, and also to those that I shared them with. It helped me to understand why Easter and the work of the cross were so important to me as a Christian. God had revealed Himself to me with those words, and I had revealed Him to others with those same words. I loved that God was using words to speak to me and I knew that He would use words to speak through me to others; just as in this book.

The next day Mr T informed me that I was required to go back to the city to help a woman detox. He told me that she was coming up from Sydney and was willing to go through the program but only if she had a female to help her through the rough first few days. I agreed to help her out, even though at the time I didn't know how long it was going to be for. Mr T was using Mark's flat for the time being, so that was where I was to be set up. The woman who I was to be helping was named Mary. She was a bit older than I was but we were actually quite similar. We didn't hit it off straight away, due to the fact that we were both very strong-willed. She wanted to do things her way and I wanted to do them the right way. Within the first few days she seemed to be getting better, and stronger. We had a few hard times, with her wanting to leave and give it all in, but I was able to talk her through each time, thankfully. On her fifth day, the day before she was due for her rapid detox, Mr T invited

Beth to come and stay with us at the flat as well. She apparently had asked for help to detox. I explained to Mr T that I was willing to help her but that it was going to be next to impossible for me to keep a watch on both of them at the same time. After all, neither of them were easy cases; probably much like me when I had first arrived. Mr T offered for me to have two helpers, Mark and Michael. I wasn't very keen on the idea, mainly because I knew that Beth knew how to play the male species; but Mr T bought her in anyway.

I had not been able to have much sleep for almost a week, due to helping Mary, and so the first night that Beth was there I told Mark and Michael that I was going for a quick sleep. It was 4a.m. and I was totally exhausted. They were awake playing a computer game and so they were happy for me to have some rest. I woke up almost two hours later and when I walked into the lounge room all I saw was the two guys still playing computer games. When I asked them where the girls were they told me that they had gone to the shops; which really was a big no-no during the detox period. They were not supposed to go anywhere by themselves. I had a feeling that when they got back, whenever that would be, that they would have used heroin and we were going to have to start all over again. That was exactly the case. It was then that I thought, for the first time in a long time, that I couldn't do that sort of work any more. It wasn't the actual detox work that I couldn't do – I loved helping people and I knew that there would always be some hard times, but I had foreseen what was going to happen if those two girls were to be bought together. As far as I was concerned these events didn't have to happen, some changes needed to take place if I was to stay working with Mr T. I felt a movement in my spirit; I knew that I was on the verge of something big with God. I just had no idea how big it was going to be.

That day I explained to Mr T what had happened and that I wasn't happy with the way things had unfolded. He told me that I just needed to get some more rest and he admitted that it wasn't fair for him to expect me to do all the hard work myself. I told him that I wasn't comfortable with a guy helping a girl detox; that I thought that there was too much sexual frustration at that time of the process. He agreed, but then told me that there weren't enough spiritually strong females and that the guys would still have to help me out. I wasn't happy with the way things were turning out, and after all of my time in the bush I think that I was finding it difficult to adjust to city life. I missed my special, quiet time with God, as that just didn't seem possible at the flat. Mr T made the guys agree to give me a break every few hours so that I had the opportunity to rest and recharge my batteries. But there was still something inside of me that wasn't happy with the situation as it was. I decided that the best thing to do was to pray about it, and then to just wait on God for the right move to make.

When I woke up from my rest that afternoon the guys told me that Beth had left, but that Mary was still there with us. I was glad – I could see so much potential in Mary, but only if she would give herself the opportunity to get clean and stay clean for a period of time. I prayed for Beth and asked the Lord to keep her safe wherever she was and whatever she was doing. About an hour later I received a phone call from one of the local hospitals; Beth had overdosed on heroin and when she had been bought back she had asked for me and for me only. I knew then that God had been right there with her the whole time and that while I had been praying He had intervened for her; I think that she knew it too. That had been one of my real experiences with the power of prayer and heeding to God's call on my life. I praised Him all the way to the hospital, thanking Him for saving her. I knew that He loved her and that He wanted me to keep her close to my heart and in my prayers. When I saw her I told her that I was willing to take her back to the flat but that she had to leave once she had found another place to stay, this time so had gone too far. Mr T had agreed that, this time around, she wasn't interested in actually getting clean; rather, she had just needed a safe haven, and that was all that we were to her at that point in her life. She was frustrated with me, but agreed. Every time that she walked out the door my heart would sink and I knew that all that I could do for her was to pray. She knew that was what I would do and she did actually appreciate that about me. That was one thing about Beth, she knew that I loved and cared for her and she understood about my love for Jesus; but she was not yet ready to accept Him into her life. I cried out to God on her behalf then; and I cry out for her now.

That night I was sitting at the table with Mark and Michael while Mary was sleeping and God showed me a vision of what He wanted me to do. As I was, and still am, a young Christian I didn't have a full grasp of God's timing and so I thought that He meant right then.

I decided to do what I always did at such a time; I wrote it down. It was about setting up separate houses, one for guys and one for girls; to enable proper detoxification to take place. I had been asking God for some time before that to reveal to me what His will for my life was; what He desired me to do. I knew that was it. It had always been a desire of mine to help people and now with God on my side I knew that not only could I help them, but I could also make a difference in their lives.

This was what He showed me:

"HOUSE OF ESTHER" – *Women's House*
Esther – rising to meet your destiny
* *trust in God*
* *willingness to lay down life for others*
* *based on keeping wisdom and patience when the pressure was on*

AIM:
A Spirit-filled household set up for women with the aim to strengthen them, get them closer to God and find confidence in Christ. Focused on Mr T's guidelines for growth.

1. Accountabilty for actions
2. Responsibilty for decisions
3. Consistency with targets

A place of warmth, love and compassion; strengthened by women living in the Word.

A safe house where women can gain a strength in themselves through God's strength. A place where they can be trained/coached to become the person that God planned for them to be – strong powerful women of destiny.

A place where these people can work quite intensively on changing their past mentalities and habits.

Allowing those that are coming in to know that we are working on a life based on sanctification.

WEEKLY STRUCTURE:
* *prayer sessions*
* *bible readings and devotions*

- *workshops – biblical/life skills*
- *daily group/house meetings*
- *fitness regime /health talks*
- *group excursions/ activities*
- *relaxation time*

The Scriptural foundation of Galatians 5:22-25:
But the fruit of the Spirit is love, joy, peace, longsuffering, kindness, goodness, faithfulness, gentleness, self-control. Against such there is no law. And those who are Christ's have crucified the flesh with its passions and desires. If we live in the Spirit, let us also walk in the Spirit.

After I had written it down, without discussion with the boys, Mark looked at me and asked me when I was going to open up my women's house. Now, there had been no way for either of them to know what I had been writing down because they were sitting at the other end of the table reading to themselves, and not once had either of them looked at what I was doing. I just stared at him; I couldn't believe what he had just said. Then he went on to tell me that God had told him, months earlier, that had been His vision for me. I laughed and thought that he was joking, but he wasn't. I was stunned. I then went on to explain to both of them the vision that God had just shared with me. They both told me that they thought I should approach Mr T with the idea; they thought that it sounded awesome. I agreed with them and proceeded to write it out for him. I decided that I would give it to him the following day when he came over. I knew that what I had just done was going to be life-changing; not only for me but for whoever entered the house, once it was set up. I felt a real sense of urgency about the whole thing, but I didn't know if it was just my flesh or the Spirit of God. I went with it anyway.

The following day when I saw Mr T I told him that I had something major that I needed to talk to him about, and so he took me for a drive. There was nowhere in the flat that was private enough to discuss all that I needed to share with him. In the car I told him about what God had shown me and just how awesome I thought that it would be. I explained to him that I had written everything out for him and he agreed to look at it, but also told me not to get my hopes up. It was then that I first felt as though my future was no longer working beside Mr T. I wasn't sure why I felt that way; I knew that it wasn't just because he hadn't jumped at my idea. I did feel as though he had shown disrespect towards me by not even looking at the proposal. I decided the best thing to do was to pray about it, to ask the Lord to reveal to me why He had shown me the vision and what He needed me to do with it. I did that; and waited.

A couple of days later, when Mr T still hadn't spoken to me about all that I had shared with him, I prayed that God would show me my options at that point in time. I knew, in my spirit, that I couldn't stay still any longer; I felt as though it was time for me to move on. The options that I wrote down were:

1. *Assist Mr T with growth – female house*

2. *Move out by myself and focus on – counselling clients/ministry aimed at women*

3. *Travel/mission ministry – Hong Kong/Thailand, and beyond*

4. *Help team in Western Australia with rehabilitation work*

I felt a peace inside of me when I looked at the list. I knew that the Lord would direct me in the right way to go and the correct way to go about it. So again I prayed and I waited.

Chapter 16

Trusting God

A couple of days later I still hadn't heard from Mr T about his thoughts on my idea, so I decided to talk to Pastor David about it. He had called me a couple of days before that to see how I was going and I had explained to him that I wasn't very happy with the way that things were turning out. I thought that the whole flat/detox issue was ridiculous and that the camp situation was getting out of control. As it was I had personally been out at Dayboro for six weeks, and the only reason that I had come back was to help people detox, otherwise I would have still been out there. He agreed to meet with me the following day to discuss where I was at and how I was feeling about everything. I looked forward to discussing everything that I was feeling, and I trusted him to be honest with me.

The following day I met with Pastor David and before anything else I explained to him that I wasn't happy about the situation at the flat. It was a small two bedroom place and, currently, five "helpers" and one person detoxing were living there. I didn't think that it was fair or an ideal situation for any of us to be in. On the other hand, I wasn't willing to go back out to Dayboro for an unknown amount of time. It was now the end of April and starting to get cooler at nighttime. Either way, he understood that I wasn't happy with things as they were. He then asked me what I thought my options were and I showed him my list of them. When he asked me what the women's house was about I decided that it was the right time to show him what I had received and written out. He read it straight away and said that he thought that it sounded like a great idea but that I would have to go to Mr T with it first. I then explained that I had done that and that he had chosen not to read it, and had actually seemed totally disinterested. I asked Dave what he thought I should do, as my pastor and someone that I trusted. He asked me to leave it with him so that he had an opportunity to pray about it, and that he would get back to me. So again, I waited.

A couple of days later Dave called me and asked to meet with me again. He told me that he had been thinking about everything that I had said to him and that he thought the best thing for me to do, for the time being, was tell Mr T everything that I had told him and explain to him that Pastor Dave and Frances had offered for me to go and stay in a spare room at their place while everything got sorted out. I agreed to do that, even though I knew immediately that Mr T would not like what I had to say.

I met with Mr T and, just as I had thought, he didn't like what I had to say and didn't agree with me going to stay at Dave's place. He explained to me that they were on the verge of signing a contract on a new house and that it wouldn't be long before we were in and everything would be back on track. I honestly wasn't willing to spend any more time either in the flat or at Dayboro, and so I told him that I was going to take Dave up on his offer. Mr T wasn't at all happy and even told me that he thought that I was letting the team down. The entire time that he was talking to me I had a real peace on the inside; I knew that I was making the right decision. I had spent years living in situations that I didn't really want to be in; I wasn't about to continue doing so. So that afternoon I went back to the flat and packed up my things, and I left. I explained to the people that were there what I was doing and I told them that I wasn't leaving the program – just changing houses. I knew, in my heart, the moment that I left the flat I would never return in the same capacity in which I had lived there. My life was about to take another major step; and all that I could do was trust God that He was walking before me and beside me.

While I was staying at Dave's place I had the freedom to spend as much time with God as I wanted to. I would wake up and pray and then do what needed to be done that day and then pray again. I spent a lot of time reading the Word of God just looking for more and more of Jesus. I needed confirmation that what I was doing was right, and so I read through the Scriptures searching for answers. I don't think that I necessarily found explicit answers, but I certainly did find guidance. The primary Scripture that I was led to was one that I had never read before nor had I heard any teachings on it. It was Deuteronomy 28:1,2(NKJV) which says: "Now it shall come to pass, if you diligently obey the voice of the Lord your God, to observe carefully all of His commandments which I command you today, that the Lord your God will set you high above all the nations of the earth. And all of these blessings shall come upon you and overtake you, because you obey the voice of the Lord your God." From this Scripture I felt a real sense of security. Now I understood that what I had received had definitely been from God, but I also knew that He knew the desires of my heart; and that had been the exact vision that I had received.

So I knew that it was all from God and I knew that if I stepped out in faith that He would bless me; but I also wanted to do the right thing by Mr T. After all that he had done for me that was the least that I could do. So I made attempts to contact him, but someone else always answered the phone and told me that he wasn't available. I then decided to let Dave know that I had felt a confirmation in my spirit to step out and expect the Lord to bless me. I told him that I had been making strong attempts to contact Mr T but that I felt as though he was making himself unavailable to me. I explained that even though I wanted to do the right thing by Mr T, as long as I was sitting around not making any progress I felt as though I would stagnate. It was a part of my character build-up to need growth and change; that had been my main reason for leaving the flat in the first place. Now as far as I was concerned, I was still a part of the program but every time I would try and make myself involved I was stopped. It was then that God showed me that I was now a separate entity; that I was no longer dependant on Mr T or anybody else there. I saw a vision of a garden with two trees in it and one was blooming and growing and the other one was stagnant and I knew it that was a view of where I was at, both naturally and spiritually. I also knew that it was time for me to decide to make a change; and I believed that God would be with me every step of the way.

Every night I would spend time in my room simply enjoying the presence of God and almost always I felt led to read certain scriptures. At the point in my life that I needed a lot of guidance and heavenly support I always got it. At the time God was revealing Himself to me in a new way. He was showing me the part of Himself that would be there for me always and that would never let me down. That loving, guiding and understanding Father's love. I am sure that that was happening with Him because in the natural realm I felt really let down by the way that I believed Mr T was treating me. God was showing me that I needed to depend only on Him, not man, for my growth; and I was.

It was then that I started to read parts of Proverbs. Proverbs is known as the book of wisdom and knowledge, and that was exactly what I needed. As I started to read through it, it was almost as though the Lord was illuminating certain parts to me; passages that were of particular significance to me at the time were:

Proverbs 14:1 – The wise woman builds her house, But the foolish pulls it down with her own hands. At the time I felt as though God was showing me that I needed to at least build the house, and that it would be foolish for me to not even try.

Proverbs 16:3,9 – Commit your works to the Lord, And your thoughts will be established. A man's heart plans his way, But the Lord directs his steps. I had a really deep knowing that God was revealing to me that He knew the desires of my heart and that as long as I put Him in charge of my life that He would guide me every step of the way. I had needed to hear that from Him and He had known that.

Proverbs 19:21 – There are many plans in a man's heart, Nevertheless the Lord's counsel – that will stand. This Scripture spoke volumes to me because it was showing me that the entire vision had come from my heart. I had lifted my dreams up to God in prayer and He had answered me – returning the vision back to me.

Proverbs 24:3,4 – Through wisdom a house is built, And by understanding it is established; By knowledge the rooms are filled With all precious and pleasant riches. I understood those Scriptures to mean exactly what they said; only with wisdom, understanding and knowledge from On High was I going to be able to make the house stand apart. I felt enabled to do so and I believed that I was doing the will of God.

Those Scriptures culminated together to guide me on my next adventure with the Lord. I felt secure in my faith and I truly believed in what I was about to do in setting up the women's house.

Two other people who believed in me and what I was about to do were my parents. They encouraged me to do whatever I felt was the right thing to do. I think that they both thought that it was a little bit risky going into something so big, especially when I hadn't even been clean for a full year. But I explained to them that I believed in the project and that I needed their support. One of the things that I love most about my parents is their ability to love me through anything. This was definitely one of the times in my life that I needed them to just love me, and to trust in my decisions. I am sure that it was much more difficult for them to do the trust bit; understandably, after all that I had put them through during my years as a drug addict. And even though they knew that I had left that life behind me and that I was now a new creation in Christ, I am sure that they still worried. After all, that is what parents do for their children, but only because they want what is best for them. One of the wise sayings that both of my parents had always said was, "To keep it, you need to give it away". Now, for the first time ever, I completely understood what they meant; and that was exactly what I was going to do.

Amidst all of this I was still trying to continue my relationship with Mark. Even though we were now apart I still cared for him and wanted to continue to build on our relationship. But, just as it was with Mr T, every time I made an attempt to make contact with Mark he would get somebody else to answer the phone and tell me that he wasn't available. I had known that leaving the rehab, and Mr T, would put a real strain on our relationship; but I was still willing to try and give it a go. However, I am sure that he had other ideas. After all, the only time that we did see each other was on a Sunday morning at church, and even then he would always find an excuse as to why he had to leave straight after the service. I began to question the entire thing, but he couldn't even answer me. However, the Lord was using that time to teach me another lesson. He was showing me that He was the only One that I could trust, not man, to satisfy my desires. He was leading me to give my heart to Him completely, only I was too stubborn to hear Him. It would take some time, and some hurt, before I would heed to His voice.

The next move that I made towards setting up the women's house was to make a financial list of all the money that I would need in order to get it set up. Doing that was a leap of faith in itself, because in the natural realm I had no money and nobody that was willing to back me financially. However, in the spirit realm I knew that God would bless me and provide for all of my needs. I prayed long and hard before I wrote anything down; I wanted it to be all God. And it was. The house that I was believing for would cost approximately $320 per week, so that meant that I would need $1280 for the bond and another $1280 for the rent in advance. Including the other expenses to set up a house, all up I was looking at needing approximately $3000 to get things started. Now at the time it seemed impossible, but I knew that with God all things are possible (Matthew 19:26); so I stepped out and started to look for a house. Ben was helping me at the time; he believed in what I was doing as much as I did, and he devoted all of his spare time to helping me make the dream a reality. I will never forget all that he did for me then, and always. Five days after we had started looking he called me up to let me know that he had found the perfect house; and it was.

When I first saw the house Ben and I were driving past so that I could get an idea of the area. As soon as I saw it I knew straight away that it was 'the house'. I had prayed that God would show me the right one and steer me away from the wrong one. With this house I immediately felt propelled inside. We made an appointment to get the keys and off we went. The advertisement for the house said this: 6 bedrooms, 3 bathrooms, separate office and sewing room, family room and rumpus, great entertaining area with inground pool, walk to shops, with yard and pool maintenance included; and the house was in Camp Hill – within 7kms of the city heart. When I read it I thought that it would be way out of my price range but, of course, God was already on to that for me. The price was $325 per week, only $5 more than I had faithfully budgeted for. I knew that it was the house for me to set up. The next hurdle was explaining to the real estate agent exactly what I wanted to do with the place. But, of course, God was on to that for me as well.

I met with the agent the following morning and explained everything to him; I even showed him my written proposal. He called the owner down to the office who happened to be Catholic, and he said that he would allow me to have the place as long as I paid for everything up front. I explained to him that it would take me seven days to get all of the money together, and he was fine with that. So I had a house and no money. But I immediately put the word out to everybody I thought could help me, and I just knew that it would all work out perfectly. Dr Reece had told a few girls about what I was planning to do and he already had four or five of them ready to move in, so they paid up front and I explained to them that we would be in the house within a week. Every word that I was speaking at the time was being spoken in faith; and God heard me, loud and clear.

The afternoon of the seventh day I walked into the real estate office with $2560; exactly the amount that had been requested, and I had enough left over to buy the first week's food. I had prayed that the Lord would provide for me and the money had come. Not only money had come in, but furniture, cleaning products, clothes and some food. God was not only providing for our basic needs, but He was choosing to bless me over and abundantly what I required. It was totally amazing to me – just watching everything fall into place around me. It was all God; and all that I could do was thank Him and praise Him for all that He was doing. It was then that I started to pray for the house and for the girls that were coming into it; and for guidance and patience for myself. Because even though I had support coming to me from other people, I was basically doing it alone. I knew that with God on my side I would never be truly alone, but this was going to be my greatest step of faith yet. And I felt ready. I believed that I could do it. I felt spiritually able to achieve the dream that God had placed on my heart. With Him firmly by my side, I leapt into it – feet first.

The first night in the house I spent alone. When the last helper left, just after dinner, I sat on the front steps and could do nothing other than cry. I was so happy, so amazed that what I had seen in a vision just two and a half weeks before, was now real. I was sitting on the front steps of this amazingly blessed house and I knew that God was smiling down on me. I had received the word from Him and I had stepped out, in faith, and made it a reality. I was in total awe of God and all that He had done in my life. All that I could do was cry. For the first time in a very long time they were not tears of sadness, but tears of pure joy. I felt so blessed, to be chosen to such a destiny. I was overwhelmed and it was flowing out of me. That night, sitting on the porch, I knew that as long as I turned to Him with all things that God would always be there for me; and peace overflowed in my heart.

When I eventually went inside I decided to walk around the house while I was praying. I had seen people anoint other people with oil before, but not houses; but that was what I felt led to do, so I did it. I prayed in each and every room and anointed each one with oil. I prayed that Jesus would be the Lord of the house and that the Holy Spirit would soften the girls' hearts to Him. I prayed that they would all come into a greater understanding of Him and that each and every thing that took place in that house would be blessed by His hand. After I had prayed I sat on the floor in the room that I had chosen to be mine. I felt the presence of God flow through there, and I felt the hand of God touch me and comfort me. I am sure that He was using that time, the last time that I would ever be in that house by myself, to reassure me that He was right there with me; and He always would be. Even though I lay on the polished wooden floorboards, I slept very peacefully that night.

The following day some of the girls moved in, and some of them bought furniture with them. The house was slowly taking form. My mum also came down for the weekend and bought with her two big boxes full of kitchen things that people had given to her for the house. Everything was falling into place. It was strange for me watching the girls coming into the house, because less than 12 months prior to that I myself had been a messed up heroin addict looking for a way out. It made me reflect on the awesomeness of what God had done in my life in such a short time and helped me to remember the pain from which He had set me free. It actually bought me into a greater revelation of just who God was to me; Saviour, Lord, friend, redeemer, strength, and provider. Those descriptions are a mere glimpse of all that He revealed to me at that time.

On that night my mum and I were lying down and we both just started to cry. Neither of us could really fathom all that had happened and was about to happen in my life. It was one of the most tender moments that we had ever shared together, and I will always hold it close to me as a very special memory.

Over the next couple of days the remainder of the girls moved in and the house became very full, very quickly. All together there were eight girls, including me. We were all very different personalities and we all came from different backgrounds, but we all had one thing in common – a problem with drug addiction. I knew, from my own experiences, that there was so much more to it than just that. The drug addiction was basically just a symptom of the underlying issue, or issues that needed to be dealt with. I knew that it was going to be hard work trying to get the girls to trust me and to work with me; but I was almost bursting with excitement at the prospect of all that lay ahead for all of us.

When they had first arrived the girls, too, had been very excited about living in a clean, safe house. They all chose their rooms just as though it was a normal share house; but it certainly wasn't that. As it was with me, all of the houses that they had ever lived in while they had been using drugs had been focused solely on the drugs. In that sense, this house was very different. Those differences became very clear to them when, at the first house meeting, I shared the household guidelines with them. I had chosen to call them guidelines as opposed to rules because I knew how I had felt towards rules of any kind while I was detoxing. I figured that guidelines would be healthier.

1. No drugs or drug activity to be taken or undertaken by any household member (inc. pot, heroin, pills, speed, alcohol etc.)

2. Naltrexone and any other medication or prescriptions are to be handed to Bronwen upon arrival and to be dispensed and recorded under supervision as required.

3. Regular urine samples will be collected upon request.

4. a) the weekly structure must be adhered to and any other arrangements must be made known and approved of ahead of time.
b) any personal activity outside the structure is to be made known and cleared before being undertaken.

5. The utmost of respect must be shown for other people and their property at all times.

I explained to the girls that these guidelines had been put in place to protect every member of the house, from themselves and from other people. They were all glad that I had explained them and said that they were willing to try and give them a go.

I knew that coordinating a house full of women was never going to be easy, but I also knew that I had the Lord on my side. They had all seen the blessing and provision for the house from day one, and they were all very curious. Getting them to explore their curiosity would prove to be the difficult part. David had agreed to come into the house one morning a week to work through the Alpha classes – the classes that I had initially attended at rehab. All of the girls would attend, as it was part of the program, but not all of them were willing to listen. The ones that did listen always had a lot of questions for him. Questions about the reality of God, the difficulty of Christianity and if He was real then why were they hurting? David knew exactly how to answer them all and he was always able to explain everything in an understandable manner. When he left at the end of the class and discussion the girls would always keep talking about whatever he had been teaching about. I always felt encouraged, knowing that if they hadn't been in the house they may never have discovered those particular things about God. I prayed that they would continue to be interested enough to ask questions. I knew that was all that I could do.

I knew that I couldn't force Jesus down their throats; because like me they needed to find Him for themselves. What I could do was live my life based on the word of God and create a place of Christian living. They would often comment about how peaceful they felt in the house and how they knew that it was because I prayed for God to be there. So even the girls who were against God seemed to be softening. It was awesome to stand back and just watch God at work in their lives. I loved watching the changes in them; more often than not they were without them even noticing. I saw them all grow in different ways knowing always that without the house, which God had given to me, they would never have had the opportunities that they were having.

One of the other Christian activities that we had at the house was a worship night. Every Friday night Frances and Ben would come over with their guitars and they would encourage us all to sing along. Some of the girls would sit and listen, some would sing and others would just fall asleep. But no matter what they were doing, again I just had a real excitement inside of me knowing that the Spirit of God was at work in the house. The house was so big and because of the floorboards, the music would resonate through the entire place. Nobody could escape what God was doing there even if they wanted to. That was exactly what I had been praying for.

It wasn't all about God and it wasn't all good. At different times over the first few weeks people were 'busting' – using heroin or smoking pot. I never judged them on their actions but, rather, we would attempt to get to the root problems, the real issues. Problems were surfacing for the girls, and they felt comfortable knowing that I was there to hear them out. I tried to always compassionately love them through their struggles although I am sure they felt otherwise. I am sure that some of them thought that I was being really hard by not allowing them to do certain things or to follow through with certain bad decisions; but what I was doing was setting a standard, a godly standard. I knew that it wouldn't be the sort of house that they could all stay in, but I knew that I was following the lead of God and I was doing only what I felt led to do.

One of the other things that the girls had to take part in, as part of the structure, was church attendance on Sunday mornings. We would all pile into a taxi-van and off we would go. I am sure that some of those girls would never have had the opportunity to attend church and so it always excited me that now they could. Not all of them liked it, and like me in the beginning, they preferred to sit out the front and smoke cigarettes. I knew that I couldn't force them to stay. The best thing that I could do for them was pray that God would meet them where they were at and that the hand of God would lead them in the right direction. As it was, I was just glad that they were there; and so was the Lord.

With the understandable hiccups during the first few weeks I was kept busy, constantly helping someone in some way. It seemed that no matter how much I loved what I was doing and as rewarded as I felt, there was still something not sitting right inside of me. I didn't know what it was, so I asked God to reveal it to me, in due time. As it was, I was spending all of my time giving out to people, and even though I asked God to fill me with His Spirit every single day, there were still times that I felt worn out, as though all I wanted to do was be by myself. It very rarely happened at the house, or anywhere else for that matter. The only time that I was on my own was when I was sleeping, or getting ready for bed; and I always used that time to pray. I would pray thanks to God for the opportunity that He had given to me, and I would pray for the girls. Every night I would ask God to reveal Himself to them in new ways. I asked that His glory and grace flow through me; and I knew that it did.

One of the other things that I spent a lot of my prayer time talking with God about was the way that I felt about leaving the rehab and how everything had happened. I felt really hurt and upset about the way that I believed that Mr T had treated me. A lot of things had been left undone and unsaid, and it was those things that affected me the most. I didn't feel as though there had been any sense of closure; it was still an open wound for me. It upset me, and angered me, that he and I had worked so closely and so well together and the moment that I wasn't willing to submit to sub-standard living he neglected me. Up until that point Mr T had always treated me with the utmost respect and he had always given me the encouragement that I had needed to break through to the next level. He had guided and supported me through one of the hardest, if not the hardest, times of my life; and all of a sudden he was no longer in my life. It was very strange for me. The positive thing that came out of that time was God revealing Himself to me as the only faithful and dependable source in my life. Once again He was showing me that I needed to trust in Him 100% because no man or woman would ever be able to love me the way that He loved me. Even though He was showing me these wonderful things, it still hurt. I looked forward to having an opportunity to sit down with Mr T and talk everything through, only I had no idea just how soon that would be.

One Sunday after church, just a few weeks after I had started the girls' house, Mark asked me if we could go somewhere after church for lunch and to talk. I hoped that he was going to use that time to explain to me what he thought was going on between us, because I had absolutely no idea. I also had no idea that Mr T was going to be there while we spoke. We went to a café and I knew the moment that I sat down that it was going to be a hard afternoon. I felt as though they had me there to drill me, like I was being investigated; and it wasn't very comfortable at all. Here were the two guys that had meant the most to me, apart from my dad, during my entire rehabilitation experience and I may as well have been having lunch with strangers. They spoke together about things that I had no idea about and I felt alienated. I wasn't sure if that was their aim, but if it was, they had definitely achieved it.

Moments before our lunch came out Mark told me that he had something that he needed to talk to me about. At the time I hadn't really spoken to him, properly, for months. He then proceeded to tell me that he felt as though we were going in opposite directions and he didn't think that we had a future together. I guess I was expecting those words to come out of his mouth, but they still hurt. After all that we had been through together; now when it suited him, he was willing to give up the fight. It was a strange feeling that I had – almost like a weight had been lifted from my shoulders yet sad at the same time. The hardest part for me to deal with was that he had chosen to do it with Mr T sitting there at the table; almost as though he had felt that he would need the back up. Both of us had leaned on Mr T over the time that we had known him; but not like this. I almost felt humiliated. It was obvious to me that they had discussed, in detail, what Mark thought that he should say. It was as though it had been scripted and I was just there to play a part. The remainder of the lunch passed by rather uncomfortably; I am sure that none of us really wanted to be there.

Chapter 17

The Goodness of God

The following Sunday at church two of the girls gave their heart to Jesus and I was reminded of where I was at and what God had called me to do. I'd had a really tough week and the Lord had used the girls to bring me back on track. After they had prayed for Him to be the Lord of their lives they came rushing up to me – they wanted to hug me and to thank me for giving them the opportunity to meet Jesus. I immediately knew that I was in the right place with God and He had again revealed His goodness to me.

The change in the girls was rapid and immediate. One of the girls, whose name was Emily, had been one of the hardest to break through to; yet she softened up and opened up to me in a way that allowed me to actually help her. My prayers had been answered – the Holy Spirit was softening their hearts to allow Jesus in, and that meant that then I could do my part. My part was to love them and guide them, and to teach them the word of God. I watched those girls, hungry for God, reading any thing that they could get their hands on that was going to bring them closer to Jesus, and at that time I had a real peace inside of me. I knew that God was smiling down on those girls, welcoming them into His kingdom. I also knew that He was smiling down on me for my obedience to His call on my life. It was an amazing time for me; and for them.

It was around the time that the girls started to get saved that God spoke to me and revealed something to me that I had known, but never understood. I was writing one day and the words that He gave me were: Use what you've GOT and GOD will use you. Those few words spoke volumes to me. I was doing that, but didn't even know it. The way that I saw it was that I needed to take to God all that I had and He would use it to bring glory to His kingdom. After all, there was no denying my background and I knew that I needed to use what I had and ask God to do the rest. I guess those words reminded me that I needed to never forget where I had come from; because if I did I ran the risk of forgetting all that Jesus had saved me from. That was something that I never wanted to happen. That day I promised to always use the talents and gifts that God had given to me; after all, He had given them to me in the first place. I decided to always give my all to Him; regardless of the cost.

Kylie came back into my life at around this time. She called up out of the blue one day and I invited her over. She was now noticeably pregnant and I was very excited for her. We talked and talked, until the next thing we knew it was late at night. I asked her to stay over and we continued talking about whatever came to mind; it was awesome. It showed me that people that I helped could also become my friend, although I had known that it would happen with her from the very beginning. No matter how different we were, we were also very similar in a lot of ways. Anyhow, I was glad for the friendship and I know that she was too. After that night Kylie would come and go whenever she could until eventually she just stopped going home. A couple of the girls had left so there was a spare room for her. She said that she felt a real peace in the house and that she was so comfortable there that she never wanted to leave. Although she never moved in there under the same circumstances as the other girls, she was always grateful for any wisdom and advice that I could offer her.

We prayed almost every night; for her and for Michael, and especially for the baby. It was very exciting for me to be so close to someone that was pregnant as I had never really experienced anything quite like it. I loved reading all of her books and magazines about the growth of the baby; sometimes it was almost as though I had taken over the role of the father because Michael wasn't in her life at that time. She had never asked me to, but I was happy to stand by her side and support her throughout the pregnancy. She already knew that she was having a girl, and she had named her Harmony – as her hope was that the baby would bring harmony into her life. I would often just rest my hand on her bump and talk to Harmony, sing to her and pray for her;

I looked forward to having the opportunity to meet her face to face. It was a really special time for our friendship and we created a healthy bond between us that we knew would never be broken.

Not long after that I had decided to have a party to celebrate being clean off heroin for one whole year. I was so excited, not just because of that, but because of all that the Lord had done in my life within that year. I was not the same person who had walked into the rehab 12 months prior. I was now a new creation and now I was a vessel for the Lord instead of for the enemy. Basically, my life was so far removed from the life that I had been leading without God at my side; it amazed me everyday. So I decided to celebrate the beginning of it with those people that I cared about. The girls were glad to help me prepare for it, and it was great to see them so enthusiastic about someone else's recovery. My parents were really glad that I was going to have a party to celebrate the event. I am sure that deep down they both never thought that I would make it. I invited everybody that had impacted my life in some way over the 12 months; and that included Mr T and the gang from rehab. It definitely wasn't easy for me to invite them, but on the other hand I knew that I needed to act out the forgiveness that I had spoken out over Mr T's life, and there was never going to be a better opportunity. So basically, everyone that I knew at the time was going to be there.

It was a great night, just celebrating being clean and the goodness of God. The part that will always remain the most touching one for me was when my parents spoke. It was a really emotional time for all of us – me especially. I also noticed that a lot of the girls were crying; perhaps they were thinking of their own parents and all of the harm they had done to their relationships with them. My dad started to explain how proud he was of me and all that I had done. He said that he knew I was special and different, and that I was definitely being looked after by "the man upstairs". It was really sweet to hear him talk that way about me and all that had been achieved in such a short time. Then he hugged me as mum started to speak. She was crying before she uttered her first word. The words that she did speak were beautiful. She said that she couldn't believe that I was sitting there and that she had asked God for a miracle and this is what He had given her. I don't think that there was a dry eye in the place. It was a very emotional time. It opened up my eyes to see exactly how much they both loved me, I mean I knew that they loved me, but it helped me to understand the heart of a parent; unconditional and pure.

One of the things that happened at the same time as the celebration party was that I attended a seminar about deliverance counselling held by a man named Dr Badu Bediako. I believed that the Holy Spirit led me to the seminar; I had heard him preach at church and his teaching had really affected me. I knew that deliverance counselling was something that God had place on my heart and so I figured it would be great. I knew that it would be difficult but I also knew that God would reveal to me what I needed to know and allow me to leave behind what I didn't need. Kylie and Emily decided to come as well. I was going because I wanted wisdom and knowledge on setting the captives free. I was really excited about it as I knew it was going to be great for my spiritual growth.

I learned so much from attending the seminar – it was totally awesome. One of the main things that I took away from it was this: a counsellor is an intercessor. I knew that God had called me to pray for other people and I had already seen the fruit of my prayers for others, but I now understood that I was actually standing before God on behalf of those people. How powerful! I was praying for people that didn't know God, and He had heard me. I was standing before Him, believing that the Holy Spirit would help to remove any blockage that stood between them and a relationship with the Lord. It sounded so simple, but it affected my spirit in a way that I knew from that moment on my prayer life would never be the same again.

On the last day of the seminar Dr Badu talked about an issue that was very close to my heart and I knew that God was using him to speak to me. He spoke about soul ties, and explained that every time unwed people attach to one another sexually that they are transferring curses, and creating ungodly bondages. I had read something about that before, but never really understood it. The way that he explained it, it was as though he was speaking straight into my spirit; actually it was the Holy Spirit talking straight into my spirit via him. I felt a move inside of me, a knowing that this was something very important for me. He then spoke about prostitution, and how it is a perfect opportunity for gangs of demons to enter into the woman. Those words struck me. After all of the counselling work that I had done with Mr T, and all of the books that I had read, and all of the prayers that I had spoken to God, this was something that I had no understanding of. After he had finished speaking I asked him what a prostitute needed to do to cleanse herself from the demons and the curses. He explained that every soul tie needed to be broken, as did every curse. He said that it would take many sessions to see it happen and even then not many of those women ever become truly free. God spoke to me then and there and said, "You are free my daughter. He who the Son sets free is free indeed"(from John 8:36). I sensed a real comfort in my soul, a knowing that He had already taken care of it all. I knew that He had seen my heart and my desires, and He had set me free. I knew that I was free, and there was no turning back. It was an amazing time for me. It was clear then just how much He loved me and how much He needed me to step out and be a light in the darkness.

When I got home and was in my room praying, God revealed something to me. It was something that I had thought about before, but had never really taken seriously. Now I knew exactly how important it was to the kingdom of God. He gave me the title for a workbook for women, entitled "Setting the Prostitutes Free". There was no such book available; I had scoured the bookshops ever since I had been saved. I knew then that God was going to use the gift of writing that He had given to me to make it real. The working girls of the world needed to have some hope, a tangible way of seeing a change; a change that only God could create. I knew that it was going to be a really big project and even though I had no idea of the timing of God; I was just glad to have a vision about it. To see that, within time, God was going to use my experiences and my testimony to turn around the lives of so many hurting and lost women, there was a real excitement in my spirit. I decided to seek God for all that I would need to know. I am still seeking.

During my time at the women's house we had been having a lot of problems with the girls using drugs, and even though we were tackling them head on they were all still very fragile. One of the girls, Eli, had done a graphic art course and we decided that in order for her to stay busy, and therefore not use drugs, that she should use her talents wisely. I had written up a mission statement for the house, calling it *Stepping Stone*.

The reason I called the house 'Stepping Stone' was that I wanted the whole idea to be about turning our stumbling blocks into stepping stones. I wanted the house to be a stepping stone back to reality for all of the women that came there. I shared that in my mission statement, to which Eli added an amazing letterhead. This is what it said:

MISSION STATEMENT

In today's society women face certain challenges and situations throughout which they need support and encouragement in order to overcome them. "Stepping Stone" has been structured as a safe place where these women can work intensively on changing their lives by focusing on their mentalities and habits. Our support house, which has been set up in Camp Hill Brisbane, is a place of warmth, love and compassion. Our focus is on the rehabilitation of recovering female drug users.

Assisting these women to discover their full potential and achieve their dreams as they work through their issues has a beneficial and fruitful outcome. Helping people out of hopeless situations and on to hope road is the ultimate fulfilment.

We are in the process of initiating a full time structure including workshops, study and group activities. We are currently searching for any form of support or input from people and organisations in order to spread our message of hope and reach as many lives as possible.

AIM

To create a safe environment to equip women choosing to break free from the torment of addiction; and to facilitate growth into living new and clean lifestyles. To guide them to become true women of destiny.

That was basically my whole dream on one page of paper. I had prayed to God for the right words and that was what He had given me. It was so perfect; so God.

It would have all been perfect, if the house wasn't seemingly falling down around me. The house wasn't, but the attitudes of the girls were. I continued to pray for them and I knew that all that I could do was leave them all in God's hands and just be there if they needed me. The best thing that I could have done was all that I did; I loved them through their struggles and directed them to the proper doctors and counsellors. There was no more that I could have done, other than that. I knew that by setting up the house I had provided them with an opportunity that they may have never have had otherwise; and I knew that I was doing the right thing.

As most of the girls were struggling with their issues and choosing to use drugs to numb the pain that they felt, Emily was becoming a really strong woman of God. She read the word every day, and other Christian books that she could gather and she had an amazing gift of revelation knowledge. She would read something and then be able to relay it to me in a really understandable manner. She was growing in leaps and bounds; it was really encouraging. Unfortunately, most of the other girls were deciding to leave the house and return to their drug lifestyles. I knew that at least by being in the house, if only for two or three months, that they had had a glimpse of Christian living and they had been introduced to Jesus. It had been up to them to accept Him, or not. That was one thing that I couldn't do for them.

So a few months after the house had been set up there were only three of us living there; Kylie, Emily and myself. We would spend a lot of our days just reading the bible or Christian books and/or listening to worship music. We were all just content and comfortable to live life like that, for however long it stayed that way. Often we would gather together and just talk about all of the amazing things that God was doing in our lives, and we would pray. Even though the house had been set up to accommodate more people, it was really encouraging for me to watch those two women becoming stronger in Christ. They were happy to work through their issues whenever challenges arose. I was enjoying working with them that closely; it was a much more intimate manner, and seemingly much more effective. It was a struggle for us financially, but somehow we always managed to pull through. We were all just glad to be clean, to be Christians and to be growing; it was a really memorable time for me.

Every now and again Emily would have a struggle with heroin, but between Kylie and I, we were always able to talk her through. She knew what was right and what was wrong and that the final decision was always hers. I watched her struggle, and amidst her struggles I saw her get closer to God than she probably ever would have. It was amazing for me to watch Him at work in her life; another answered prayer.

During this time of what I considered to be solitude I got a call from Mr T telling me that Jason had left the rehab and gone back to heroin and asked if I would consider calling him up to encourage him. My immediate response was to think about what a waste it was for him to throw his life and his wisdom away on drugs. He had so much to offer the kingdom of God – he knew that there was an incredible call on his life – yet he was choosing to walk away from it. I couldn't understand it. I couldn't comprehend walking away from God once I had found Him. But, realistically, Jason had been running away from God, and his call, for years. I called him up the following day and, suprisingly, he was there. I told him that Mr T had told me that he had left and had explained the circumstances to me. I then offered for him to come to the house any time that he needed a friend or encouragement. He was quite dazey but said that he would get back to me. Funnily enough he called back, within half and hour, to ask if I minded him coming over that day.

When I got off the phone I started to praise God and ask Him for the wisdom to know what to say to Jason when he arrived. After all, he had been one of the people that I had learned from about the Lord, and now he was lost. I was led to the Scripture in Galatians 6:1,2 which says, Brethren, if a man is overtaken in any trespass, you who are spiritual restore such a one in a spirit of gentleness, considering yourself lest you also be tempted. Bear one another's burdens, and so fulfill the law of Christ. I knew that it was the perfect way for me to deal with the situation; gently and with patience.

Jason came to the house almost every day for nearly two weeks. The house was now quite obviously no longer the house that it had intended to be – but was still a refuge for those in need of love and care. I think that Jason found it to be a peaceful house and a place where nothing was expected of him. I knew how it felt to be free of the load of helping others, only I had not chosen to use drugs to celebrate that freedom the way that Jason had. He and I would spend a lot of time just talking – I was trying to work out why he had made the choices that he had, and he always tried to avoid the answer. Some days he would come over and he had obviously been using heroin. I didn't like seeing him like that. I had been so used to seeing him alert and aware it was strange for me to see him dulled on drugs. I told him that I didn't like it, and then we didn't see him for a few days. When he did return to the house he started sleeping in one of the spare rooms; and much like the way that Kylie had entered the house, he basically never left.

Around the time that Jason basically moved in, one of Emily's old school friends made contact with her. That girl happened to also be my old friend from private school days, Melinda. The one girl that I had made a real connection with way back in Grade 8 and 9 was now re-entering my life. She had just come back from China and wanted to see Em. Emily explained to her where she was living and told her that I was running the house. Melinda couldn't believe that I was back in her life, and visa versa. The moment that she stepped out of the car, the very first time that she came to the house, I knew that it was a God-ordained appointment. She too had her own struggles with heroin, and now she was back in Brisbane needing support and encouragement. She knew that she had found the perfect place. Immediately, we started talking and I told her about the life that I had been living since we had last seen each other; which was actually about six years prior to that, at a party. She couldn't believe that I had allowed heroin to get the better of me; she said that she had always remembered me to be a really strong person. I explained to her that I had allowed heroin to be stronger than I was after the very first taste of it. I knew that she had been placed into my life at that point in time for a reason; I just had no idea as to what that reason was.

As she always did, Melinda affected everybody that she met in an unforgettable way. She had a warm and loving smile and a really big heart. She started to call me up just to talk and then eventually we would end up having an impromptu counselling session. She was very curious about my relationship with Jesus, and was continually asking me questions that I was more than happy to answer for her. Our friendship was blossoming, and it was really nice to have her in my life again. I had been asking God for a special friend, someone that I trusted, to just hang out and spend time with; and He had chosen to give me Melinda.

Chapter 18
No Turning Back

One day Kylie needed to go to her old place at Albion to pick up some of her things and Jason had offered to drive her there. Emily and I were sitting on the verandah and they asked us if we wanted to go for the drive. Emily did, but I didn't – I just felt like lounging around. They all spent a while trying to talk me into getting out of the house and eventually I gave in and agreed to go with them. The easiest way to get there was over the Gateway Bridge, but Jason had decided to go through the city – for no reason other than he wanted to go for a drive. So off we went, the long way round. After we had been in the car for about fifteen minutes I realised that the way that he was going was going to take us through Spring Hill – my old stomping ground. I hadn't been anywhere near there for years, and was quite happy to continue to avoid it. God obviously had different plans for me and was using Jason as a vessel. The closer we got, the more uncomfortable I got. I am sure that if everyone else had looked closely they actually would have seen me squirming in my seat. When we reached Spring Hill the route Jason took went down the back streets, which meant that we actually drove down the street that I used to walk my clients down and straight past the house that I used to live in and work at. I just stared out the window; there was nothing that I could say. We then drove up the hill and came out directly opposite where I had stood night after night, selling my body to complete strangers. It seemed a world, and a lifetime, away, and yet so eerily close. The hardest part for me was actually driving past the spot and realising that I had been prostituting myself in front of a church. I hadn't even thought, or cared, about it at the time; but now it was the straw that broke my back.

I just stared out the window, unsure of what I felt or how I was going to address my feelings. Then Jason reached over to me and touched my hand which made me jump. Then he quietly asked me if I was okay. I couldn't respond, I couldn't speak. I felt as though I was reliving a horrible nightmare, but it was a reality for me. I don't know how long it took us to get to Kylies old place, but it felt like an eternity. When we got there I got out of the car and just stood there. I didn't know how I felt; I couldn't understand all that was going on inside of me. I knew that I wasn't alone, but I felt like a stranger in my own body. I wasn't sure if it was God or the enemy bringing up memories that I had repressed about that time of my life; all I did know was that they were hurting me. I am not sure what happened next but somehow I ended up walking out to the back yard, and just sitting down on the ground. I had my eyes closed and when I eventually opened them up Jason was standing next to where I was; he was praying for me. That is a vision that I will never forget. Regardless of how I was feeling I knew that I could trust him and I knew that he wouldn't hurt me. He encouraged me to stand up and asked me how I felt. I told him that my head was aching – it was throbbing with the pain; though I'm sure that it was actually emotional pain. He then told me that I needed to pray against what was happening to me, that I needed to verbally rebuke the demons that were at work inside of me. But I couldn't; again I couldn't speak. It was a horrible feeling and an experience that I will never forget. Then I remember seeing Kylie out of the corner of my eye. She was holding a glass of water and had her hand outstretched towards me in prayer. I don't know what happened next but I do remember Jason wrapping his arms around me, and I was shaking. He told me that Jesus loved me and he encouraged me to see Jesus standing right beside me as I visualised my life in Spring Hill. It was difficult to do, and I knew that it would take some time.

I don't have any idea how long we stood there for, or how long the ride home was, but the moment that I sat in the car I closed my eyes; I didn't want to look out the window anymore. Instantly, I felt hands reaching out to touch me, in a very gentle manner, as everyone in the car prayed for me the whole way home. When we got home

I went straight into the bathroom for a long, hot shower. I wanted to wash away the way that I felt, even though I knew that the only way I could do that was with the blood of Jesus. I felt unable to connect with God, regardless of the intimacy in our relationship. I felt very distant from Him at that point. So instead of praying I decided to play worship music while I was in the shower. Once again I felt as though I was in a time warp. I don't know how long I was in the shower, but I do know that when I got out I felt as though a change had taken place inside of me. I am sure that the others had continued to pray for me while I was in there. The music that I had been playing had reached into my soul and been like a soothing balm over my wounds.

The song that I had chosen to play, on repeat, was one that had touched my heart earlier on in my walk with Christ. But I don't remember choosing it, so the Lord must have done it for me. It is a song called Within Your Love, and I feel strongly led to share the lyrics with you.

> Oh Lord you have searched my heart
> You have known my thoughts my ways
> You guide each step until it leads to you
> And I am found safe within your love
>
> Hold me now
> Safe within Your arms
> Hold me closer
> Safe within Your love
> Touch me now Lord
> With the power of forgiveness
>
> Hide me now
> In the brightness of Your love
> Oh Lord where can I hide
> From this love that can know no end
> I am found in this state of grace
> I am found safe within Your love*

That song, and my friends' prayers, radically transformed how I felt. I had already known that God loved me deeply, but I now also

---

* *WITHIN YOUR LOVE Words & Music Geoff Bullock © Word Music/Maranatha! Praise. Licensed courtesy of CopyCare Pacific Pty Ltd*

understood that there was nothing that He wouldn't love me through. I now had the revelation that He had always loved me and there was nothing that He didn't know about me. He had found me and loved me from where I was then to where I was now. I was always going to be safe within His arms and His love. I knew that He was going to see me through this trial. God loved me so much that He had revealed Himself to me on an intimate level before allowing me to return to the scene of my crimes, so to speak. I was so grateful that I had the relationship that I had with God before I had returned to Spring Hill, because if I had gone back any earlier only God knows what may have happened.

Unfortunately, at around this time Emily had started to use heroin again. It had taken her by surprise, so she said. She had had it once and then couldn't shake the desire to keep using it. She would ask me to pray with her and would then be okay for a day or two, and then she would be off again. I told her that she couldn't keep staying there as long as she was doing drugs. Sadly, as with all of the other girls, she chose drugs. It was sad for me to see her leave as we had become quite close and I had seen so much potential in her. As with most people I concentrated on the potential within her – I never looked at how far she had come but instead chose to look at how far she had to go, into her God-given destiny.

The incident with Spring Hill had stirred so many emotions inside of me that led me to do three things. Firstly, it made me run to God. Whereas, in the years gone by I would've run to heroin to numb the pain, this time I ran to God to heal the pain. Secondly, it encouraged me to start keeping another prayer journal so that I could commune with the Lord in the most expressive way that I knew how. Thirdly, it forced me to work on, and deal with, my issues regarding the men in my life and how I felt about them. I knew that there was still some very painful stuff that I needed to deal with; and the Lord had provided the perfect opportunity and timing. I knew that these steps were all going to help me to grow in my relationship with Him; but that didn't make doing them any less painful.

The easiest one for me to do was run to God. Since I had met Him I had turned to Him through everything up to that point, so it was the obvious thing for me to do. I felt so raw and so hurt but I knew that He would see me through; He always did. My prayer life took a turn and became something that I was again very passionate about. I prayed continually; some days just waiting to hear from the Lord. My relationship with Him became so strong during that time that I knew the entire incident had occurred for a reason; a heavenly reason. God had seen a need in me, in my spirit and in my heart, and He had made a way for me to turn to Him with it.

Whenever I read the bible during that time I always found myself in the Psalms. I had read the Psalms a lot when I had first been saved; I found a real comfort in them. I found them to be really heartfelt and in line with where I was at, at the time. Again I found myself in need of that comfort, but on a different level. It was during this time that one particular Psalm became the cry of my heart, and one that I found myself meditating on daily, as well as singing to God. It was Psalm 51 (NIV).

Have mercy on me, O God,
according to your unfailing love;
according to your great compassion
blot out my transgressions.
Wash away all my iniquity
and cleanse me from my sin.

For I know my transgressions,
and my sin is always before me.
Against you, you only, have I sinned
and done what is evil in your sight,
so that you are proved right when you speak
and justified when you judge.
Surely I was sinful at birth,
sinful from the time my mother conceived me.
Surely you desire truth in the inner parts;
you teach me wisdom in the inmost place.

Cleanse me with hyssop, and I will be clean;
wash me, and I will be whiter than snow.
Let me hear joy and gladness;
let the bones you have crushed rejoice.
Hide your face from my sins
and blot out all my iniquity.

Create in me a pure heart, O God,
and renew a steadfast spirit within me.
Do not cast me from your presence
or take your Holy Spirit from me.
Restore to me the joy of salvation
and grant me a willing spirit,
to sustain me.

Then I will teach transgressors your ways,
and sinners will turn back to you.
Save me from bloodguilt,
O God, the God who saves me,
and my tongue will sing of your righteousness.
O Lord, open my lips,
and my mouth will declare your praise.
You do not delight in sacrifice,
or I would bring it;
you do not take pleasure in burnt offerings.
The sacrifices of God are a broken spirit;
a broken and contrite heart,
O God, you will not despise.

In your good pleasure make Zion prosper;
build up the walls of Jerusalem.
Then there will be righteous sacrifices,
whole burnt offerings to delight you;
then bulls will be offered on your alter.

Those passages affected me in a way that no other Scripture had ever done before. Even though I had only been saved for around twelve months I believed that I had quite a deep understanding of the Word. I had always prayed for revelation knowledge and God had granted my requests. But this Scripture changed the way that I saw God, for then and for always. I had always known of His love for me and that He had forgiven my sins, but now I also knew that I needed to continually ask for His mercy on me. He wanted to continually give it, but I needed to ask for it. It was something that I suppose I just took for granted from Him but now I felt as though I understood Him a little more. I also now understood that I had a really deep desire to confess and receive forgiveness for all of my sins. I wanted God to do for me what He had done for David in the psalm; I wanted Him to "wash away all my iniquity and cleanse me from my sin." That was an interesting revelation for me, because up until that point I had thought that I had already asked for that to happen. But God had just shown me a part of my life that I had not yet received total forgiveness for, I felt forgiven but I didn't have the assurance of total forgiveness, which was Gods deepest desire for me.

Another way I got closer to God during that time was through my prayer journal. God showed me that He had given me a gift in my writing and now He wanted me to use that gift, purely to get closer to Him. I couldn't think of a more beautiful way to use the gift. Some days I would write pages of prayers to Him and other days I would write Him letters. They were letters of thanks and of praise, for all that He had done and all that He was going to do. I always loved to just thank Him for all that He had planned out for me – it always excited me. It seemed confusing to be thanking God when deep down inside of me I was still hurting. I had just been through a very painful time emotionally. Although I did believe that praise would be one of the keys to my breakthrough. I needed to not just dwell on my current circumstances and feelings, but to focus on the future and promises of God for my life. It was so healing and releasing to keep the journal. It helped me to see my answered prayers, when I would reflect on what I had previously written. It also helped me to see the true nature of God, through what I had written about Him. Every time that I sat down to write I would always pray for the Holy Spirit to fill me and then I knew that what flowed out of me was of God. It was an awesome experience and exercise for me at the time. Although in the natural I felt pain, in the spiritual I felt joy. It was amazing what God was doing in me and through me, purely because of my obedience in keeping my journal. It was another way that He revealed Himself to me; blessing me in my spirit for my obedience and sacrifice. I fell in love with Him all over again during that time; it was so beautiful.

This was the very first entry.

Father I come before your throne of grace of which I am only worthy through the precious blood of Jesus. I thank you Father for the powerful spirit of adoption, that through your grace and mercy I can call myself a child of God. I thank you Lord for all that you

*are doing in my life. Protect me Jesus, come into the painful parts
of me and cleanse me from my shame with Your blood. I thank
you Jesus that you died so that I could fall in love with You. Help
me know and believe that I am free and cleansed; speak it into
my heart. You are so good to me. I came to you in despair, and
filled with guilt shame and strife, and true to your word you are
removing those mountains from my path, in the name of Jesus.
Gracious, loving, pure, compassionate, healing, true, protector,
strength. You are so merciful; Father forgive me for my sins, my
disobedience, my self will not Your will. Pour the blood of Jesus
into those wounds that I created. Father I come to you broken and
I want to be made whole made complete by your love. Glory to
you for all that you have done, are doing and will to do in my life.
You've taken me from the snares of death and made me new. Lord
I love you, make me whole. I know you took my shame to the cross
now I just need to believe it, forgive me for my unbelief. I am your
child, I pray that you will take hold of me in this time of healing,
teach me how to receive Father. Show me You. I am a child of
God, thank you Jesus.*

*Hebrews 4:16 Let us therefore come boldly to the throne of grace,
that we may obtain mercy and find grace to help in times of need.*

Over the following few weeks I went to places with God's help
that I had been avoiding and dealt with things that I hadn't realised
were issues for me. It was an amazing work that God was doing in
me at the time. Only He knows whether I would have been willing
to confront so many painful issues, if I hadn't been for that trip through
Spring Hill. I may have continued to run from them. God knows
what we are able to cope with and when during our walk with Him.
He will never give us more than we can handle. He loves us too much
to allow that. As long as we call on Him, He will hold us up and
love us through our pain. That is something that I still continue to
pray for everyday.

One of the biggest revelations that I received during that time
was that we wouldn't understand victory if we didn't have trials, trials
are something to gain victory over. I discovered this when the third
issue to come from the Spring Hill trip arose. This happened when

God encouraged me to use the time of healing and cleansing to work on my issues regarding the men that had been in my life. I knew that it was going to be a difficult time, but I was willing to do it. After all, I knew that He was with me through it all.

It was during this time of growth and healing that I realised my closest friend at the time was actually Jason. He and I had had our ups and downs, but we had come through it trusting one another and I was really enjoying our friendship. We would often just sit up all night and talk. We talked about everything from Creation to Revelation and everything in between. During this time the bond between us strengthened and I think we were both really comfortable with the way things were going between us. Jason had been there to help me work through my recent bout of challenges, and that had meant so much to me. I had been so grateful for his wisdom and his guidance at a really difficult part of my walk with God. He had proven himself to be a trustworthy and reliable friend. I discovered also that the words that he had spoken to me when we first met, the ones that I had thought were harsh and rude, were actually exactly what I had needed to hear; I just hadn't been ready to hear them. They had been the right words in the wrong season for me. But now those words were enabling and promoting growth inside of me, and I was more than grateful for them.

It was also around this time that Melinda was in desperate need of help. She called up one night and asked if we could go and pick her up; that she needed to get out of the house but she needed to go somewhere safe. Jason and I drove over to pick her up and on the way home she wouldn't stop squeezing my hand – it felt as though it was going to burst. I knew then that she was desperate. All that she really needed was love – not a human love, the kind she had always been hurt by; but a heavenly love, a pure and real love. Melinda and I went into my room when we got home and she immediately started talking to me and asking me questions about how I had been able to get so strong in such a short amount of time. I then felt led to share about the love of Jesus and make the offer for her to receive His salvation. We had been working through some pretty tough issues that night and I am sure that she knew that choosing Jesus was the only way that she was going to find the peace that she longed for; the peace that she saw in me. She desired to be cleansed and to be forgiven for all that she had done wrong, but first she needed to confess that she had sinned against God. That was the hardest part for her, because at first she said that she knew that she had sinned but that she didn't want to confess it, because then she would be admitting responsibility for her actions. I explained to her that was what she needed to do and after we had sat there and listened to worship music for some time, she reached out and took a hold of my hand and told me that she was ready to be saved. She later told me that during the time of silence she had been confessing her sins to God, and that after she had done that she actually felt forgiven. She felt clean, and because of that she knew that she had to give her heart to Jesus right then. It was a very special moment for her, and for me; it was like welcoming one of my very special friends into the kingdom of God, and into heaven. At the time I had no idea of how true that would be, but I would soon find out.

Without me realising, my friendship with Jason was blossoming into a romance. We were starting to spend all of our spare time with each other and really enjoying one anothers company. One night we were sitting on the front verandah and I decided to kiss him. I don't think that he was expecting it and afterwards he asked me why I had done it. I simply told him that I had felt like it. He then went on a big spiel about living by feelings as opposed to living by the Spirit. I knew that what I had done was not of the Spirit, however it did feel right. At the time I didn't understand how that deeply grieved the heart of God. I had crossed the line between friendship and beyond, and I wasn't turning back.

There was so much about Jason that I had grown to admire. That in itself was a first – before I had always just fallen quickly for someone; but with Jason I had slowly grown to love him. I knew that he still had feelings for his ex-girlfriend, but I also knew that he definitely felt something more than friendship for me. One day I sat down with my notebook and decided to write down the reasons that I was attracted to him, and to work out whether or not it was worth pursuing. The aspects of his heart and his personality that I admired were; strength, integrity, heart for God, gentle, honest, knowing, thoughtful and understanding. They were some of the things that I had, at first, not liked about him and now I found myself falling in love with him because of them. There was nothing stopping me from pursuing my relationship with him; except him.

While I was busy trying to understand and comprehend my feelings for Jason, he was busy trying to think of ways to use heroin without me asking him to leave the house. It was a difficult time for both of us, because he was doing what he claimed that he didn't want to be doing, and I was trying hard to stop myself falling in love with him. Both of us were, seemingly, unable to stop what was happening in our lives. All the while the Lord had totally different plans altogether. He was going to enable us to fall in love regardless of our present circumstances. Once I realised that was what He desired, I knew there was no way to stop it.

One of the young guys from the rehab, Dane, called me one day and told me that he needed help and somewhere to stay and asked if he could come and stay with us. I explained to him that I would have to ask Kylie, as the baby was due in only a few weeks; and I didn't want to create any unwanted discomfort for her. She knew how I felt about Dane; he was like a little brother to me, and she also knew that I thought he had great potential – so long as he was encouraged to stay on the right track. Anyhow, she agreed that he could come and stay for a while. He moved in two days later.

For the first couple of weeks everything seemed to run quite smoothly at the house. Kylie had started her maternity leave at work and so she was at home, preparing for the birth of Harmony. Jason was busy either trying to work through his feelings for me or plotting his next drug using adventure. I was still busy working through my issues, spending time working on my relationship with the Lord and also looking forward to the birth of Harmony. Dane just kind of plodded along. It was nice having him around the house; I always thought of him as being very special, especially in the eyes of God, and I believed that he was in the right place for the time being.

Unfortunately, he and Jason started using drugs together, as often as they could. They were bad influences on each other and, because they both knew how I felt about them, they thought that they would be able to get away with it. And they did, for a little while. It was difficult for us because we knew what the house had been originally intended for, it now seemed more like a half-way house. Kylie and I both spoke to them and they told us that it would stop. Because we had been there ourselves, we knew better than to believe them and they both stayed at the house for quite some time in that state. It was difficult for me, because even though I continued to pray for them, I just wasn't sure what the best thing to do for them was. I continued to love them and care for them, but even that was difficult at times. Kylie and I spoke together about standing firm, but one of us would always back down and let them stay. They were both such special people (they both are special people) – they were just lost and confused.

Even with all of the drug activity going on in Jason's life, there was still something inside of me that felt as though I was falling in love with him. It wasn't that I wanted to rescue him, because I knew that he would never let that happen. I suppose a lot of it was just being able to see where he was at compared to where God wanted to take him, and holding onto the hope that he would one day choose to turn back to God and see it too. In the meantime, I continued to pray for him and believe for him to be protected by the Holy Spirit at all times, regardless of the choices that he was making. It was difficult for me to watch him disintegrate as a person, after having seen him so strong and able. But I knew that I had to let him go, and leave his destiny up to him, and God.

During this time I had to make a few really difficult decisions; but one of the toughest was regarding Dane's future at the house. Unlike Jason, when Dane had first moved into the house Kylie and I had sat down with him and told him what we would and wouldn't tolerate. Unfortunately, he had pushed us both too far too many times and eventually we had to make the decision to ask him to leave. It was hard for me because I knew that he was struggling with heroin, and I also knew that if he left the house he would wind up worse off than when he had arrived. But he reaped his own consequences by choosing to use drugs. Kylie and I had gone out of our way for him and allowed him to stay there but he, and Jason, had continually disrespected our requests. He knew that his time was up at the house, and he graciously left. Saying good-bye to him was very hard for me; after all, he was like my little brother. When he left it was like saying good-bye to the Dane I once knew, knowing that in the drug world, things were only going to get worse for him. But it was not up to me to try and protect him from himself; only God could do that, and that was what I would continue to pray for.

Jason, on the other hand, stayed at the house on the understanding that he also would stop using drugs. It was definitely a struggle at first, but I could see that he was making an effort. He eventually detoxed off heroin and then started to drink more. I had been having a few drinks of an evening, a couple of beers here and there. I knew that it wasn't really what the Lord wanted for me, and I justified it in my own head by telling myself that I had just been through some really hard stuff. It was no excuse, but that was what I told myself. Jason started to join me and eventually he was drinking as much as he could afford to, and sometimes more. Together we would sit and drink and talk, and drink some more. It was strange for me – because of my dad's alcoholism I had never really enjoyed drinking. I was just using it as a tool of relaxation; a very worldly tool. Instead of running to God for my peace and rest, drinking was what I chose to do. I knew that it wouldn't be forever, and so we just kept on doing it.

One night Melinda, and her partner Matt, asked me out for dinner and some drinks. I hadn't seen her for a couple of weeks, even though we had talked on the phone almost every day; so I jumped at the opportunity to spend some time with her. It was a great night out; we talked about whatever came to mind with a knowing that we understood each other. I loved spending time with her; she was very special to me. At one stage during the night we decided that we needed to go to the bathroom at the same time. On our way back to the table I told her that I thought that I was actually in love with Jason. She smiled and told me that she already knew that, that it was very obvious just from watching us together that we were in love. I then explained to her that I wasn't sure what to do about it, and of course she encouraged me to simply tell him. We giggled about it for the rest of the night. It was like being in grade nine all over again.

One of the other things that we discussed at the table that night was where Melinda was at and what she wanted to do with herself. She told me that she thought that she needed to be held accountable for her actions because, left to her own devices she kept slipping up, and she was really ready for a change in her life, and lifestyle. I asked her if she would consider moving into the house and she told me that she had already been thinking about it and hadn't known how to ask me. We both started laughing again. We both knew that it would be the best place for her and probably the only safe place for her at the time. She, just like me when I had entered rehab, needed to be protected from herself and her own decisions. She decided that she would move in the following week. That allowed her a week and a half to do her own thing before committing to getting clean and staying that way. I was very excited for her. We all were.

That week another couple of guys moved in. One of them was a young guy that I had met, and helped, during rehab. The other was a friend of Jason's from church who came from a similar background to all of us, but who just needed a clean house to live in. Kylie and I had been trying to work out how we were going to be able to afford to stay at the house, and then all of that happened. We believed that they were a blessing to us, but time would tell.

Melinda had called me that Thursday night to tell me how excited she was about moving into the house. She told me that she had been using heroin, but only because she knew that as of Monday she wasn't going to be able to. She justified it as making the most of her freedom. I encouraged her not to do that because when she did come to stay it would be much harder work for her to detox. She eventually agreed and said that she would call me the next night and maybe come over for the night; so as to keep safe from herself.

She never called me. I received a call from her sister on the Saturday morning to tell me that Melinda had died. She had overdosed on heroin.

I was shattered and I was angry and I was upset, but I also had a strange peace inside of me knowing that she had received Jesus and that she was now in heaven.

Her sister went on to explain to me that Melinda had told her that she was going to be staying at my place and then asked me if she had ever made it there. I told her that she had planned to call me, but never had. Her sister was understandably very upset, and so was I, so we agreed to speak later on in the day. I walked out to the lounge room and Kylie was sitting on the couch just staring at me. She had heard me crying while I had been on the phone and I told her what had happened. She too started crying. She had only known Melinda for a short time, but they had shared some real quality time together; and, as always, Melinda had left a mark on Kylie's heart. Then Jason came downstairs and I told him what had happened. He just came to me and held me in his arms. It was exactly what I needed at the time. I knew that the Lord was there with us as we cried for Melinda; I could sense His presence in the room, comforting us.

Over the next few days I was on an emotional rollercoaster ride. One moment I would be okay and peaceful about Melinda's death, knowing that she was in heaven; and the next moment I would be angry and confused as to why the Lord had chosen to take her then. Just as she had made a decision that may have positively changed her life, how could He do that? It was then that He revealed to me that He had loved her and protected her, and that she had made one crucial decision that had actually saved her life; she had accepted Jesus into her heart. And because of that decision she was now in heaven with Him, dancing on golden streets and laughing; a laugh unlike any that she had ever laughed on earth. She had, perhaps, finally found the peace and comfort that she had been searching for. I was happy on the inside, but very sad on the outside. I spent a lot of my time just crying. I am sure that some of the tears were for her, and some were just for me. Unfortunately, it had taken her death for me to realise that she had trusted me so much that she allowed me to share my love for Jesus with her. And because she had been so trusting and so open she was now in heaven. I decided the best thing that I could do was to write her a letter. A letter that I knew I would never share with her in person, but one that I needed to write into the spirit realm. I needed to say thanks to her for trusting me; and I needed to say good-bye.

The funeral was beautiful, and very difficult. Her family was very kind to me and they thanked me for all of the hope that I had given Melinda over the past couple of months. They said that they had seen a real change in her and her attitude everytime she spent any time with me. It was really encouraging, and under different circumstances would have made me very pleased. But this day was set aside for all of us to say good-bye to Melinda. Her sister had invited us back to her place for a good-bye party; she didn't want to call it a wake. When we arrived there I saw a lot of girls that I had been friends with in high school, and that was very strange for me. None of them understood addiction and its power, so they were all asking me questions about it. I am glad that I was there to answer them, to give them a little bit of insight into Melinda's life. Even though it was difficult, I knew that I was there for a reason. After I had spoken to them I started to drink more and more and before I knew it I was very drunk. Again I had chosen to drink to allow the alcohol to numb the feelings of pain that I had. Sadly enough, so had everybody else that was there. Everybody except Kylie, whose baby was due the following week. Kylie had to basically drag me to the car. It was a pity that I had allowed myself to get so drunk, even though I later justified it as having been my way of saying good-bye to my friend, Melinda. I knew that wasn't true, because I had already said my good-byes in my letter to her and in my prayers for her.

It was after that day that I decided that I definitely needed to cut back on my alcohol intake. Jason and I had started to do more physically than just kissing, often after we had both had a couple of drinks. Deep down I believed that my relationship with him was too important to waste it away on alcohol, and perhaps destroy it.

When Jason and I did start sleeping together it was a really big deal for both of us. We both knew that it wasn't the right thing in God's eyes, but for some foolish reason we chose to do it anyway. Our self-control was lacking at the time and we both chose to run with our emotions, instead of being led by the Spirit. The weakness of our flesh got the better of us. We were being outright disobedient and it was wrong. Deep down I felt very ashamed of what I was doing with Jason. After all that God had bought me through I was still blatantly disobeying Him and His word. I knew that there would be consequences for our sin – I just had no comprehension of what they would be.

Chapter 19

Gifts From God

Jason continued in his struggle with drugs and I realised that it wasn't my love, or anything else that I could do, that was going to change that; only the Lord could change it. I prayed for him daily, as often as I thought to do it. I know now that those prayers may have played a part of the role in saving his life. As I am now aware of, there had been a couple of circumstances where he had gone out and used heroin and then dropped (overdosed) and had to be bought back around. All the while he knew that God loved him and he knew that he had a big calling on his life; but he couldn't get past his desire for heroin, the very drug that had almost destroyed my life. It was difficult for me to really understand how he couldn't stop, but at the time all that I could do was pray for him; and I did.

One night he came home, after not having used for quite some time, and he was pinned. I got angry with him and we eventually went for a walk to the park. I had told Kylie to call me if she needed anything, she was over her due date and I wanted to be there for her. While we were at the park Jason and I were discussing the future. I explained to him that I thought God had bought us together for a reason and that we needed to honour Him in all that we did. I also told him that it was going to be difficult for me to continue having a relationship with him if he was going to continue to use drugs. After all, I knew from my own experience that an active drug user definitely couldn't be trusted. Just as he started speaking to me, and attempting to explain himself, my mobile phone rang. Kylie was in labour and had called a taxi to take her to the hospital. I told her that I was on my way straight back home to go with her.

When we arrived at the hospital Kylie told me that she would understand if I needed to wait in the waiting room. She knew that I had a very unhealthy fear of hospitals, for no reason that I knew of or understood. I told her that I wanted to be there for her, to encourage her and pray with her and that I would brave it and go inside with her. Once we actually got inside the delivery suite the whole reality of Harmony being there very soon was imminent. Kylie had been praying that God would chose to bless her with her baby daughter on her one-year-clean anniversary, which was the 18th of November. It was currently just after 11 p.m. on the 17th, and her prayer seemed sure to be answered. She had always considered her baby to be a gift from God and she said that having Harmony to remind her of how far she had come, with the Lord's help, would be the most amazing blessing.

God answered her prayer and Harmony Mikayla was born a very healthy little girl just after 10 a.m. on Saturday the 18th of November. When I held her for the first time something incredible occurred on the inside of me. Here was this precious little girl, a gift straight from the heart of God. Because of Kylies love for the Lord she was going to have an amazing start to life, as opposed to life that she may have had if Kylie had have stayed on drugs. The entire experience was amazing. It felt so awesome to hold one of God's little miracle babies in my arms. I loved her from the moment I held her. The first time that I held her I told her how much Jesus loved her and that I looked forward to being able to share His love with her. Just having her in my arms gave me a sense of joy that I had never known before; I knew that the Lord was doing a work in my heart.

I guess that holding Harmony in my arms, and seeing the glory of God in her eyes, reminded me of the two previous pregnancies that I'd had; and what had happened with both of them. I knew that God had forgiven me for the abortion, but I saw then as the perfect time to receive the forgiveness that I already believed that I had. I knew it in my head, now I needed to know it in my heart as well. I had basically the same feeling with regards to the missed miscarriage that I had suffered. So while Kylie was in hospital I cried out to God to heal those old, open wounds that I had. I wanted that to happen then, so that I felt able to love Harmony in a whole and pure way.

Again, God answered me.

When they came home from the hospital I let Kylie know that I was there for her whenever she needed me. It was so awesome having a brand new baby in the house. Harmony was, and always will be, a very important little girl to me. When I held her I understood unconditional love. There was nothing that she did that I got angry about, or upset with; I just loved her. I was actually blown away by the way that I felt when I was around her; it felt very natural to me to have a baby in my arms, and in my care.

Having Harmony in the house softened all of our hearts in a new way. Sometimes Kylie and I would be in the kitchen and we would hear Jason talking to her, very softly and sweetly. Then we would pop our heads around the corner and he would be dancing around the room, holding her gently in his arms. Every time that I saw that, my heart would melt. I saw a whole new side of Jason that I had never seen before; a very soft and tender side. I saw that he would one day make a great father and I wondered if he would be the father of my children.

Exactly a week to the day that Harmony was born I was admitted to hospital myself. I was suffering from abdominal pain that had become unbearable. Jason and Kylie took me into the emergency department and after we had been there a short while they found a bed for me to lie on. I couldn't actually lie down without the pain increasing. After much internal debate I eventually agreed to have morphine to ease the pain, as my previous lifestyle choices caused me to be extra cautious; but the nurse explained that easing pain was actually what it was created for. I ended up staying there overnight, still with growing pain. In the morning they did some tests and discovered that I had appendicitis and that they needed to operate. I wasn't at all keen on hospitals and I could see why I had been so brave with Kylie the week before; I had been in training for needing to be there for myself.

I explained to Jason that I was scared of being operated on and that I wanted him to pray for me. I asked him to pray for strength for me and for God to watch over me during the operation. God answered his prayer in an amazing way. It turned out that the surgeon who operated on me was a Christian himself Jason discovered this when the surgeon came to check up on me and told us that he was on his way to church and had felt led to come by and make sure that I was okay. Then, just to bless me even more, my main nurse was also a Christian. She saw my bible next to my bed and we started to talk about it. I even discovered that her favourite bible book was the same as mine; Esther. God had been so good to me, showering His grace and mercy over me in my time of need.

Something else I discovered during my stay in the hospital was Jason's desire to care for me and nurture me. He was there every morning when I woke up and left at the end of the night when the nurses basically threw him out. He told me that it was very hard for him to see me in pain and in need, and that he wanted to be the human response to God's desire to fill that need. After the operation I could hardly walk, and Jason had to push me around in a wheelchair. He was very sweet to me and I saw an even deeper level of the tenderness that had been shown during his time with Harmony.

When I came home from hospital Jason and I went to stay at my parents place at Maroochydore for a few days. They had encouraged me to go there so that I could have a proper rest; and that was exactly what I did. It was awesome to spend time with them and to watch them getting to know Jason. They too had seen him at his best and at his worst and I know that they had concerns about our relationship because we both had addictions in our past. But that week they had the opportunity to see Jason in a new way. He did nothing but care for me, and I think they realised the seriousness of our relationship together.

I enjoyed spending time with my parents that week, as I had every time that I had seen them since I had stopped using drugs. My relationship with them was very different now; we all had a mutual understanding of the battle that I had gone through, and from that our respect and love for each other had grown to new levels. I had always loved them; that was something that I had never stopped doing, regardless of my circumstances. But now I had a new freedom in showing them that love and sharing myself with them. I loved just sitting and talking with them about whatever we decided to talk about. I especially loved sharing my love for Jesus with them. They always listened to me and they knew that without Jesus I definitely would not have been where I currently was. They saw me and they saw a walking, talking miracle; and that excited me.

While Jason and I were at my parents I had a phone call from Kylie telling me that the two guys that had been living there, Matt and Chris, had had a violent fight and that the police had been called. For the first time in a long time I had no desire to rush back and calm the waters; I just prayed and asked the Lord to watch over the house for me in my absence. My main, and only, concern was for Kylie and Harmony. But about an hour after the first phone call from her she called back to tell me that they had both decided to move out. I knew that that would be the best outcome for all of us, especially with Harmony in the house. I also knew that it would place an unnecessary financial burden on us, but I knew that we would manage. Kylie, Jason and I all got along very well together and I knew that that was one of the reasons that it would all work out.

Not long after we got back to Brisbane it was nearly time to head back up to my parents place for Christmas. I was really looking forward to sharing my Christmas with Jason. I knew that the message of Christmas was as important to him as it was to me and I also knew that there was going to be something very special about that Christmas. We went to see my parents for a few days before Christmas and, again, we had a really lovely time there with them. On Christmas Day we dropped Jason off so that he could spend the day with his family and I spent the day with my parents at Uncle Peter's house. For the first time I shared an understanding with him about the meaning of Christmas; it was Jesus Christ's birthday and that was why we chose to celebrate. When he made his speech before lunch, he mentioned Christ and the true meaning of Christmas; and I nearly cried. I had always loved Peter, he was my uncle, but on that day I felt as we grew closer as we shared a love for Jesus; and that was very special to me.

When I got back home that night I found Kylie sitting alone in the lounge room; she said that she had had a terrible day. She had always envisioned her first Christmas with her daughter as being the opportunity to spend it together with Michael as a family. But sadly, that dream had not come to pass, and she was very upset by it. I sat with her and we started to talk about Jesus and the true meaning of Christmas, and we ended up laughing together. It was a very special moment for our friendship and I am sure that the Holy Spirit was there with us in the room, pouring His anointing healing oil into Kylie's wounds. Because after that night she was never the same. From that moment on she seemed more at peace and content with accepting her life as it was; for the time being. She knew that she loved Michael and she believed that one day they would be together again.

Just after Christmas I decided that it was time to find a new church; one that I could call home. Ever since the girls had left the house I had stopped going to David's church and I really missed it. Not only that, I knew that I needed to go. I needed the teaching that I received there; and the fellowship I desired I knew I would only find in church. The only church that I really knew of in the area was called Citipointe Christian Outreach Centre. I had already been there a couple of times to hear guest speakers when I had still been in rehab. I knew that it was a big church, but I also knew that I could meet with God there. The couple of times that I had been I had received some awesome revelations, so it really was the place for me at the time. I did go and I don't remember what the pastor was preaching on, but I instantly felt comfortable and at home. I had needed exactly what I received there that night so from that moment on I decided to go there every week, and to call it my home church. Jason and Kylie came most weeks with me too. Even though it was a big church I instantly felt like a member. They had people to follow-up my visits, and when they called me to see if I needed any information about the church and to encourage me to continue on there I knew that I had found the right place to call my spiritual home.

Soon it was New Year's Eve. Kylie had been spending a lot of her time with Michael again and so we had all decided that we were going to buy a couple of bottles of alcohol and spend the night in the pool. We did that for the first part of the evening, but as the night drew on and we got quite drunk, Jason and I started fighting. I cannot remember how it started, as is the way with alcohol, but I know that we ended up yelling and screaming at one another; and not having a very nice welcome into the year 2001.

The next day I declared to the Lord that I was going to stop drinking alcohol all together. If the night before had done anything positive, that was it. I also declared into the spirit realm that I was going to have an awesome and amazing year with the Lord. I prayed that God would reveal to me any open wound that needed healing. He showed me that by drinking I had opened up my old addiction wound and the enemy had stepped right in there and pressed me to do things that with the Holy Spirit I should never have done; things such as sleep with Jason and lose my temper. I cried and cried. I believe that they were tears of healing, because from that moment on, God showed me the way back to right- standing with Him. The one and only way back to true right-standing with God was by me asking for forgiveness and repenting of my sin. Repentance is the decision to ask for forgiveness and then actually turn away from that sin. It is choosing to not do that sin any more. Again it had to be my choice. God never forces us to change but He challenges us to grow. I knew that there was no other way to please God – what I had been doing had grieved His heart and I needed to make things right with Him.

God knew that I had loved Him all along, but unfortunately I had again been led by my fleshly nature. I loved God but not in the 100% sold-out-to-Him way that He desired me to. After beginning again on the road to repentance He showed me a Scripture that I grabbed a hold of as one for the year 2001. It was Romans 8:27,28, which says: Now He who searches the hearts knows what the mind of the Spirit is, because He makes intercession for the saints according to the will of God. And we know that all things work together for good to those who love God, to those who are called according to His purpose. I chose to receive that Scripture as mine and in doing so I knew that God would help me to make it a reality. I knew that all things worked for good for those who loved God, but I had failed to properly understand the rest of the verse. I now knew, in my spirit, that regardless of what I had been doing in the natural, God knew my heart and that the Holy Spirit had been praying to Him on my behalf. Now here I was renewing my love and my heart for Him. I knew that I needed to seek only Him for my pleasure, nothing or no-one else; for He was the only true source of my joy and my salvation.

Jason and I had spoken about the events of New Year's Eve and agreed to cut out the alcohol and the sex. We both knew that our relationship could only get stronger by committing to holiness, so we both pressed into it together. At the time I wasn't sure how Jason really felt about me. He knew that I believed that I was falling in love with him. The relationship between us was definitely able to grow stronger once we followed through with the quest for holiness – together. Thankfully because our lives were about to again be shaken up.

In the third week of January I told Jason that my period was late, and that I actually felt as though I was probably pregnant. He told me that if I was he would stand with me and do the right and honourable thing by me, by God and our child. The day that I went to the doctor for my pregnancy test Jason had gone out of town to help his family. So I was alone in the doctor's office to get the results of the test. The doctor told me it had come back positive; that I was definitely pregnant. I just sat there, silent, unsure of how I felt or of what to say. I had known in my spirit, before I had even done the test and now it was real in the natural as well. She asked me what I was going to do and all that I could think to say was tell Jason and thank the Lord. She laughed; she had heard me talk that way before, because one of the things the doctors had told me when I had my appendix removed was that during the testing procedure they had found something wrong with my fallopian tubes and they thought I would have difficulty ever falling pregnant. Now, I needed to share my news with Jason.

I felt as though I ran home. I was so excited and eager to share my news with Jason – I knew that I loved him. I called him up and told him that I loved him and that I was definitely pregnant. Jason told me that he loved me too and that he looked forward to coming home to hold me and share in the joy with me. I went to my room and just started crying before God. I knew that we had done the wrong thing and sinned before God, and I knew that saddened God's heart. He wanted the best for His children. I understood that it had been wrong to have been having sex with Jason outside of marriage and I also understood that living in sin removes us from the real blessings that God has for us. I believed, and accepted, that falling pregnant was a consequence of our sin. However, I had decided to accept the situation with open arms. I cried before God. I was on my knees; desperate for the forgiveness that He had been so willing to give to me.

So when Jason got home he came to me and just held me. We sat together and cried, talked about being pregnant and shared our joy, our fears and our excitement. Neither of us was really sure that our relationship was ready for the next big step that we were about to take. But both of us knew, and believed, that we wanted to get right before God and that we wanted to accept our responsibilities together. We wanted God to take our failures and our mistakes and forgive us for our wrong doing. We knew that we had been living our way and now we wanted to again live God's way. We agreed that now was the best possible opportunity to get married and declare our love before God. We both would have run from commitment and the whole idea of settling down, but by me becoming pregnant God had shown us that He wanted us to be together. We knew that He had a very big plan for us together, and that marriage was the first step that we needed to take in order for everything to fall in line with the Spirit

The person that we chose to share our news with first was Kylie. After all that we had been through with her, and Harmony, it seemed obvious. When I told her she just smiled knowingly and told me that she thought something special was going on. She was so happy and excited for us and she told me that she knew that we would both be great parents, especially after all of the training that we had had with Harmony.

A couple of days after I found out that I was pregnant I decided to keep a journal of the experience – I wanted to bless my child by sharing with them all that I felt while they were in the womb. This was my very first journal entry to my unborn baby:

> *I don't quite know how to express the deep and intimate love that I already feel for you. Knowing that such a seed of pure joy has been planted to grow inside of my body is such an incredible blessing. You are so precious and loved by me, baby. I am so looking forward to this unforgettable time of growth in all of our lives. 21.01.01*

The next step that Jason and I had to take together was to tell our parents the big news. We wanted to tell them in person, so I knew that I would have to wait to tell mine. Jason called his mum and step-dad to invite them over. But he couldn't contain himself and ended up telling them on the phone. They came straight over to see us. When they walked into the house they both just hugged me and told me that they would be there for us, to support us and to love us through the whole experience. They let us know that, regardless of the circumstances, they were glad for us and excited at the prospect of being grandparents. It was a really special time for me. I was very glad to know that they were going to support us, and pray for us.

The next time that my parents came to visit was only a few days after that. I had spoken to mum on the phone and it had been very difficult for me to not tell her the news. But I knew that when I told them that I was going to need to hug them as well, and just have them hold me. That day we were moving house as we had found a smaller house that was perfect for us, now that we no longer had a house full of people. We were moving in with Kylie. She was now spending most of her time with Michael and Harmony; they were working hard at being a family together. My parents came down to see us and to lend a hand. Jason and I took them over to the new house so that they could see it. While we were there we waited until we were all in a room together and then told them that I was pregnant and that we were getting married. I don't remember their reactions; all I do remember is my dad reaching out to hold me, and my mum doing the same; they were excited. It was a very memorable time for me.

Chapter 20
New Beginnings

A few days after that Jason went out for the day with his mum, and when he got home he came and sat next to me. I had been having a bit of morning sickness and was resting as much as I could. He sat down and told me that he loved me and that he was very glad that I was going to be his wife, and the mother of his child. Then he gave me the most beautiful engagement ring that I had ever seen. It had two blue sapphires that were pear shaped, with two diamonds next to them. It was very different, and as someone who didn't wear jewellery I needed that. He placed it on my finger and it felt so perfect. The Lord was doing an amazing work in us and we were just so happy to be sharing in the experience together.

So I was going to be Jason's wife, and somebody's mother. The reality had not really sunken in, and every time I thought about it, which was nearly all the time, I was amazed at all that God had done in my life. As it was, I had only been clean off heroin for just over 18 months, and here I was living a totally new life. He had blessed me with His promise of making me a new creation and I had more than willingly accepted. It was a really special time between the Lord and myself. I couldn't stop thanking Him for the blessing and protection of the unborn baby, and for Jason being obedient to His word and asking me to be His wife. I spent entire days, sometimes, just worshipping Him; it was amazing time of breakthrough for me. I reached a new level of intimacy with my Creator, and it was magnificent. It was definitely a time in my relationship with Him that I will never forget, and I will always seek to do what I learned then; the most important thing for me to do everyday is to spend time with Him, just dwelling in His presence.

Just after we moved to the new house Jason started at Bible College. We were both going to go, but when I discovered that I was pregnant I decided that was my main priority at the time, and so I chose not to go. Jason was going to get closer to the Lord, but also to get some godly discipline in his life. He knew that the Lord had a big call on his life, and in order to prepare for that he was going to need to be more disciplined. And he was. He would go every morning and when he would get home he would tell me of all of the wonderful things that he was learning, and then he would do his homework. It was strange watching Jason being a student. I had always known him to love his spare time, and as it was he didn't have much of it, but which also meant that he wasn't able to have time to think about life before Bible College. He knew that he needed to continually work through his issues and together we prayed that his time at Bible College would enable him to do that. His character grew so much in such a short time. He became very determined to learn and grow while he was there, and it helped our relationship grow as well.

So while he was at college, growing in the Lord, I was at home doing the same thing. We would come together at the end of our days and discuss where we were at, and pray together. It was a time of reflection, and of gratitude; for all that the Lord was doing in our lives and all that He willed to do. It also helped to create a real sense of unity between us; we were growing stronger in our love for one another as we grew stronger as individuals with God. It was a real lesson for both of us; as long as we love God and each other, God will always work things out for our good. That was, and is, His promise to us.

I had decided to do the counselling course, at the church, on a part-time basis, as I knew that it was something that was important to me and my own personal growth. The classes were held on a Monday night at the college and I knew that without a car it could be difficult for me to get there. However, after a lot of prayer, someone was always able to pick me up and drop me home. The classes were awesome. I learned so much during the first module, not just about counselling, but about myself. Every week after class I would come home and Jason would sit up with me while I talked to him about all that I had learned. It was great for me to be so mentally stimulated. I had always loved being a student, but hadn't actually been one for many years; though my excitement for knowledge had obviously not disappeared. I craved to know more; more about what we were being taught and more about God.

Our prayer life together, at the time, was nothing short of wonderful. Every night we would come together and pray for each other, and for the life of our unborn baby. It was a really special time in our relationship and an awesome time of growth for both of us.

Just after I had started the counselling course we spoke to one of the pastors at our church and asked him to perform our marriage ceremony. So we were now officially on our way to being married. It was such a big step for both of us to take and one that, without the Lord behind us, I am sure neither of us would ever have made together. We decided to have pre-marriage counselling with a couple from the church who had a lot of wisdom and love to impart into our lives. We happily attended the sessions, and always left knowing more and questioning more about one another. We were able to learn so much about marriage and our roles as husband and wife from the counselling. The sessions with them helped me to get a proper grasp on all that God required of me as Jason's wife, invaluable knowledge that would always be relevant and vital. I will never forget the loving and honest manner in which our counsellors shared themselves; and I will remain grateful to them for all of my days.

I had asked Kylie to be my bridesmaid, and she had lovingly said yes. I only wanted one person to stand by me, and I wanted that person to fully understand all that being married to Jason meant to me; and Kylie was that exact person. She was so excited for me, and Jason, and she looked forward to the day almost as much as we did. Kylie had been such an incredible friend to me, she had stood by me when others wouldn't and she believed in me and the call on my life. She also believed that I would make a great wife for Jason and a wonderful mum to our baby. Her believing in me meant so much to me then, and it still does now.

The next step towards getting married was actually organising the wedding. We had set the date for the 24th of March, which was only a few weeks away. My parents had spoken to me and told me that they would pay for and provide anything that I needed. Jason and I had spoken about it and all we wanted was a very simple wedding;

more than anything we just wanted the opportunity to declare our love for one another before God and our close friends. We prayed about the wedding and the preparation for it and we knew that the Lord had it all under control.

Firstly, we spoke about having it in a park; and then Jason's Aunty Gem and Uncle Ray offered the use of their house. Their house is a magnificent place overlooking the river, and as soon as I saw it I knew that it was the perfect venue. Our next decision was, who we were going to invite? There were about 35 people that we really wanted to be there with us to celebrate our special day with us. These people had all impacted our lives in one way or another, and they were all very special to us for their individual reasons. So I found some beautiful invitations and sent them out to those people.

Our next decision was food; we decided to have a simple, but special, barbecue; so that everybody could be catered for. We wanted to have food that people could relax with, and be able to interact with other people while they ate. So that decision also was perfect. Then we had to decide on decorations. We had decided on navy blue, silver and gold as our theme colours and my mum set about organising all of the balloons and things. Jason's parents had offered to provide the drinks for the day. We had decided that we didn't want to have any alcohol, other than the toasting champagne, for obvious reasons. That was about all that we decided at the time. The rest, and the best, was yet to come.

Unfortunately, at around this time we had a scare with the pregnancy. One night I lost quite a large blood clot, and felt very weak and frightened. I called Jason in and he stood by me and told me not to be afraid. When I came out to the lounge room we prayed together, and it calmed me down slightly. But then something rose up inside of me and I opened up my bible and prayed for the Holy Spirit to reveal some life giving Scriptures to me. I needed the word of God to stand on, when in the natural I felt like crumbling in at the knees. I knew that the word of God was all that I needed; and Jason praying beside me that God would reveal Himself to me through His Word. It came almost immediately. A promise from the Lord that He was going to keep me and my family safe in His arms. The Scripture that we stood together and declared into the spirit realm was Exodus 23:25,26, which says: "So you shall serve the Lord your God, and He will bless your bread and your water. And I will take sickness away from the midst of you. No one shall suffer miscarriage or be barren in your land; I will fulfill the number of your days." At the time that I read it I started to cry; I felt a break in the spirit and I knew that my wound and my pain had been filled with the Holy Spirit of God. I continued to search the Scriptures; I knew that was the most important thing that I could do at that point in time. The next passage that I was led to was Psalm 139:5, You have hedged me behind and before, And laid Your hand upon me. As soon as I read that I knew that God, who loved me, was right there with me; loving and protecting me through my experience. I had such comfort inside of me just knowing that to be true. Then I discovered Jeremiah 1:5, which says: "Before I formed you in the womb I knew you, Before you were born I sanctified you." Again I started to cry. I knew that God was trying to reveal to me that He had created the baby that I was carrying, and He had created a destiny just for that child; and He was going to make it come to pass. I instantly knew then that the Lord had a very big call on this child's life, and I knew that I would see His plan for their life become a reality. It was a magnificent revelation for me, and one that I will never forget; and one that I continue to pray over that child's life.

I went to bed that night in absolute comfort knowing that God, the Creator of all things, had blessed us with an incredible gift with the life of this precious child. I will never forget the peace that He bestowed upon us that night. When we ran to Him He drew closer to us; closer than we could have ever imagined.

A couple of days after that I went to see my doctor to tell her what had happened. Jason came with me and we told her together. She sent me for an urgent ultrasound, even after I told her that everything was fine. She needed to see that it was fine, medically. It was a perfect description of the world; needing proof, needing to see the facts; as opposed to faith, believing in God. The one incredible blessing that we received from following her instructions was that we had the opportunity to see our baby on an ultrasound screen for the second time; but we also got to hear the baby's heartbeat for the first time. It was absolutely amazing. I felt so blessed, and so in awe of just how magnificent God is. When we heard it we just looked at each other in amazement – we could hear our special baby.

We knew that the enemy had been trying to use the entire incident to scare us and to try and tear us apart, but instead it bought us closer together; to one another and to God. We then stepped up our prayers for protection over the baby and the family and we reached a new level with our faith. It was incredible what God had done with our faith in Him through that experience. He had created a new and deep understanding of His love for us, and He had granted us the peace and comfort that we had desired.

Just after that Jason and I went to stay at my parents for the weekend. While we were there my parents asked me what else needed to be organised for the wedding. It was only then that I realised that it was only two weeks away and that I needed to get myself prepared. That weekend mum took me out and I selected a ring to give to Jason. It was beautiful; just plain gold with a small patterned band around the edge of it. I knew that he would love it, and I looked forward to the day that I would be placing it on his finger.

When we got back to Brisbane I decided to start thinking seriously about what else I needed to organise. A friend of Jason's mum offered to do our make up; so that was under control. I never wore make-up so I had no idea about what needed to be done, anyway. It was, again, one of the blessings that we received towards our preparation. Then the Monday before the wedding my mum came down for the day and we searched until we found the perfect outfit for me to wear. I had been believing God to show me the perfect thing for me and He did. We had been looking nearly all day and found nothing, and just as we were about to give up the search we found a small shop that we hadn't been into before. I saw some beautiful two piece outfits in the bridesmaid section and I knew that it was going to be the one for me. I tried on one in powder blue. It wasn't a colour that I would have chosen normally but when I tried it on, it was perfect. When I looked in the mirror at myself I felt like a princess, and I knew that was exactly the way the Lord wanted me to feel. I looked forward to walking down the stairs and seeing Jason see me. I knew that it was going to be perfect; God wanted nothing less for our special day.

That night Jason sat up until all hours writing. I had gone to bed early and so I had no idea what he was doing. But the Holy Spirit had inspired him to write some declarations that He desired for us to speak out to one another at the wedding; in front of Him and our loved ones. When I woke up the following morning and read them, I cried. They were the most beautiful words that I had ever read.

Jason told me that he had been inspired to translate, into his own words, from one of the Psalms in the Living Translation of the Bible. They were absolutely perfect, absolutely God.

Jason

May this marriage be a holy institution that stems from the heart of God.

Today God had given unto me a jewel for my crown, causing grace to be on my lips,

our union forever blessed by the Lord.

I shall always keep God's word at my side to protect you, also walking in honour and integrity daily.

May prosperity follow as I lead with truth, humbleness, and righteousness in our union, together accomplishing tremendous things in God's kingdom.

No strife formed against us shall ever prosper as I lead you with love and God's statutes.

I proclaim Christ Jesus is Lord over our house, having confidence that we will live righteous lives together.

I love righteousness and hate evil; therefore, Joy shall strengthen us in any adversity we face

And heavenly Peace shall accompany our union as we grow together with love.

You, my love, being a woman of honour at my side, bring God's favour to our union.

These words are my promise to you Bronwen.

Bronwen

Your instruction my Love, I shall listen, submit, and consent to; leaving behind all independence, so that you will always desire my beauty. As my husband, I will continually hold you in reverence,

I will be a noble and gracious wife, who brings honour to our name;

standing by you always.

Today, I say farewell to my father's house, as he brings me into your house.

I present myself to you as a virtuous wife, and with me I bring joy and gladness.

I will bear you children who will be royalty in God's kingdom.

Our name will be remembered in all generations, for it shall bring glory to God forever and ever.

These words are my promise to you Jason.

Every time that I read them I found myself crying. Never would I have thought that I would be getting married. Never would I have ever thought that I would speak words like those, especially to a male. Never would I have thought that I would have become a Christian. But I had given my heart to Jesus, and He had given a brand new life to me.

The day before the wedding my parents came down so that they could spend the day with me, and so we could finalise whatever was left to organise. My dad had made a booking at Rydges, a hotel near Southbank, but when we got there they had no record of a booking in his name; and they were booked out for the weekend. My mum flipped out a little bit, but I decided to just remain calm and prayed, under my breath, that the Lord would sort it all out for us. Not only did He sort it all out, we got upgraded at another hotel, for the same price, and they gave us a bottle of champagne for the inconvenience. When we got to the new hotel it was perfect. It overlooked the city and the Story Bridge. Our room had awesome views; again it was perfect, and God.

That night we went out for dinner and my parents kept telling me they couldn't believe how calm I was. I was so calm because everything just felt so right, so perfect; so God. I was really excited about my wedding day but I knew, deep down inside of me, that God was in control and that there was nothing for me to be concerned about. That was a real testimony to them about the peace of God; and He knew that.

When we got back to the hotel room and I went to hop into bed, my parents had left a card on my pillow with a small gift. The gift was a little angel, an angel of Love. My mum had always said to me for as long as I could remember, "angels on your pillow" whenever it was time to say goodnight. That was her special way to say goodnight, and I had always loved it. So the angel was her way of showing me that there was then, and would always be, angels on my pillow. When I opened it I started to cry. I think that at that moment it struck me just how special my parents were to me. They had loved me through some of life's toughest circumstances and now they were seeing me come through the other side in a way that they had never imagined possible. It was a very precious moment for me; and for them.

The next day, Saturday the 24th of March, was my wedding day. I couldn't believe how perfect the weather was; but I should have known that God wanted nothing less then the best for us; even after all that He had done for us already! When I woke up my parents were already awake and my mum started crying. She told me how proud she was and that she loved me more than words could say. Then my dad came out and gave me a huge hug and told me that he loved me and that he wanted only the best for me. It was a huge revelation for me; my earthly dad wanted exactly what my Heavenly Father wanted for me; the best for his daughter. It was a beautiful memory; waking up and having Mum and Dad there with me to share in the memory of my special day.

Then Kylie came to pick me up to take me to the beauty salon to have my hair and nails done. So when I said goodbye to my parents it was the last time that I would see them before being made-over as a bride. It was a very precious good-bye. At the salon the hairdresser asked me if I had thought about what I wanted and I told her that I trusted her to do whatever she felt to do. I ended up with an incredibly beautiful hairstyle. She had curled it and put little white pearl drops in it. It looked totally amazing. After I had finished there I walked around the corner to our house to have my make-up done. She was finished within half and hour and after she had gone Kylie and I sat there in awe of the fact that it was my wedding day; I was getting married. Not only was I getting married, but I was getting married to Jason; the man that the Lord had chosen for me. It was an incredible feeling.

Then we went back to the hotel to get ready and my parents arrived soon after us. Both of my parents were in shock at how their little girl had become an amazing, beautiful bride-to-be. They couldn't believe just how beautiful I looked; and neither could I. But as with everything else, God wanted nothing less than perfect for me. When it was time to get dressed I went into the bathroom and prayed. I prayed that the Lord would shine through me on that day, and all days. I prayed thanksgiving for all that He had done in my life, and all that He had done in preparation for my wedding day. I prayed thanksgiving to Him for choosing Jason to be the man that I would grow old with. And then I thanked Him for saving me. When I had finished praying tears started to well up in my eyes and I knew then just how pleased He was with me. I knew that He loved me, in a deep and Fatherly way. I felt so blessed; it was amazing.

When I walked out of the bathroom my parents and Kylie were standing there, waiting expectantly. They couldn't believe that it was me. I knew that the light of the Lord was glowing out of every part of me, and I was so excited. My parents fought back tears. Their little girl had become a beautiful woman. All their years of love and hard work was standing right there before their eyes; and they were amazed. It was such a special moment for me to see them so happy and at peace.

Then we made our way over to the house on the river. The moment had come. I was only a short walk away from becoming Jason's wife; from becoming Mrs Bronwen Healy. Even when we arrived at the house and I received my flowers and people started taking photos, I was still calm. I had an incredible peace inside of me; a peace that can only come from the Lord. When I got out of the car my dad came to me and took my arm, then he told me that he loved me and that he thought I looked wonderfully beautiful. Then we started our walk through the house to the backyard. I had chosen the song 'Butterfly Kisses', by Bob Carlisle, as my wedding march. It is a beautiful song about a father's love for his daughter and handing her over to become somebody's wife. It was an incredibly touching song, and one that now will always hold very special memories for me.

When we got to the backyard I looked down, and all I saw was Jason. I didn't see the other people sitting there to witness our marriage – all I saw was him; and my heart melted. When my dad let go of my hand and Jason held it in his I felt an awesome sense of unity and love. The Scriptural foundation that we had chosen for pastor Tim to speak out over our marriage was Romans 15:5-7, which says: Now may the God of patience and comfort grant you to be like-minded toward one another, according to Christ Jesus, that you may with one mind and one mouth glorify the God and the Father of our Lord Jesus Christ. Therefore receive one another, just as Christ also received us, to the Glory of God. After those words had been spoken over our marriage we exchanged vows, and while we were doing so we were also squeezing each others hands very tightly; it was very sweet. Then we exchanged rings. It was so incredible looking down at my hand and watching Jason place the ring on my finger. I knew that the ring was a circle; an eternal, never ending circle like our love for each other, and it was just awesome. Then we spoke out our declarations to one another and I felt the presence of God rise up and hover over us; under the shadow of His wings we were. After "you may kiss the bride" (which lasted quite a while) we had decided to have communion. We wanted communion to be the first meal that we shared together as a married couple and we wanted to partake in the symbols of the blood and body of Jesus together as one. We had asked our parents to join us for that monumental time in our lives. We also had chosen to play a song about the beauty of the blood of Jesus – to show everything that we believed it had done in our lives; it was an incredible moment. After we had partaken of communion we signed the register, to the song 'One Hope'. It is a song about being one together, and that was our prayer. Then Stuart, Anne and Tim prayed for us and spoke words of love and life into our marriage. That was a very important time of the ceremony for us; sharing and receiving prayer as a married couple. Then we were presented as husband and wife, "Mr and Mrs Healy". It was an incredible feeling for me – I was Jason's wife! We had declared our love and our hopes for one another; and we were now husband and wife. All I could do was smile – a smile that spoke of Jesus' love; a smile that will remain forever.

It was then, and only then, that I turned around to see all of the special people that had come to share our wedding day with us and witness our marriage. They all came to us and hugged and congratulated us one by one. It was such a precious time for me. To see, and hold, all of the people that had helped to make my life what it was at that time. As I was greeting them I sensed the arms of God wrapped around me also; it was a hug from Him that I will never forget.

The day continued on into the night. Jason and I spent a lot of our time having photos taken, and then we spent the rest of the evening talking to people. I am glad that it was such an intimate wedding, because it gave all of the people there an opportunity to talk to one another while we were elsewhere. It also meant that we were able to talk to everyone there, if only for a short time. I wanted to personally thank each and every person for coming and sharing our awesome day with us. Just before dinner was to be served one of our friends from church, Tim, came up to us and told us that he had a word from God for us. Tim is gifted in prophecy and he wanted to share that with us, as his gift to us. We went upstairs with him and Jason and I sat down and held hands while he prayed over us. I held one hand on my stomach; I wanted the baby to receive the word as well. It was an awesome word about our ministry together, our calling and our family; but above all of that it was spoken out that that day, our wedding day, was a God-ordained day; that He had orchestrated the entire day just for us. When I opened my eyes and I saw my husband sitting next to me, I was so humbled before God. That He had chosen for us to be together and prepared the day for us; what an awesome God, and what amazing love He has for His people.

After dinner it was time for the speeches. Jason had asked for Ben to be the Master of Ceremonies and he spoke of how amazing it had been to watch Jason and I grow to love each other; it was very sweet. Then my dad spoke. He spoke of how he welcomed Jason into our family, and that he was grateful that I had chosen a man that would be able to look after me the way that a father wants his little girl to be looked after. Then he said that he was grateful, "to the man upstairs"(as he called God) for seeing me through the hard times, and for all that He had done for me. It was a lovely speech. It was good for me to hear him speak those words out in front of such special people. Then it was my mum's turn. That morning she had told me that she didn't want to say a speech, but I had told her that it would mean a lot to me if she could; so she did. She started to cry as soon as she spoke. She spoke about her love for me and how glad she was that I had found a man like Jason. Then she said what she had said at my one-year clean party – that she thanked God for me everyday; that she had asked Him for one miracle and He had given her so much more. It was absolutely beautiful. Then Jason's grandpa said a short speech about Jason growing up. Then he played a tune on his harmonica; it was a song that he had played to Jason as a child. He said that now that I was a part of the family, and a welcome addition at that, that I needed to hear his playing. It was so sweet. Then Jason's mum read a passage from the bible and shared about how glad she was to be a part of such a special day. Then Jason spoke and thanked everybody for coming, and thanked my parents for handing me over to him, and that he would always look after me. It was all very beautiful and very special.

The night passed by very quickly, and before we knew it we were saying goodbye to people. As it turned out, we were basically the last to leave as we had to hug everybody goodbye and thank them for being there with us. Just as we were about to get into the taxi to leave my brother called on my parents' mobile and I had the opportunity to speak to him. He told me that he was sorry that he couldn't be there with us, and that he loved me and wanted the best for me. I was really glad that we had been so late in leaving, I was so glad to have spoken to him; it had helped me to feel as though the day was complete.

That night Jason and I sat up quite late talking. We were sharing with one another for the first time as a married couple; and it was awesome. We talked about the day that we had shared together, about our future, our family and about the prophecy that we had received. It was a beautiful time of unity. Together as one. How awesome our God is to us.

The following morning we picked up our hire car and drove to the Sunshine Coast to a small bed and breakfast in Buderim. Jason's parents had blessed us with three nights there as our wedding gift. It was a lovely place and we thoroughly enjoyed being there together as husband and wife. Every night we would sit together and pray and talk about every possible thing that we could think of. Often we would get inspired to read from the bible. When we did that we would write down the Scriptures that we had been led to – we saw them as words for our marriage. We read a lot from the Psalms and there was a lot of love and healing between us over those few days. The Lord had chosen to use our honeymoon time together for His glory; and we were very willing vessels.

Chapter 21

Brand New Life

Once we got back to Brisbane, and reality, it became apparent to us that we were going to have to start thinking about somewhere else to live. After all, we were a married couple now, with a baby on the way and we needed our own space. While we contemplated our options and time passed by, my belly started growing at quite a rapid pace; and I absolutely loved it. I saw it as an incredible gift from God that He had chosen me to be somebody's mum, and that He was watching over the baby that was growing inside of me. The whole sensation was absolutely awesome. About a month after the wedding I was sitting in church one Sunday morning and during the worship time I felt the baby kick. It actually felt more like a gentle pressing on the inside of my tummy. At first I thought that it was my imagination, but it continued to happen throughout the day. I was so excited – it felt wonderful. It was only a week later that I was lying in bed one night, and just after we had prayed together I felt the baby moving again. I quickly grabbed Jason's hand and placed it on my tummy; he felt it too. It was so wonderful and so special. I was grateful that Jason was right there with me to share in the beauty and the wonder of all that was happening; to witness the miracle of the baby growing inside of me. I lay there for a long time that night, in absolute awe of all that God was doing inside of me; and I am sure that I fell asleep smiling.

It was around this time that Jason and I discussed me going for some counselling of my own. I still had a lot of issues to work through and we knew that we also needed to break off any spiritual bondage that may be on our baby's life, having been conceived in sin, and I just wanted to start afresh; spiritually and emotionally. I had spent a lot of time in prayer about the issue, but I knew that I needed to seek counsel as well; to really sort through the depths. Every time I went for a session I left feeling as though a huge weight had been lifted from my shoulders. We talked about so much. Allowing me to let Jesus into the situations, as Jason had encouraged me to do that day after our drive through Spring Hill. Because of my willingness I was being released and set free on a whole new level. God was using my time in counselling to show to me, and reveal to me on a deeper level, all of the unresolved issues in my life that needed to be dealt with. I was so glad that I was doing all of this hard work with Jason right by my side. Whenever I would come home from a session he would ask me all about what had happened, and we would often pray together. We always prayed the blood of Jesus over our lives, and our baby's life, because we knew that the enemy would not like the fact that I was being cleansed and set free on a whole new level.

It was at this time that I really started to recognise the deep, godly wisdom that Jason had been gifted with. He would see things in me that I would never have seen, and he would always be able to explain everything to me in a way that I could understand it. I realised then that the call on Jason's life was absolutely huge, and that the Lord had placed me by his side to love him through to his destiny in Christ. I felt honoured to have been chosen by God to love someone that was so precious to Him; just as Jason was chosen to stand by my side too. Our destiny together was going to be so special, and just as we had spoken out in our declarations to one another at our wedding, we were going to do great things for God's kingdom. The future seemed so exciting to me at that time; and does to this very day. I knew that we had a long way to go, but it was going to be a journey that would grow us up into who God had chosen for each of us to be; and that seemed so awesome to me.

At this time we also started to attend classes on a Sunday after the church service that were about forming your life around God, people and the church. I really enjoyed learning more about Christianity and relationships, especially now that I had been a Christian for a little while. I just loved being a student and learning whatever I could. The classes were set up to help people understand the church, their giftings and their destiny. During the third section of the classes we had to fill out questionaries to discover our spiritual giftings. Not surprisingly, my key ones were counselling, teaching, prophecy and mercy. When I saw what they were I got really excited. I knew that God was already leading and teaching me in the way that I should go. I got excited because I saw then that He was walking the path before me, and all that He needed me to do was follow Him. I saw that as such an honour.

At the end of the third series of classes we were all taken aside and prayed over and prophesied to. Because Jason and I were doing the classes together and we were now married, we were kept together, thankfully. When the two ladies started to prophecy over us, the baby started kicking sharply (not painfully) and I thought that the baby was jumping for joy at the word from God. The word included confirmation about where we were at – learning and studying the word of God, and went on to also confirm where we were going; to teach and preach. The word also confirmed for me something that God had placed on my heart quite a while before that; that He had chosen to bless me with the gift of healing. Not just physical healing, but the healing of wounded hearts and emotions. It was definitely a word in season for me. I knew that God was going to use that gift to speak to people in need, and it was at this time that He first gave me the idea for a book. Now here He is bringing the vision to pass, right before your very eyes. What an awesome God.

At that time, Jason and I didn't really have very many friends, other than people that we had met through rehab. It didn't bother us, because we were both so busy with God and preparing for the baby but every now and then we would crave other people's input into our lives. Jason had made friends with a lot of people through Bible College and, thankfully, some of them started to come over to our place for meals. I always really enjoyed meeting them; they were all such interesting people. One night the girl who gave Jason lifts most mornings came around for dinner. Her name was Ellie. As soon as I met her I could sense her tender heart; a heart soft for people and the Lord. She was so open and honest with us and I had a wonderful time sharing with her that night. She and I very quickly became friends; we both just needed real people in our lives – people that weren't afraid to speak the truth in love, and people that we could count on to encourage us to grow with God. For me, at that time, that was Ellie.

Another young couple came around for dinner the following week and they, too, struck me as very genuine people, people that I knew would become friends to me and to us. I knew that they were special and different when I told them a short version of my testimony and they never flinched. They never judged me; they both just sat there and praised God for all that he had done in my life. They were amazed at the enormity of what He had done in me, and all that He willed to do. I knew immediately that Becky and Aaron would become people that I could trust to speak the truth to me, and love and encourage me through to a deeper relationship with God.

These three people all played music for God, and for His people. They all loved to worship Him. And so much of my life was spent in worship to Him. I knew then that God had placed them into my life for a reason and a purpose. One of the very special things about my friendships with these people is that I trust them to touch my spirit, to speak to my spirit; and that is exactly what their music does for me. I will always be so grateful to God that He chose to bless me with such wonderful people to become my very special friends.

Not long after that we decided to start really looking for somewhere else to live. Kylie was spending all of her time with Michael and we both just felt as though it was time to move on. Jason drove past a block of townhouses everyday on the way to college; they were literally just around the corner from the church. When I called up they told me that the rent was going to be $35 a week more than the house that we were already in, and there would only be Jason and I making the payments. So together we prayed that if it was God's will He provide a way to make it happen. Thankfully Jason had just accepted a casual job driving buses at the church school, it wasn't a lot of money but it would certainly cover our living expense increases. So within the next 48 hours we were released from our current lease, our application was accepted, we paid two weeks rent in advance and we told Kylie what we were doing; all of which we had thought would be nearly impossible.

So the following weekend we moved into a beautiful and modern three-bedroom townhouse that also happened to be a short walk to church, which was awesome because we didn't have a car at the time. Everything that we needed for the new place we either had, or God provided for us, especially by people giving things to us. It was amazing just watching the blessing that we received when we moved in there;

He was blessing us over and above what we needed. Jason and I are both firm believers of passing on the blessing, so of course, anything that we didn't need we gave to the opportunity shop at the church, knowing that God would bless us and provide for us.

The same weekend that we moved house we were also both doing a deliverance seminar through the church. It was being held by an awesome couple who I had never met before, but they both knew Jason from the times when he had needed deliverance. The whole seminar was absolutely awesome. I learned so much about a whole new realm of the spirit; a realm that I knew God was going to use me in. Those three days, and nights, of classes helped to set me free on a deeper level. I found myself praying through things as they were being taught; as God would reveal to me what needed to be broken off my life, and the life of our baby. It was absolutely amazing what God did in my life over that time. I am sure that it changed my life. On the final day we had a group deliverance session. During the session, an evil spirit got a hold of Jason and tried to take control of him, and the session; but wise counsellors that were in the room praying at the time carried him from the room and prayed for him elsewhere. But at that time I felt a stabbing in my stomach and tears streamed down my face. God used that opportunity to show me that Jason and I truly were one flesh; and at that moment I was experiencing his pain. But that also meant that a short while later I was also able to experience his freedom. For me, during that session I was released and delivered from spirits that I didn't even know existed, especially not in my life. It was absolutely phenomenal what God did in me during the time that I was there. It is definitely a time in my life with God that I will always remember as feeling truly free. God loved me so much that He led me to the seminar so that He could set me free, free to the deepest level that I had known.

The following day I lost some blood and instead of panicking I prayed. I asked God to reveal what was happening to me. I knew from the previous scare that I'd had that God was not going to let anything trouble my baby, or me. I felt led to ring the Christian lady who is also a midwife. I told her what was happening and she told me to place my hand on my stomach and then she prayed for me. I felt instantly better. She also encouraged me to get Jason to pray with me; for a hedge of protection to be around us and the baby. She told me to pray in tongues over the baby, and to plead the blood of Jesus into every single open space that was created in my spirit the previous day. As soon as I had done that I felt relief inside of me; I had no more bleeding after that and I felt so content, so at peace and so in love with the Lord.

It was at this time that I started to really pray for some more female friends. I was believing that God would place the right people in my life at the right time, just as He had always done. I knew that I needed more input from other females; people that I trusted to speak into my life. When the baby was born that I wanted to have some women that were already mothers in my life. I knew that I would just have to keep praying and that God would direct my steps in His timing. I knew that I could definitely trust Him.

Not long after that, Jason and I were at the shops one day when we saw Mark and Jane there. Mark was my ex-boyfriend and Jane was an old counselling client of mine. They had gotten together not long after Mark and I had broken up; and she too was pregnant. I knew that it was God that pointed them out to us that day, for a purpose. Jane and I were at about the same stage of pregnancy, and we quickly became friends again. We would talk on the phone about where we were at and how we were feeling. It was awesome that I had someone that I knew, and cared for, to share in the whole experience. We talked as often as we could, just sharing our joy. It was so God. Mark and I had cleared the air about the break-up, and I was glad to have him in my life again; he had always tried to be a good friend to me. So Jason and I saw them whenever we could, and we all shared in the experience of pregnancy together. God had blessed us with friends who understood us; past, present and future – what an awesome God! Jane and I would joke about being pregnant at the same time and so close together; we even joked that we would probably end up in the hospital together – which would be God's sense of humour shining through. We would just have to wait and see.

I absolutely loved being pregnant, and even when I got bigger and sometimes uncomfortable God still showed me that I needed to count it all joy. He had blessed me with the amazing gift of a new life and I knew that He would keep me close to Him through it all. I prayed as often as I could for the baby and for our family. God always let me know that He was there with me. It was a wonderful time of growth in my life; physically, emotionally and spiritually. I knew that God was building me up into motherhood. He was using my relationship with Jason to teach me to be patient and kind, and always loving. It was sometimes a struggle to be all of those things, but the struggles only drew me closer to God. It was magnificent what He did in me over the final stages of my pregnancy. He was training me to step into my destiny as a mother. It has been spoken over my life a number of times that I will be a mother to many, in the spirit, and God was using my first pregnancy to train me up in the way that I should go – and I was a very eager student.

I had decided to defer from the second half of my counselling course to complete it the following year. I just knew that being at home and preparing for the baby was where God wanted me to be at that point in time. Jason had also decided to defer from his studies as he believed that he needed to be at home to prepare for fatherhood, and to develop further as a husband before the baby arrived. I didn't necessarily agree with him because I had seen the incredible growth in him during his time at college, but the final decision was his. So we were both at home together all of the time. I really did enjoy having him around and we talked all the time about marriage, parenthood and God. We were both looking forward to our baby arriving and turning our marriage into a family; and it was getting closer with every passing day.

It got to the point where instead of counting down the months until the baby was due, I was counting the weeks; and I was so excited. I had never expected to be alive myself, let alone have God bless me with a life to give birth to as well. It was a firm declaration of the blessing of God over my life, that He loved me so much that He would choose to give me the desires of my heart; a husband and a child, and a brand new life. It was at that time that I came into a whole new realisation of just how powerful my precious Lord was in my life, and just how much I loved Him. I felt so honoured to be chosen by Him to be the mother of this baby – a baby that I loved so much; a breathing and growing miracle inside of me. I couldn't describe the love that I felt then; for God, for Jason and for our precious baby. A love beyond human words.

A couple of months before that Becky had asked me if I was having a baby shower. I told her that I hadn't really thought about it and she told me that she would organise one for me. I suppose that I just thought that a baby shower was the pregnant lady getting together with her friends and people giving gifts for the baby, and at the time

I didn't really have that many friends. But God used that as an opportunity to show me that it wasn't the number of friends that He had blessed me with that mattered, but that I needed to look deeper into the hearts of those I did have. It was quality not quantity. The people that I did invite were people that were very special to me, and it turned out to be a very intimate gathering; much like our wedding and that was how I liked it. All together there were 8 women, including my mum. I had a fantastic day. I was special to all of the people there and they were all there to celebrate the life that was growing inside of me; and I felt so blessed by their company. The baby got a lot of gifts – lots of toys and teddies and bath stuff. The provision for our baby had been nothing short of phenomenal. I had written out a list of everything that I believed that we needed and God had provided everything through the people in my life. I basically just watched the blessings pour into the nursery. Everything on my list was provided for, and much more; and I could do nothing but thank the people and God for it all. It was truly amazing.

I knew then that our baby was going to be blessed over and abundantly, just as God had promised in His word; not just in the natural, but in the spiritual as well. I prayed that the baby I was carrying would serve God all of its days. Every time that I played praise and worship it felt as though the baby was dancing, even though I couldn't tell what was arms and what was legs. I had always played praise and worship music as often as possible, but even more so once I found out that I was pregnant. I knew the importance of praise in God's eyes, and I wanted to do nothing but praise Him for the gift of our baby; and the baby obviously loved it!

Very soon my counting down the weeks turned into counting down the days. I had had my labour bag packed for weeks it seemed; as I am sure most first-time mothers do! Wanting to do everything that the magazines and books tell you to do, because you yourself have no real idea of what to expect. My excitement turned into anticipation as it really sunk in that I was very soon no longer going to be a pregnant woman; but I was going to be somebody's mother. I was very eager to finally meet this little person, just to see them face to face. I longed to hold them and to love them. I knew that the time was drawing very near for me, and I could do nothing but pray for it all to be in God's perfect timing.

My due date was Saturday the 22nd of September, but I had a

feeling that it was going to be before that. On the Wednesday before that date I felt quite strange for most of the day. At the time I just thought that it was nerves or perhaps just reality setting in; and so I prayed. I loved the fact that God had given me the gift of prayer; a time when I could just pour out my heart and He would lovingly take heed to my needs and my desires. I asked Him to reveal to me why I was feeling so strange, and He did. At four thirty the next morning my waters broke.

The time that Jason and I had been reading about and preparing for was dawning on us; and all we could do was wait. Even after all of the things that I had read about waters breaking and people going into labour, I still felt totally unprepared; but Jason kept me very calm, regardless of how he was feeling himself. After all, he was very soon going to be somebody's dad. Even though he didn't have to endure the actual childbirth himself, to me he was as much a part of the birth as I was. So we just sat around at home and he encouraged me to have a shower to try and ease some of the pain. It worked – for a little while. I didn't know if the pain that I was experiencing was actual contractions or not so I decided to ring the hospital. I described how I was feeling to the lady and she very calmly told me that I was definitely in the first stages of labour, but that the best thing for me to do was stay at home and try to relax. I attempted to relax, but it got more difficult when I realised that Jason was going to need to leave to go to work. As he was driving buses for the church school, and he couldn't just not show up. So just before he left I called Kylie and asked her if she would mind coming over and she said that she would love to. I already knew what a wonderful friend she was, but it was confirmed then when she came to sit with me at 6:30 in the morning!

While I was waiting for Kylie to get there I decided to ring my mum. I knew that she would definitely not be awake, but I had a real desire to share my experience with her. She groggily answered the phone and said that she knew that it would be me. I told her what was happening and she told me to keep in touch with her and that they would come down later in the day. Even though she was very tired I could hear absolute excitement in her voice. After all, she was about to become someone's nana and dad would be their poppy. I am sure they would never have expected to be grandparents; how amazing God is to me, and to them. Then I called Rhonda to let her know what was happening as well and I told her that I would keep her informed as well. When Kylie got there I had just stepped out of the shower, again. She couldn't believe how calm and relaxed I was. I was glad for her to say that she thought that I was, because I didn't feel very calm. Even though I had prayed for God's comfort, I felt as though I was struggling to receive it.

The strange pain continued off and on and when Jason got home he encouraged me to call the hospital back to tell them. When I did they told me to come in for an examination, and to bring my labour bag with me as they didn't think that I would be going back home before having the baby. Jason quickly called my mum and his to tell them what was happening; they were both so excited. Kylie drove us to the hospital, and every little bump in the road felt like a mountain! There was so much going on inside of me, and all I could do was pray for the peace of God to be over the baby's life, and mine. Once we got to the hospital they placed me in a delivery suite as they suspected that I was in labour. I certainly felt as though I was, or so I thought. A few hours later the doctor decided that he would send me to a normal suite as things seemed to have slowed down a bit. I didn't mind, I just wanted to understand what was happening. Jason and I kept praying in tongues, asking God to keep us in His peace. I couldn't believe how calm Jason was. Even though this characteristic was one of the things that attracted me to him originally; now I loved it, and him, more than ever.

At one stage in the afternoon after I had well and truly lost track of time, Jason and I went down to the cafeteria for some food. Not long after we had sat down (well, I kept standing up, and then sitting down, then standing up again-I couldn't get comfortable!) my mum and dad walked in. I was so glad to see them; it was a joy beyond words. They had shared in the hard times of my life, now I wanted them to share in the good times as well. A short while after that we went out to the front of the building so that Jason could call his mum. While we were out there we saw Mark and Jane. I couldn't believe it; it just seemed so surreal. She and I had joked about being in hospital together, and here we were; Jane overdue, and me not quite due! I had spoken to her the day before and she had told me that they were going to induce her, and I jokingly had said that I would see her there; God obviously knew all along. So after we all stopped freaking out about what was happening they left and said that they would be back when her labour kicked in. I told her that

I would see her very soon.

By this stage it was late afternoon. Jason had been keeping me calm all day, but when intense contractions started up there was not much calm left inside of me. I knew that people had told me to pray in tongues when that happened, but I actually felt as though I couldn't; so I asked Jason to do it for me. The nurse took me back over to the delivery suites at some stage; by then I had well and truly lost track of time. All I did know was that the baby was definitely on its way towards coming out! Mum and dad had come back and they were in the waiting area; being very excited and very patient. At one stage Jason went out there to tell them where I was at, when the midwife told him that it would definitely be quite a few hours away. When he came back in he was laughing. I was in no laughing mood and I demanded that he tell me what he was laughing at. After all, here I was feeling as though I was about to explode, or give birth to a watermelon; whichever happened first! He told me that my parents had seen Mark and Jane come back in, and that she was in labour too. Not long after that I heard her, screaming and calling out to Mark; she was in the room next door. That was definitely God's sense of humour shining through, just as we had joked that it would.

At around that time, whatever time that would be, I started telling Jason that all I wanted was praise and worship music. Unfortunately, the only thing that I had forgotten to do was pack my music. Fortunately, though, the midwife had borrowed a radio out of one of the other rooms and we had it on the Christian station. At exactly 10p.m God answered my cry when late night praise and worship came on the radio. I was sure that it was one of the few things that would have calmed me down at the time. I had become quite worked up by this stage; after all, it had now been 18 hours since my waters had broken and I was quite tired. I have always been known to become quite short with people and grumpy whenever I get tired, so imagine me tired and in labour! Every time that Jason would help me onto the bed I would tell him that I needed to go to the toilet again, and every time I would get to the toilet I would tell him that I wanted to lie down. And all the while he remained very calm and very patient with me and it was then that I realised one of the reasons that God had chosen him to be my husband, and the father of our children, was that together we made a wonderful team. Just after the worship finished the nurse asked me if I wanted anything to help me with the pain. Because of my past, I had put off taking anything. But Jason very quickly pointed out to me that that was exactly what painkillers were for, killing pain! He also told me that he thought it might be good idea, just to take the anxiety away. Before he said that I hadn't realised just how worked up I had become. So I agreed and was glad that I did. The pain definitely wasn't killed, but it was eased. I was able to sit down for more than 10 seconds at a time; much to Jason's relief.

The next few hours passed by in what seemed like minutes. All I knew was that time seemed to have no meaning to me, other than the fact that I knew I was about to meet our precious little baby very soon. I don't really remember how it happened or when, but all of a sudden I felt a great urgency to push. The midwife kept telling me to wait as she didn't think that it was quite time, physically; but I couldn't help it. I knew inside of myself that God was the One in control, not any of us, and I knew that it was time to push. Jason stood right beside me holding my hand and encouraging me every moment. Regardless of all that I was going through it was a relief to look up and see him standing by my side. I knew that with him, and God, on my side that I was going to be okay.

I was more than okay when at exactly 3:30 a.m. on Thursday the 20th of September, 2001 the midwife passed me our little baby. As soon as I saw that the baby was a girl I said, "Mummy loves you baby Grace." I held Grace in my arms and just stared at her – smiling the biggest smile that I have ever smiled, I'm sure. I felt such intense love for her; a love that exists between a mother and a daughter. It was then that I truly understood the love that my mum has always had for me; an unbreakable love, an unconditional love, a phenomenal love. I kept staring at Grace, and at Jason. It was so awesome to think that God had gifted us with such a perfect and beautiful little girl. She had big eyes and a wad of dark hair, and an incredibly peaceful nature. She never cried when she was born; I am sure that she was as glad to be with us as we were to have her with us!

As I was holding Grace in my arms, I started to thank God for her; and for Jason. Having him with me and comforting me, reconfirmed in my spirit the deep love that I felt for him. He had been a real strength to me, both during the pregnancy and the birth, and it helped me to understand why the Lord had chosen him as my partner. He had showed such courage and wisdom in knowing how to treat me during such a tender and incredible experience. My love for him grew in a totally different way when I saw him hold our precious baby Grace for the first time. It was almost as though I could see his heart melting; his eyes said it all. All that he could do was stare at her and tell her that he loved her. It was such a special moment for me; to witness the love between father and daughter. I wept tears of absolute joy.

After the reality of all that he and I had accomplished together had started to sink in and we had done all that we could do in the delivery suite it was time to head over to the mothers ward, where I would stay for a couple of days. It felt so amazing to be walking down the corridor, one hand holding Jason's and the other hand pushing the crib that held Grace. Such an awesome gift – Grace Healy.

Just after we got to our bed and Jason picked Grace up to hold her close to him, Jane came in holding baby Joshua. It was a really emotional time for all of us as we sat there in awe of all that God had done in our lives. Jane had a smile on her face – one of absolute joy; and I knew how she felt. Her baby boy, Joshua, had been born at 2:19a.m. It amazed us that God had chosen for our babies to be born on the same day.

That morning Jason started phoning people to share with them our news. I sat on the bed holding Grace, and I just watched him talking. He was so proud, and so full of joy; it was beautiful to watch him. He called his parents and Rhonda said that she was going to come straight up to the hospital; I knew that she couldn't wait to hold her baby granddaughter in her arms. Then he called my parents. They were both so excited. They, too, were looking forward to coming to the hospital to meet Grace in person. I am sure that my mum would have cried; amazed at all that God had done in, and through, me. Then he called Kylie to let her know that Harmony's little playmate had been born and she too said that she would come up as soon as possible. I had written up a list of all of the people that I wanted to share the news with and Jason started to call them. He was just so excited; excited to be a dad and excited that he had such a precious baby girl to love and call his daughter. I will always remember the joy in his voice as he shared the news with everyone that he could; it was just so sweet.

That day passed by so quickly, as we had visitors coming and going for most of it. Rhonda held Grace and told her how special she was, and that God had an amazing destiny planned for her. My parents both held her and couldn't stop smiling at her; at how beautiful she was, and how perfect she was. My mum stopped holding her long enough to give me a big hug and tell me how proud she was of me, and then she started crying. It was very special for me to watch my parents holding my daughter; it was definitely a time that I will always hold very near to my heart.

When Kylie got there she smiled at me; a knowing smile at the joy that I so obviously had on my face. Harmony just kept staring at Grace, unsure of what she was – she must have thought that she was a little moving doll or something. It was very special for me to watch her with Grace; they were two very precious girls in my life and I looked forward to the time that they would play together.

People kept coming and going all day and all that I could really think about was just how incredible it was to be holding my baby in my arms, with my husband at my side. I spent the day in total awe of my Lord, thankful for all that He had done in my life and amazed at the depth of the blessing that He had given to us. After Jason left that night I lay on the bed just staring at Grace sound asleep in the crib next to me. I cried tears of joy and relief – she was so perfect, so beautiful, so God. I was crying because I was thinking about all that God had done in my life since I had given my heart to Jesus. It had been just over two years and God had taken the troubled life that I had given Him and given me a brand new life, a fresh start, a clean slate; it just made me so grateful to Him for all of the love that He had shown me, and all of the blessings that He had showered over me; I was in absolute awe. I fell asleep with my hand resting on her, just as I had done every night that I had been pregnant, only now she was here with us. She was, and is, a true testament to the love of God for His people.

Chapter 22

In His Hands

Once we had arrived home I couldn't believe how easily I had slipped into motherhood. It felt so natural to me, and I honestly couldn't remember life before Grace; neither could Jason. It was an absolute joy to have her there with us. She was such a peaceful baby, and still is to this day. I would say to Jason that she was a living testament to the power of prayer. I loved being a mother, I loved being her mother and I loved that Jason was her father. He was such a strength to me in those early days; always encouraging me to do whatever needed to be done for her, and doing whatever he could to make the transition that bit easier. Jason was a wonderfully understanding husband and a very loving and giving father; and is growing in amazing ways, to this very day.

One day someone asked us why we had chosen to call our baby girl Grace. It was easy for us to explain; she was an undeserved blessing and without God's grace in our lives, we wouldn't be there and, therefore, neither would she. It seemed like such a simple explanation, but that was it. She was a testament to the grace of God in our lives, and her own. The word grace means favour of God, undeserved blessing. That was what He had given to us, and what Grace was to us.

Not long after that we realised that we needed to decide on a second name for her, for her birth certificate. We had talked about it but just hadn't found the right one yet. One day Jason was looking through a naming book and came to me and told me that he had found the right one; Laura, which means virtuous one of beauty and wisdom. Immediately, we both knew that it was perfect for her, as we had always prayed those virtues over her life. So on that day she officially became Grace Laura Healy; our precious baby girl.

In our lounge room we had a coffee table that was piled high with all of the gifts that had been given to Grace. The blessings that she had received astounded me. Through other people, God had met every single need that we had for Grace, and more. Every time I walked passed that table it reminded me of just how awesome He was to us. That is still how I feel every time that I walk past her nursery, which is filled to the brim with everything that she needs, and loves. And that also is a testament to God; He gives us not only what we need, but also what we desire as well. That is one of the ways that God has used Grace in my life to reveal Himself to me on a deeper level. Through her He has shown me His blessing, His love, His grace and His mercy. After all that He brought me through, He chose to give her to me just because He could. That is a gift that I never forget to thank Him for, as often as I can.

While I had been in the hospital my brother Adam had called me to congratulate us on the birth of our beautiful baby girl. At the time Grace was only a few hours old and I was still very emotional and started crying. I suppose that it was the fact that my brother was calling me all the way from Thailand just to tell me how proud he was and how much he loved me. After all of the ups and downs that we had been through as siblings, we had finally reached a level of maturity and friendship that we could tell each other that we loved each other and really mean it. Anyhow, once we had been home for a few days he called again, and once again we had a really lovely conversation. He told me that he was a really proud uncle who had been telling all of his friends about his beautiful niece. It really touched my heart that he was telling me all of these things, as we had never really been very intimate with our words to one another. I knew that my relationship with him was another facet of my life that God had entered into with His healing touch. I have always loved my brother, but now I could tell him; and that is so special to me, and only something that God could have achieved in my life. Yet another reason to be thankful to Him; another blessing in my life. I look forward to the time that Adam can come back to Australia and meet Grace face to face. I know that he loves her now, but I also know how much she will melt his heart with her smile when they finally meet each other. I am praying for his safe return home, knowing that it will be in God's time, not mine.

One of the decisions that we had to make about Grace's future was when to have her dedicated at church to the Lord Jesus, and whether to ask anyone to be her godparents. We knew that we wanted to have her dedicated as soon as possible, as it was very important to us to publicly give her back to God; something that we had done in private just after she had been born. We understood that to have her dedicated was us giving back to God the life that He had blessed us with; for Him to lead her and guide her and to always love her. So we planned for it to be exactly two and a half weeks after she was born. I am sure that she would have to be one of the youngest babies that I have ever known to be dedicated, but to Jason and I it was very important that it was done so early. After we had decided when to have the ceremony, it was time to decide who we thought would make good godparents to her. We saw the role of godparents as being like spiritual mentors. As soon as we started discussing it, we both just looked at each other and said "Beck and Aaron". We knew that part of the role of a godparent is to assist the parents to raise the child spiritually and we both knew that the giftings on their life were very different to the gifts in our lives. We wanted Grace to see the full spectrum of the spiritual giftings, so they were our obvious choice. We invited them over to ask them and they looked at each other and said that they would be absolutely honoured. We already knew of their love for her, which had been obvious to us the first time we saw them with her. I was so glad that they had agreed to stand with us in raising her up into her God-given destiny; and so were they.

The day of the dedication ceremony we had invited Jason's family and my family to join us, so that there would be a lot of people there to witness Grace being prayed for and given back to Jesus. It was a beautiful service, and very memorable. We had asked for Beck and Aaron and another special couple to join us on the stage when Grace was being prayed for. They had all played integral roles in my life during my pregnancy and I believed that they would also all have a great affect on her life. Thankfully, they all agreed. Rhonda, Ian and David, Jason's brother, came up also, to offer their love, support and prayers. I had invited my parents up as well but they had decided that they would be more comfortable watching. I respected that decision.

When we were up there I remember looking over to where my parents were sitting and just thinking of how glad I was that they were there. Just as days like my baptism and my wedding had been very important to me, spiritually, so was this day. And there they were, loving and supporting me and my family. The prayer over her was very special, and I particularly remember the pastor praying for her to come into a very close relationship with Jesus from a young age. That was very important to me, because that was something that I had prayed for her from the time that she was in the womb. I looked forward to watching her grow up, but I especially looked forward to her growing up in the Lord. I am so thankful that I know Him, and can therefore offer her the best upbringing possible; and I am so thankful that He is willing to show me how!

My relationship with my parents had grown so much over the previous two years, but it grew in leaps and bounds after Grace's birth. I suppose that I had a new and deeper level of respect for them, now that I had an understanding of the relationship between a parent and a child. I spoke to my mum most nights, as she would always ring to find out how our day had been and to tell me, "angels on your pillow." I loved speaking to her, and hearing her and dad talk about their love for Grace. I saw a side to my dad that I had never seen so intensely before; a very tender heart. I had grown up knowing that he loved me, but watching him love my daughter was something that seemed even more special to me. It definitely bought out the best in him, and mum. Both of them just absolutely adored her; every move that she made they raved about, every look that she gave them spoke volumes of love to them. I have never really known my grandparents, on either side, and I am determined to always allow my parents, and Jason's parents, to build loving relationships with Grace and any other children that the Lord chooses to bless us with. It is very important to me that she grows up to know them as very special people; thankfully, it is just as important to them as well.

Jason and I spent the next couple of months growing as a married couple, and as a family. We spent a lot of our time just watching Grace; it seemed that just as she was growing and changing so were we. I was continually amazed at how well we both coped with parenthood; it just seemed very natural to both of us. I was then reminded of prophesies that we had had spoken over our lives – that we both had parent hearts and a desire to watch people growing, in the natural and the spiritual. Those words couldn't have been more true than how we were with Grace. She had always been a very advanced baby; for example, she held her head up the first time that I ever held her. Watching her was, and is, absolutely awesome. When I watch her I am always reminded of the verse of Scripture where Jesus blesses the little children. The verse is Mark 10:16, And He took them up in His arms, laid His hands on them, and blessed them. I knew that to be abundantly true of Grace. Not only was she a blessed child, but she also blessed anybody whose life she encountered. Everybody that came into her presence left blessed. It is a very special gift that she has, and one that I am sure the Lord will nurture with time, as will we as her parents.

Towards the end of November, when Grace was just over two months old, I was in the mothers' room at church one Sunday and a woman came in with her little boy and sat opposite me. Her little boy's name was Nathan, and he was only a few days older than Grace. We started talking about our babies and then I started to share my testimony with her. I had never before felt so strongly led to do so. After we had spoken for a short while I realised that we didn't know each other's names. She gladly told me that her name was Deanna. I knew that God had ordained our meeting but wasn't sure why. When I got up to leave I got all the way to the door and then turned around, sat down and wrote our details onto a piece of paper. When I got home I told Jason all about the woman that I had met in the mothers' room and that I knew that I would become friends with her. He told me that he had actually been to a few creative arts meetings at her place a couple of years before that. I knew that God was answering my prayers that I had been praying earnestly for months, and blessing me with female friends. I just had no idea to the extent He was going to bless me with them.

The following Sunday Deanna and I both ended up in the mothers' room again, and again, we started sharing stories with each other. I told her that I wasn't sure why I had given her my details the week before and she smiled; we both knew that God knew exactly why. After we had been talking for a while, I realised that I felt as though I had known her all of my life. I was sharing with her very openly and honestly, and I was normally slow to trust people; I knew that she was different. As we were talking she asked me what I did during the week and I explained to her that most of my time was spent just being Grace's mum and Jason's wife; which I thoroughly enjoyed. She told me that she went to a home group on Tuesdays where there were a lot of awesome women and also quite a few babies there. They were having a special Christmas get-together at her place that week and she asked me if I would like to go. I didn't think twice, I knew that God was urging me to go, to enable Him to answer my prayers. I explained to her that I didn't drive, and she happily offered to pick me up. Once again, when we got home I told Jason all about it. He was very excited for me as he knew my desire for more female friends. He encouraged me to go with an open mind and heart. I was very willing to receive what God was offering me.

That Tuesday I had one of the most wonderful days that I can remember. Deanna picked me up early and we went to her place to prepare for the party. Even being in her house I felt so comfortable, as though I was where I was meant to be at that point in time. Grace was comfortable as well, as there were other babies to play with. She didn't actually play with them yet, but she was more than willing to make an effort to interact. As the ladies arrived Deanna would introduce me to them. They all seemed very warm and welcoming; just as I had believed they would be. Over lunch everybody shared stories and laughter. I don't think that I can remember ever seeing a group of women having so much fun just being together. I knew that God had led me in the right direction; as He always did. After lunch everybody gathered in the lounge room to exchange gifts and to play some games. The group leader, a lady named Christine, offered me a gift and welcomed me to become a regular member of the group once it resumed the following year; and I immediately agreed. I knew that I didn't need to pray it through; after all, God had placed me there in the first place. After that she asked them to all gather around me to pray for me. Deanna led the prayer, which was full of love, warmth and friendship. After they had prayed for me I gave Deanna a big thank-you hug. I wanted to thank her for being in the right place at the right time for me, and for hearing God's plea to her to talk with me initially. She received the hug gladly and told me that she could feel the Lord's love flowing out of me. Afterwards, on the way home in the car, I told her that I knew that God had placed us in each other's lives for a very big purpose and she agreed; and we both laughed, amazed at just how awesome He is. It was a joy that

I will always remember. Because he loves me, I knew that God had gifted me with a friend that will always be very precious to me. What an absolutely awesome God!

I was really looking forward to sharing Christmas with Grace and Jason; our first Christmas as a family. I often thought about how it would be when Grace was a little bit older, when I would be able to explain to her what the real meaning of Christmas was. I was always so excited when I thought about sharing Jesus and His love with her. It made me feel as though having her in my life was such a big part of my calling; knowing that whatever knowledge of Him that I passed on to her would also help to build the foundations of her own ministry.

A few days before Christmas Jason went out one night for some time to himself. He had expressed anxiety to me about his desire to use drugs again. I knew that all that I could do was pray for him, and some days I would spend all of my spare time in prayer for him. God showed me during those times with Him that I could not protect Jason from himself; only God could do that. He told me that I needed to give control over to Him and trust that He would watch over him. Even with the peace that I had inside of me about knowing that God was with him, I still prayed as soon as he left the house and also while he was out. Every time I looked at Grace that night I thought about what Jason might be doing, and wondered how he could choose to do anything that might upset our family life and growth. However, he did, claiming that he just felt like doing something for himself. He called me just before midnight to tell me that he had played up and used drugs again. I was silent; I didn't want to say anything to him in case I said something that I would regret. I told him that I would talk to him when he got home. I fell asleep crying that night; I couldn't understand why or how he could have chosen to do what he had done. He had talked to me previously about knowing that he abused God's grace and now I felt as though he was abusing mine as well, and I knew that it was not right. It wasn't right in my eyes, or God's eyes. I felt so angry with him, because I just couldn't understand. I didn't know how someone could know God and His love for them, and still choose to sin against Him. I prayed then that God would instil in Jason a fear of God; the type of healthy fear that keeps His children on His path, and off the enemy's path. That was all that I could do.

The following morning when I got up to be with Grace I heard that Jason was home. He was on the computer doing something. We avoided contact for as long as we could that day. I still felt very angry with him and I didn't want to explode at him; so I continued to pray until I felt able to be calm. On the other hand, I think that Jason felt ashamed of what he had done and, therefore, didn't want to make contact with me. It seemed so ridiculous, I couldn't understand living in the same house and not talking; but that was what we did for most of the day. By dinner time we both realised that we had to talk, so after Grace had gone to bed for the night we sat down together and spoke. He asked for my forgiveness and I gave it to him. After all that God had forgiven me for, I couldn't not forgive my husband for what he had done. He told me that he was very sorry and that it wouldn't happen again. He asked me to understand, but that was the one thing that I couldn't do. God had removed me from the drug lifestyle because I desired for Him to do that. I wanted the same for Jason, even though I knew that he needed to want it for himself. We ended up having a big argument about how we both felt, and while I was screaming at him about how angry I was he told me that the only thing that we could do to resolve the issue was to sit down and pray together. It was definitely the last thing that I felt like doing; and that was how I knew that it was the right thing to do. God needed us to put Him first in both of our lives. God needed us to give the control back to Him. He needed us to love Him above loving ourselves; and we did. It was the most difficult prayer that I had ever spoken, but once I had started it became much easier to do. Through that prayer to the Lord I spoke love and life into my husband and our marriage; and so did he. It was very special and, regardless of the circumstances, we knew that God had taken us to a new level of intimacy with each other. I fell asleep that night totally exhausted, but holding my husband's hand; knowing that God was holding us in His.

A couple of days later it was Christmas Day. I was so excited when I heard Grace wake up. I couldn't wait to take her in my arms and tell her that today was Jesus' birthday. She smiled at me; whether she understood or not, I believed that her spirit was dancing. I still felt a little animosity towards Jason, but I had declared that I was not going to let his behaviour spoil my celebrations. We spent the morning at home as a family; enjoying each other and sharing our love with one another. It was very sweet. I knew that I was acting out of my spirit not my natural self when I told Jason that I loved him and that I was glad to be sharing our day together as a family. Even though I said it I didn't necessarily feel it, and he knew that, but he told me that he loved me too. It took me back to the days of rehab where I learned that I needed to live by what I believed not what I felt. I knew that was what I was going to have to do to make it through the current trial. I knew that with God I could do it; all I had to do was depend on Him to make the way for me, and He did.

That day we had planned for Jason's family and my parents to all go to Ray and Gem's house, where we had been married; that way everybody could share in Grace's first Christmas with her. It was a really lovely day and even though Grace didn't know what was going on, she did seem to understand that most of the special people in her life were all in the same room. Everywhere she looked there was someone to smile at her and tell her how wonderful she was; she had a great day. It was quite a hot day and she ended up falling asleep just before lunch and not waking up for about three hours. No matter how hard I tried to be polite to Jason I found myself reacting to a lot of what he was saying. Even though I knew that I needed to control myself that seemed difficult to do based on how I felt. I needed to ask God to help me – I knew that was the only way I would be able to do it. I didn't, and the day ended up being much more difficult for me because of it. My mum picked up on how I was feeling and told me to just be patient with him, and with myself; that all good things come to those who wait. I knew that, I just had to follow through with it. When we arrived home that night I asked Jason to sit and pray with me; after all, it was Jesus' birthday and we needed to stand together and give thanks for all that He had done for us. We did and I felt the presence of God surround us and cover us. I fell asleep in the presence of God that night and I experienced a peace that I never had before; a peace that can only come from Him.

We had decided to have a very quiet New Year's Eve at home, together as a family. We knew that Grace would go to bed early; she had been sleeping through the night since she was 7 weeks old, and so we sat together after she had gone to bed and just watched the fireworks on television. We laughed at how different our night was now; with God and without drugs. We sat together on the couch and prayed a prayer of thanksgiving for all that He had done in our lives that year. He had gifted us with each other, with being married, with having Grace; He had done many miracles in our lives, and for that all we could do was thank Him. It took me back to the promise from the year before, and showed me that He had kept His promise to me. That promise was founded on Romans 8:28, And we know that all things work together for good to those who love God, to those who are called according to his purpose. I knew that all that had taken place in my life that year worked out for good; I knew that the trials built my character and made me (and my marriage) stronger. All that I was able to do was sit in awe of Him and thank Him; thankfully, with my husband by my side.

The next couple of weeks were spent in anticipation of our first family holiday. We had made plans to go to Melbourne and we were very excited about the trip. Everything had fallen into place perfectly – the tickets, the accommodation – God had been with us every step of the way. Rhonda drove us to the airport when we were leaving. Jason and I had prayed that Grace would be fine on the plane, and she was more than fine. She spent her time feeding, sleeping or looking out the window with her daddy. I am still not sure who had the most fun, her or him. It was very sweet watching them together, and God revealed to me during that time that they both shared the same sense of adventure and it was something that I was going to have to encourage and help to cultivate as she grew up. I was glad for the revelation, as I always was. When we arrived in Melbourne Lynda (my brother's ex-wife) was there to pick us up. Regardless of all that she had been through with my brother, I would always love her like a sister. She was so excited to meet Grace in person and had organised everything that we would need for her during our stay, for which I was very grateful. We were all very glad to be there to begin our first holiday as a family.

That night I decided that I needed to call a few people to let them know that we were there. After all, I hadn't been to Melbourne for many years. I spoke to some of my relatives and they immediately made plans to come over the following night. They were so excited – they couldn't believe that I grown up so much and that I now had a family of my own, as they had both babysat me when I was young. I looked forward to seeing them. Then I knew that it was the right time to try and make contact with Rani, my very special friend. My mum had looked on the internet and found a number that we weren't sure was hers, but I felt to call it straight away. Rani answered the phone and she screamed down the line when she heard my voice; she couldn't believe that I was there, in person, after all that time. She asked me if I was there with my mum and I told her that I was actually there with my husband and my daughter. She thought that I was joking. After talking to her for quite awhile, we both realised that after everything that we had been through together we were still so close; as though we had just spoken the day before. I know that there are very few people that I will ever have such a relationship with; and I was glad that she would be one of them. I knew that God had made the way for us to reconcile, after I had treated her so badly in Brisbane on her visit to me a couple of years before. She told me that the number that I had called was an unlisted one, even though my mum had found it on the net, and that she normally never answers that phone but felt an urgency to do so when it rang that night. We both laughed and knew that our friendship had just made its way over yet another hurdle. I knew that only God could have done what had been done, and I knew that He would make an opportunity for me to share that with her. We made plans to see each other the following day. I was so excited at what God had in store for us while we were there.

The next morning my special friend Ellie came over to loan us her car. She was my friend from Brisbane who had moved to Melbourne for a few months, and had offered for us to use her car while we were there. That in itself was an incredible blessing, as we didn't have to use our money for a hire car. I was so glad to see her – I hadn't seen her for quite awhile and she, too, was excited to see us. She hadn't seen Grace for a long time and couldn't believe how much she had grown. We spent a lovely morning together with her then made our way to Rani's place. As soon as I got out of the car and hugged her I knew that it was a God-ordained appointment. I asked her for her forgiveness for the way that I had treated her and she gladly gave it to me. We spent the remainder of the day getting re-acquainted and she was also able to get to know Jason and Grace. All in all it was a very special, and memorable, afternoon. We spoke about our lives and she was glad that Christianity had had such a huge impact on my life. We spoke about our ups and our downs, and everything in between. It was an awesome time. When we left we agreed to all go to the Melbourne Zoo together on the weekend. I was looking forward to sharing in that experience with my family, and with Rani.

That night my relatives, Nance and Shirl, came around to meet Grace. Instantly they were amazed at just how incredible she was – they thought that she was beautiful. They were also glad for the opportunity to meet Jason and thought that he was lovely also! They couldn't believe what an absolute turnaround my life had been, in just two and a half years. I told them about how I had met Jesus, and how He had blessed me with a new life. They were glad for me; I could see it in their faces. I loved spending time with Nancy and Shirl; I felt as though I had just seen them the week before, even though I hadn't seen them for years. They loved me so much, and I them, and my time with them will always be very special to me. Thankfully, they happily accepted Jason and Grace into the big extended family, so it was a great time with them.

The rest of our time in Melbourne was mostly spent time catching up with people, so I had the opportunity to share my faith with them. Jesus was, and is, the only explanation that I can give to people when they ask me how I went from being a drug addict to a family woman. We also caught up with Ellie again, which was great. I was glad that she was such a special friend to me, that regardless of where we were or what we were doing I could be happy that I was simply sharing it with her. I know that God placed her in my life for a purpose, and I am excited about discovering what that is; in His time.

We spent a couple of days driving down the Great Ocean Road. It was something that I had always wanted to do, and so had Jason, so we decided to just go ahead and do it. It was an incredible adventure, and once we reached the 12 Apostles we knew that it had all been worth it. It was so special for me once we got there, taking photos of Jason and Grace looking out over the Apostles; creating memories of our first family adventure.

We were all so grateful to Lynda for having allowed us to stay in her home and for making us feel so welcome. She had also spent some quality time with Grace, which I was very glad for. All in all God had blessed us, over and abundantly; as usual.

When we did get home I sat back and thought about all that had been achieved during our holiday. God had made the way possible for us, and then opened up doors of opportunity to share our faith with people that I cared very deeply for. It showed me that when He goes before you, all things are possible (Matt 19:26). A lesson to always remember.

Chapter 23
Forever Altered

After we had settled back in at home I decided that I needed to sit down with God and write down my plans and purposes for 2002. After a lot of prayer and worship time with Him I wrote down five things God laid on my heart; I didn't understand all of them, but I wrote them down anyway. They were: write book/cell group/finish counselling course/daily devotions with Jason and strengthen personal prayer time. God had given me a peace in my heart when I wrote the list down, even though in the natural I didn't understand how it would all happen. I knew that all that I could do was to trust Him and know that He would guide me in the way that I should go; so long as I yielded to Him. So then I also knew that my major aim was to: trust God with all of my heart, knowing that everything else would come in His time.

The cell group started up when school went back and I was very glad to finally be a part of it. For the first few times that I went I knew that God had me there for a reason, but I wasn't sure what that was. So I started to ask Him, and He showed me that He had me there as a part of the Body of Christ; He showed me that He had me exactly where He needed me to be for that point in my life. He asked me to simply love people with the love that He had bestowed on me, and to show them the compassion He had shown to me. He later showed me that if I could be faithful to do those things, that He would raise me up to be faithful in other things. So I decided to be faithful in what He had called me to do for the time, and I loved it. It meant that I could hug people and tell them that I was thinking of them; and they would tell me that they felt better after it. I knew that because I was following God's instruction to me, that He was blessing those around me with my obedience.

I loved being in the home group, and having a focus for my Tuesdays. I always looked forward to spending the day with the girls, and Grace being able to spend time with the babies there. I had asked God for female friends and for an opportunity to minister His love to people, and He had given me both. I have a very special place in my heart for all of the women in the group and whenever I see them all together I can visualise the separate parts of the Body of Christ that they make up to form one being. Together, I know that the group will always reach great heights for God's kingdom. Each woman in the group has diverse gifts that nobody else offers. It always amazes me just how perfect God's plan for His people is; and I am thankful to be a part of it. Sharing with so many wonderful women, it is a very special place for me to be.

My friendship with Deanna grew strong in only a short period of time. God knew why then. She has shown me so much; how to be a strong and godly wife and mother, and how to be willing to step into the destiny that God has laid out for me. She had been such a source of love and inspiration for me with this book – she was the first person that I ever asked to read the book – as it was being written; and her words of wisdom and encouragement have had an enormous effect on me. She has helped me to push through the tough parts (as they were happening in the book) and to focus on the finish line. Her prayers have held me up when I felt as though God had given me too big a project, and her tears have helped me to push on to complete it. I will always thank God for answering my prayers with such a special friend. A friend who I know He has placed in my life for His purpose.

I had also struck up a friendship with one of the other women in the group, Viv. It started one day when I invited her over for a coffee. We spoke to one another about our love for God and how we had been saved. When I told her my story she cried tears of joy, for me and for all of the people whose lives she knew I was going to touch with my story. Within the first month of us spending time together I felt as though I had always known Viv. It has been a very special friendship to me; Viv has always been there when all I needed was a cuddle, or a word of encouragement, or just a good laugh.

At this point Citipointe started up 'Girls Church' – church specifically for women. At that first meeting I had been prayed for and it was spoken out that it was my time to step into the spotlight that God had turned on for me. In my prayer time I started to ask God for a deeper revelation of those words. He encouraged me to step out in my giftings and share my testimony with others. When I asked Him how to do that He told me to use what He had given me; and so I decided to write a book. At the time I didn't know what I was going to write about, or how I was going to do it with Grace here so all I could do was trust Him and know that He would enable me to achieve great things for His kingdom. Once I received the revelation about this book I started to wait on God; knowing that His timing was perfect.

Just before the second 'Girls' Church' I sat down at the computer one day and started to write this book. Before I started writing I prayed for the Holy Spirit to reveal to me everything that I needed to write. I also prayed that the Lord would inspire me to write down His words with my hands – that I would be a vessel through which could be shared the message of hope in Jesus Christ. Finally, I prayed that He would open the doors for me with the publishing and distributing of the book – that He would make a way where there seemingly was no way. I have continued to pray for those three things every day that I sit down to write, always knowing that He is walking before me and writing through me, and showing me all that I need to know. I have such an internal peace about this book, knowing that it is God's book – a book for His glory and His kingdom. I felt then very honoured and blessed to share my testimony with people in such an incredible way; for people to read of the transforming power of God's love, grace and forgiveness.

Just after I started writing the book I attended the second girls' church and Aureole (my midwife friend) introduced me to a friend of hers by saying, "This is Bronwen, she is a trophy of grace." With those three very precious words the Lord had spoken my book into reality. As I mentioned at the beginning of this book I knew immediately that the Lord had given me the title for this book. Two nights later He showed me a vision in my sleep; it was the cover of my book, including the title. When I woke up I knew that I had to ask Jason to design the cover of my book for me, at is was a gift that only he could give me. He agreed.

After that vision, and receiving the title, the writing of this book just started to happen. God was blessing me with the words to write. I knew that He was doing that for me because I had asked Him to, and that excited me immensely. It also was an opportunity for Him to again reveal to me the power of earnest prayer; the fact that you are holding it in your hands right now.

Writing this book, looking after Grace, and being a good wife to my husband took up nearly all of my time. The spare time that I did have was spent organising things for cell group on Tuesdays. Christine had asked me to prepare a few things over the months, such as communion, the teaching lesson and the worship time. I especially loved to do the worship time. I had always seen worship as the time for people to enter into and sense the presence of God. I knew that it was a big responsibility, but I believed that I was prepared for it. After a few weeks of doing whatever it was that Christine asked of me, she took me aside and asked me to assist her. Deanna was her co-leader, but she said that she also needed someone to call on at other times; a person to fill in the gaps of the meetings, if there were any. I was honoured to be asked, but I also knew that it would be an even bigger responsibility. God, and Jason, were happy to release me into it, knowing that it would be great training ground for my destiny. That is exactly how I have always viewed my time at cell group; as a training ground for me. I am so grateful that God chose such fresh, and anointed, soil for me to be planted in for the time being.

As I was writing and the book was growing, so was Grace. She gave my dad, her poppy, the greatest birthday gift when she started crawling on his birthday. She was exactly six months and one day old. She has also always been a very contented baby, happy so long as she is able to explore her surroundings. Sometimes I just sit and watch her and am totally amazed at just how precious she is to me. She affects everybody whose life she enters, which is a real answer to my prayers for her life. I know that God has her destiny laid out before her and I feel so honoured that He has chosen me to be her mother. I know that God is building Jason and I up to be strong parents based on both her, and our own, destiny. Everything about Grace is so awesome to me. She is the most treasured blessing that God has gifted me with, and I am very excited about teaching her His ways and watching her grow up in the Lord. Often I spend time dancing around the house with her, or singing to her, and she just laughs with me. She is such a joyous little girl; a little girl whom I love very much.

The day before my 27th birthday was the next 'Girls Church'. I had organised for some of my friends to join me after the service for some cake and coffee to celebrate my life. The speaker shared on friendship and what a gift it is. I was sitting next to Deanna and Arlene (my friend and prayer warrior), who had come to the service especially for me, and I knew how true that was. I felt so blessed to be surrounded by such awesome women of God, who were there to share their love and appreciation for me; on my special day.

It was the most wonderful birthday that I can ever remember having. The day started with big birthday hugs from Jason and Grace. It was my first birthday as a mum, and Jason made it very special for me. He had drawn a card for me and signed it from Grace and himself; it was very sweet. Then the phone started ringing – my parents, Jason's parents, friends – all with birthday greetings. Everybody in my life knew how important the day was to me, because when I had been a drug addict I had thought I would never make it to 27; but here I was turning 27 in an amazing way. Then Deanna and Christine came over to visit me. Deanna had been searching for a gift for me but had been unable to find the perfect one. Then she had asked the Lord to show her what He wanted me to have, and she obediently bought each thing on His list. Not only that, but He had given her a prophetic word for each gift. It was the most precious gift anybody could have given me that day. Each gift spoke straight into my spirit as she read out the word attached to it; it was totally God. Rhonda also came around with a gift and some flowers for me. Everything that anybody said to me, or gave me, just made me realise that God really wanted me to step into my womanhood. I knew that I was God's special girl, I was His princess – and He wanted me to live accordingly. He wanted me to truly live as the new creation that I was in Him – He wanted me to be set completely free, to be the whole woman that He had created me to be. I knew that he was using my special day to encourage me to step into that role; and a new level of my destiny.

The day continued on in much the same way, the phone rang and people came over; it was lovely and I felt so special. When Jason got home from work he told me that he was taking me out for dinner and that his mum was coming over to babysit Grace; so I needed to get ready straight away. When we left I asked him where we were going and he told to be patient and wait. We ended up driving to the water at Wellington Point. Once we were there he stopped the car and gave me a present from him. He had printed up his wedding declaration to me and written on the top of it that his renewed understanding of the words was his gift to me. It was perfect and it really touched my heart. Then he told me that he loved me and that he looked forward to sharing the rest of our lives together, with the Lord by our side. It was very sweet. Then we headed off for what I thought was our dinner date, but half way there he told me that he had forgotten his wallet and that we would need to go home and get it. When we got there he asked me to go inside and get it and when I got inside people came out of the spare room and shouted "Surprise!!." My precious husband had organised a surprise party for me; knowing how important the day was to me. I couldn't believe it. He had known all of the special people in my life and asked them to come and share the night with us. He is so wonderful to me.

The night was fantastic. Jason and Ian served us all, which I thought was very special. We all just spent the night talking and laughing and listening to worship music. I was glad that Jason knew me well enough to know who to invite. As my parents had been down the day before they didn't come, but I knew that they would have loved to have been there to meet all of my special friends. Halfway through the night Beck and Aaron came over; they were on their way home from Youth Church. They both gave me big hugs and then Beck told me that they were giving me a full registration ticket for the Women's Conference, '4Her', that was on at church the following week. I knew how special attending the conference was going to be for me so I thanked them immensely for their gift. The night ended with Jason and I sitting on our couch reaffirming our love to one another, we agreed to seek God in all of our ways and to love one another above all else; except God.

The following morning I was sitting in my room, just thanking God for the day that He had given me and He gave me a Scripture that spoke volumes to me. It was 1 John 4:4, *You are of God, little children, and have overcome them, because He who is in you is greater than he who is in the world.* With this word God showed me His deep and intimate love for me, by revealing to me that because He is with me I have overcome my past and all of the pain that went with it. I believed it in my heart, now I just needed to also receive it in my spirit – God was already planning that part for me. I felt so blessed by Him. It is such an awesome feeling to know that the Creator of all of creation loves you as His child; His very precious child.

He again showed this love to me in a way that I will never forget, the following week, at the '4Her' conference. I had prayed to receive an incredible blessing during that conference, and He gave it to me in a very profound way. On the very first night the guest speaker was a lady called Helen Burns. She spoke many words of wisdom that night but the words that she spoke that affected me immensely were; "God takes our mess and gives us a message." As soon as she had spoken them I knew that I received them deep down in my spirit. God had shared the same principle with me a few months before that and then inspired me to write this book; so I knew that the word was directly from Him to encourage me to push through to the finish line that He had already laid out for me. I know that nobody else had a message exactly like mine, and I believe that it is my God-given responsibility to write it down; to share with people everywhere.

The following morning Trish McDonald spoke and she too had words that were aimed directly at my spirit. Those words were, *"God only ever gives you a job that is too big for you so that you need to depend on Him to achieve it."* I knew that those words were directed at me with regards to this book. I knew that God had given me such a big project because He wanted to share in it with me. I knew that I needed Him to be with me, in every word that was written in order for His anointing to reach those who read it.

For the remainder of the morning Helen Burns spoke again. The words she spoke impacted me profoundly: "Make the enemy sorry that what ever happened, happened." I knew straight away that was what I was doing with this book. The enemy thought that he had me for good, that I would never find God in my mess; but God knew exactly where to meet me when I needed Him the most. In turn, He is making the promise of His word come to pass. The specific Scripture that He is revealing at the moment, through this book, is Genesis 50:20 which is: "But as for you, you meant evil against me; but God meant it for good, in order to bring it about as it is this day, to save many people alive." God gave me that promise at the beginning of this book, and now I understand it completely. Through me sharing my testimony, He is taking the years that the enemy stole from me and turning them around for good; for the good of His people – that includes you!

That night of '4 Her' Christine Caine spoke. The times that I have heard her speak I was always left feeling thoroughly blessed, and that night was no exception. Again I received a specific revelation. Of all of the awesome words that she spoke God chose just a few to speak directly to me. "Let your past give someone else a future." I knew that this book would speak words of life into the people that would read it. When I got home that night I told Jason what had happened. I told him that when I had received prayer that night the woman had said, "allow Heaven's destiny to collide with your hope, to let your future come to pass." I knew that was exactly what I was doing by writing this book, and I had a real peace inside me about that.

The following morning I had a real sense of expectancy when I entered the auditorium. I felt as though God had shared some really tender words with me so far, and any extra would be a wonderful bonus. (But I had no idea of the bonus that He had in store for me). Helen Burns was the speaker that morning and I thoroughly enjoyed her entire sermon, and I received a lot of revelation from her wisdom. Toward the end of her message she started to speak about sexual connections; that if there is shame and brokenness there then the enemy has control, and we must give that control back to God. As soon as she said it, I knew that was me. Even though I had done a lot of really tough work with God to be released from the way I had felt as a prostitute, I realised that since I had been married to Jason I wasn't totally free. I had been living in freedom, to an extent, and God had forgiven me and now it was time for me to receive it completely and choose to walk in it. I felt a stirring in my spirit to stand up, even though I knew that she hadn't called people to stand for prayer. I knew that there would have been a lot of people looking at me, but as far as I was concerned I was standing directly before the throne of God's grace. I don't remember what she prayed, but I felt a break in my spirit. I cried the most releasing and passionate tears that I had ever cried (similar to after my drive through Spring Hill) and I knew that my Father God was catching every one of them. I knew that I was being set free; delivered from the fragments of shame and the guilt that I had carried with me for such a long time – completely and finally. After the pain had subsided I sat down and Deanna and

Viv came and sat by me and held me close to them; just as the Father urged them to. I felt so loved, and so free. Just after that Helen came over and prayed for me – she spoke words of life and love into the broken and empty parts of my soul and she spoke out that today was the first day of total freedom for me, the wall inside of me had been totally smashed down. I knew then that I had received what the Lord had desired for me to receive. He had set me free and had totally cleansed me from all unrighteousness, and I had received it – deep down within.

The following day He gave me a vision to help me understand what had happened to me during the prayer for release. This is what He showed me:

There was a sea of mens faces and I was standing on the shore and between me and them was the blood of Jesus, flowing like a waterfall. I was crying and when I looked up Jesus was standing high up above me; His hands were dripping the blood for me. With Him was an army of angels, they looked golden. He reached down and picked me up and held me in His hands – and washed me with His precious blood. Then He wiped away my tears with the cloth of His robe. He placed me back down and I knew that I would never be the same, I had been touched by the Holy Spirit of God.

I had received the forgiveness in my spirit that He had been so desperate to give to me: NEVER TO BE THE SAME AGAIN!

I knew that God loved me; He has always loved me, just as He has always loved you!

Currently, I am so thankful for where the Lord has me. I am amazed at all that He has done for me and in me. I truly believe that He has raised me up to be a trophy of His grace – raised up from the enemies spoils and set apart to shine His love, grace and mercy out for others to be touched by. He has blessed me with a wonderfully loving and understanding husband in Jason, a precious and beautiful daughter in Grace and he has given me the two most giving and special parents in Margaret and John. He has taken me from where I was and loved me through to where I am; willing me on to where He wants me to be. I look forward to living out my God-given destiny and fulfilling my God-inspired dreams; together with Him,

Jason, my family and friends.

Every day I praise Him for all that He is to me, and today I thank Him for you. He has chosen for you to share in my testimony for a purpose; His purpose. With Him, I hope and pray that this book will alter you and your destiny; just as He has forever altered mine.

Revelation 12:11 – "And they overcame him by the blood of the Lamb and by the word of their testimony, and they did not love their lives to the death."

Prayer for a Personal Relationship with the Lord Jesus Christ

What God has done for me He wants to do for you; and more! The choice is yours. He loves you so much that He sent His Son to die for you; so that you could have everlasting life.

If you are reading this now and you don't know Jesus, or you need to renew your relationship with Him; please pray this prayer out loud, to Him. He wants you to let Him into your life; He's just waiting for you to invite Him in!

Father God,

I thank You that You love me so much that You sent Your only Son to die for me, so that I won't perish but will have eternal life (John 3:16).

I believe and confess with my mouth that Jesus Christ is Your One and only Son. I believe that He died on the cross, and with Him took all of my sins – wiping my slate clean. I believe in my heart that He rose from the dead (Rom 10:9,10).

With that faith, I confess my sins to You and I thank You for Your forgiveness (1John 1:9).

I thank You for washing me as white as snow, with Your precious blood (Eph 2:13).

I confess that Jesus is the Lord of my life and that from this day forward I will live for You (Rom 10:9,10).

I thank You for Your grace, by which I am saved (Eph 2:8,9).

I give You my heart and I thank You for Your salvation and Your love for me. I thank You that I am in Christ and that I am now a new creation (2Cor 5:17). In Jesus' name I pray. AMEN.

Now write down the date that you prayed this prayer. This is now your spiritual birthday – the day that you gave your heart to Jesus and He gave a brand new life to you!

Also, call a Christian friend or your local church and tell them that you have just given your heart to Jesus, and ask them to pray for you.

BLESS YOU, OVER AND ABUNDANTLY.

Scriptures Relating to Salvation Prayer

John 3:16 – "For God so loved the world that He gave His only begotten Son, that whoever believes in Him should not perish but have everlasting life."

1 John 1:9 – If we confess our sins, He is faithful and just to forgive us our sins and to cleanse us from all unrighteousness.

Ephesians 2:13 – But now in Christ Jesus you who once were far off have been brought near by the blood of Christ.

Romans 10:9,10 – That if you confess with your mouth the Lord Jesus and believe in your heart that God has raised Him from the dead, you will be saved. For with the heart one believes unto righteousness, and with the mouth confession is made unto salvation.

Ephesians 2:8,9 – For by grace you have been saved through faith, and not of yourselves; it is the gift of God, not of works, lest anyone should boast.

2 Corinthians 5:17 – Therefore, if anyone is in Christ, he is a new creation; old things have passed away; behold, all things have become new.

Afterword

Since I completed this book in July 2002 the Lord has continued to do a wonderful work in my life. To start with He had me take over the leadership role within the ladies cell group in September 2002, thankfully with Deanna standing right by my side. He also blessed Jason and I with another precious little baby girl, Rebekah Joy, who was born on May 19th, 2003. Jason and I have also been leading a Young Family home cell every second Wednesday night, which has really encouraged us to step up together and reach for our destiny! We, also, both took part in a short course called, 'Submitting to God' in which we discovered our personal prophetic profiles and declared our mandate as a couple; to be a bridge to liberty.

Together, we want to see broken hearts made whole and people set free to live the lives that God has called them to live. Our heart's desire is to see people surrender their all to the Lord and to worship Him with all of their heart, mind, body and soul.

I pray that this book will be a step towards our destiny. That as you hold this book in your hands you feel as though it has been for you a bridge to liberty.

Bless you all, over and abundantly.

Resource Information

DOCTORS:

Dr George O'Neil – *Perth, Western Australia*
For treatment of heroin, alcohol, benzodiazapines, amphetamines addiction.
Ph: (08) 9381 1333 (surgery)
(08) 9388 1991 (enquiries)
Email: gomedic@iinet.net.au

Dr Stuart Reece – *Brisbane, Queensland*
For treatment of heroin, alcohol, prescription and amphetamines addiction.
Ph: (07) 3844 4000
Email: asreece@bigpond.net.au

Dr David Hunt – *Brisbane, Queensland*
For treatment of heroin, alcohol and amphetamines addiction.
Ph: (07) 3849 6868
Email: djhunt@bigpond.net.au

First Step – *St Kilda Melbourne*
Dr Simon Rose and Dr John O'Donoghue.
For treatment of heroin, alcohol and amphetamines addiction.
Ph: 03 9537 3177

REHABILITATION SERVICES:

Victory Outreach Recovery Home
"Reaching treasures out of darkness" – Isaiah 45:2-3
Ph: Melbourne (03) 9352 6684
Sydney (02) 9720 0234
Brisbane (07) 3299 4173

Teen Challenge
Live-in residential program, also provide counselling services.
Ph: QLD (07) 3422 1500 (Male – 16-30 years)
NSW (02) 9644 7737 (Male – 16-35 years)

VIC (03) 5852 3777 (Male/Female – 17-35 years)
WA (08) 9309 5255 (Male/Female – 16-35 years)
SA (08) 8287 1685 (Male/Female – 18-28 years)

Sherwood Cliffs Christian Community
Residential rehabilitation farm. For 8 men and 2 families at one time.
Ph: (02) 6649 2139

<u>Salvation Army</u>
William Booth House Recovery Services Centre
Residential program for alcohol, drug and gambling dependant men.
Ph: (02) 9212 2322
Catherine Booth House
Residential program for alcohol, drug and gambling dependant women. Age 18+.
Life skills. Counselling/group work/work therapy.
Ph: (02) 9211 7300
Fairhaven – Gold Coast Recovery Services Centre
Residential rehabilitation program for males and females.
Ph: (07) 5594 7288
Fax: (07) 5594 7218

The Buttery
Residential rehabilitation program for males and females. Age 20+.
Ph: (02) 6687 1111
Email: info@buttery.org.au

ArcHouse
Residential rehabilitation program for men. Age 18-35.
Ph: (03) 9558 0488
Email: archouse@optusnet.com.au

Cross Roads Lodge
Drug and alcohol residential program for men. Counselling, prayer healing and life skills training.
Ph: 0412 508 794
Email: johncrossroads@yahoo.com.au

COUNSELLING SERVICES:

Drug Arm Australasia
Counselling, resource centre, home visitations.
Ph: 1300 656 800
Email: library@drugarm.com.au

Someone Who Cares
Counselling support agency for individuals and families with drug and alcohol problems.
Ph: (03) 9878 6099